The Essential Guide to

Early American Home Plans

Over 330 Classic & Traditional Home Designs

GAMBRELS / SALT BOXES / CAPE CODS / HERITAGE HOMES / *PLUS* HISTORICAL NOTES

 HOME PLANNERS, INC.

Zoning for Complete Livability

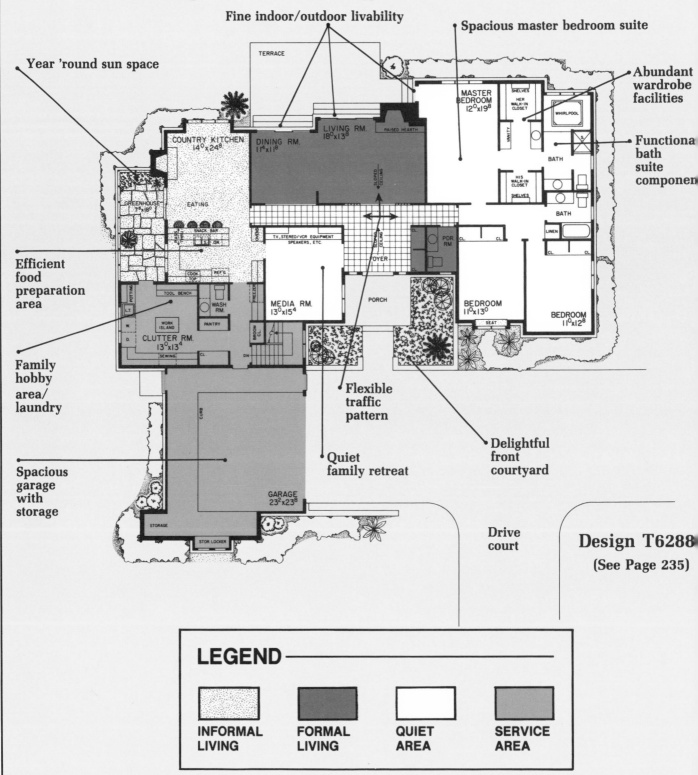

Fine indoor/outdoor livability

Spacious master bedroom suite

Year 'round sun space

Abundant wardrobe facilities

Functiona bath suite componen

Efficient food preparation area

Family hobby area/ laundry

Spacious garage with storage

Flexible traffic pattern

Quiet family retreat

Delightful front courtyard

Drive court

Design T6288

(See Page 235)

TERRACE

COUNTRY KITCHEN 14⁰x24⁸

DINING RM. 11⁴x11⁸

LIVING RM. 18⁰x13⁸

RAISED HEARTH

MASTER BEDROOM 12⁰x19⁸

SHELVES

HER WALK-IN CLOSET

WHIRLPOOL

VANITY

BATH

GREENHOUSE 7⁴x18⁰

EATING

HIS WALK-IN CLOSET

SHELVES

BATH

SNACK BAR

OVENS

T.V.,STEREO/VCR EQUIPMENT SPEAKERS, ETC.

SLOPED CEILING

LINEN

CL.

COOK TOP

REF'G

PDR. RM

CL.

CL.

CL.

CL.

POTTING

TOOL BENCH

WASH RM.

FREEZER

FOYER

MEDIA RM. 13⁰x15⁴

PORCH

BEDROOM 11⁰x13⁰

L.T.

WORK ISLAND

PANTRY

W

D.

CLUTTER RM. 13⁰x13⁴

BROOM CL.

SEAT

BEDROOM 11⁰x12⁸

SEWING

CL.

DN

CURB

GARAGE 23²x23⁸

STORAGE

STOR. LOCKER

LEGEND

| INFORMAL LIVING | FORMAL LIVING | QUIET AREA | SERVICE AREA |

HOME PLANNERS, INC.
23761 RESEARCH DRIVE, FARMINGTON HILLS, MICHIGAN 48024

The Essential Guide to

Early American Home Plans

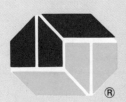

HOME PLANNERS, INC.
23761 RESEARCH DRIVE, FARMINGTON HILLS, MICHIGAN 48024

Contents

Guide to Early American Style

This guide to Early American styles is a window to the many classic home designs that continue to charm Americans today. In the book's illustrated chapters, readers easily can identify these ever-popular styles and trace the roots of American period architecture.

Basically, immigrants brought their European home-building ideas with them to the new world. The accent of their architecture stayed with them. Most early settlers here emigrated from England, France, and Germanic states. Consequently, most Early American homes resemble building styles from these mother countries.

Formal styles went through many changes in this new world, marking Americans' breaks with their past. Some Americans, however, built huge mansions to rival classic Georgian, Greek, and Gothic styles.

American homes also developed from Victorian styles, as design concepts evolved. Our illustrations show this evolution of design.

Our English Roots

Our English styles today vary from the simple Cotswold cottage to the lavish Elizabethan. These sub-styles, plus multi-gabled Tudors and classic box form Georgians, actually have much in common. Most English homes have high-pitch roofs, large chimneys, light leaded windows, and masonry siding.

Early English settlers here built familiar, simple homes of saddle-notched whole logs laid horizontally. (That's true also of many German, Finnish, and Scandinavian settlers.) The typical English house was half-timbered with wooden exposed framework and wall spaces filled with brick nogging or a mixture of mud, clay, and plaster.

Soon new kilns enabled brickmaking in Jamestown and Plymouth. Brick was used mainly in fireplaces and chimneys. Softer brick was used as nogging behind clapboard or outside walls. Brick was used for entire construction only when plentiful. It also was used as a new filler in timber frames or else set in decorative patterns.

The Tudor style (born during the House of Tudor reign) became popular in this country in the late 1880s. The Elizabethan style, with its half-timbered overhanging second floor, is only slightly less formal.

Of all English styles brought to this country, the Georgian style (born during the reign of four kings named George) became the most copied by the early 1770s. Houses based on this style later evolved into the Williamsburg and Southern Colonial styles. Our presidential White House, in fact, can claim Georgian descent.

Late Georgian (often called Early Federal) was the predominant style in America just after 1790.

The Clapboard House, popular in early Virginia, derives its name from the timber-frame structure that encases the building. The hall was the main living area of medieval English cottages. Commonly, rooms are flanked by a central chimney with a staircase that rises from an entry or porch into two upstairs chambers. This design became popular in early New England. The overhangs or "jetties" that grace the exteriors of the house echo medieval English styling.

In typical English construction, large stone buildings became the haven of wealthy landed gentry, while wooden homes became the lot of lesser personages. Today stately English churches and some elegant stone homes remind Americans of this early class distinction.

The manor house replaced the castle approximately five hundred years ago, marking another break with the past. Stone, along with brick and wood, gradually became more common in lesser buildings. By American times, all three building materials were commonly used when available.

Whether built of wood, brick or sometimes stone, most Early American dwellings reflect a common English heritage. Distinguishing characteristics include a single file of rooms, sharply angled gables, steep (sometimes thatched) roofs, tiny casement windows, lean-to additions, and asymmetrical quaintness. All of this reflects our medieval roots.

Most of the first settlers in New England were thrifty, hard-working English immigrants from middle-class backgrounds. Most came to the new world in quest of religious freedom more than wealth. Later a civil war in England in the mid-17th Century brought even more of them. Most of these English settlers came from fishing and farming villages, including Norfolk, Suffolk, Essex, Cambridge, Hertford, Middlesex, Surrey, and Kent in southeastern England. They also hailed from small townships and cross-

Design T62101, Pg. 18

1. English Medieval House with Overhang

This design recalls in faithful detail the medieval manse built by the Rev. Joseph Capen, who became the minister of the church in Topsfield, Mass. in 1682. It is typical of houses of 17th-Century English colonists. Snug Garrison style dwellings commonly featured a prominent second-floor overhang, a feature of English houses in the Middle Ages. The overhang protected the wattling and timbers on the floor below from rain and also customers of Elizabethan townhouse shops. The Parson Capen manse featured second-floor bracketed overhangs on front elevation, third-floor overhang on gable end, heavy carved pendant drops at corners, huge pilastered center chimney, and cedar-shake roof.

roads, such as Haverhill, Sudbury, Ipswich, Dedham, Toppesfield, Wethersfield, Braintree, Maldon, Canterbury, Billericay, Hadham, and Wickford. These are names familiar today to New Englanders, whose pioneer forefathers often renamed their new communities after their old.

The 17th-Century villages these settlers left behind were still entirely medieval in architecture. Houses were predominantly timber-framed, with stone used sparingly on only most expensive buildings. Brick was reserved for wealthy manors and churches in places like Kent, Suffolk, and Essex. This is the medieval world these English immigrants attempted to recreate and build upon in their new world.

Architects today even disagree on labels for design styles. Our illustrations, however, depict historic homes in renditions from the nation's popular creator of home designs. These illustrations capture the flavor of America's homes. Historic homes blueprints are available for each design at a modest cost.

Design T62191, Pg. 27

2. A Tudor Translation

This version of a 1675 gabled salt box house in New England combines Medieval and Tudor styling. It's a Medieval salt box design, because the roof line of the main house is carried low in the rear to cover an added lean-to. Tudor styling is apparent in the multiple gabled roof lines. Cross gables are stepped out in a series of projecting overhangs, common in early English houses. Narrow clapboard siding also was commonly used for exteriors. Double-leaded and triple-leaded casements are proportioned to set under overhangs. The massive pilastered chimney in the center also is typical of the period. The pictured design is a faithful adaptation of a house built by Jonathan Corwin of Salem, Mass. in 1675.

Design T62654, Pg. 20

4. Transitional Salt Box

The long, low rear roof line that is characteristic of so-called salt box houses resulted from addition of a lean-to in the rear of an otherwise simple two-room or four-room Medieval house. This change created more room, one reason this age-old design remains popular today. The rear wing of colonial salt box homes often enclosed a kitchen, flanked by a bedroom for child care and a pantry. Figure 4 above illustrates a transition from a simple, functional salt box to Georgian symmetry and refinement. The updated house still retained its basic salt box shape nonetheless. Classically inspired exterior detailing also marked the beginning of the new Georgian Period.

Design T62688, Pg. 181

3. Typical Georgian Townhouse with Tudor Chimneys

This design is based on Williamsburg's historic Red Lion House (1730). Its clipped gables and pyramidal chimneys are reminiscent of Tudor dwellings of the late 1600's. The symmetrical windows, bracketed cornices, and classic porch are nonetheless 18th-Century Georgian. Planters in 18th-Century Virginia built townhouses in Williamsburg, Virginia's colonial capital after Jamestown, and also the port city of Yorktown. Examples of this period architecture are still evident in modern Williamsburg and Yorktown. Early planters would leave their plantations to reside and conduct business in these substantial houses. Virginia was wealthiest of the colonies in the 18th-Century, and Williamsburg served as Virginia capital from 1699 to 1799, a period when Georgian style architecture flourished. Most of Williamsburg's Georgian houses were built of brick with grand simplicity.

Gambrel Roofs

The gambrel roof became popular soon after introduction in the colonies in the middle of the 17th Century. In fact, it soon became a prominent feature of New England homes. The roof is believed to be French in origin. The term "gambrel" likely comes from the early French term "gamberel" for crooked sticks used by butchers. The gambrel roof has double slopes on either side of the house. It has a sharp upper slope of low pitch and a long lower slope of steep pitch.

Soon colonial homes sported gambrel roofs on cottages, stately houses, and farms. They were fairly common on houses of Williamsburg, Virginia.

The gambrel roof enabled almost a full second story of floor space. The style was an improvement over space allowed by designs of one and a half stories.

A substyle of the Early American gambrel roof design is the Dutch Colonial which came later in history, probably wasn't truly Dutch in origin, and was more bell-shaped.

Design T62320, Pg. 53

5. Typical Connecticut River Valley Gambrel Design

This rendition of typical early Connecticut design illustrates gambrel roofs in the colonies. The charming facade of our adaptation exhibits balance between narrow clapboard siding and a shingled roof punctuated by triple dormer windows.

6. New Hampshire Gambrel

Design T62556, Pg. 165

Figure 6 illustrates the adaptation by New England colonists of Georgian styling when it made its way north. This faithful interpretation of the historic John Paul Jones home in Portsmouth, New Hampshire, features symmetrical windows capped by angular pediments, classical doorway with segmental pediment, and two-light transom – all capped by a gambrel roof.

This historic boarding house, built in 1730, housed the legendary Revolutionary War captain. It is generally typical of New England homes of the period. Note the dual corbelled chimneys, typical of much Georgian architecture, and the dormers, typical of Late Georgian or Federal styling. The house is wood construction, typical of New England Georgian, as opposed to predominant brick construction in Southern Georgian.

Gabled Houses

Design T62685, Pg. 110

Design T62668, Pg. 98

Design T62640, Pg. 138

7. Pennsylvania Stone Gable
Reminiscent of Washington's Valley Forge Headquarters.

8. Southern Colonial Gable
Reminiscent of the historic Vaughn House.

9. New England Clapboard
Reminiscent of historic Deane - Barstow House.

Cape Cod Cottages

This ever-popular Cape Cod cottage design finds its roots in Medieval England. American colonists adapted the hearty structure to New England, particularly the Cape where harsh winds swept over the low profile of these clapboard structures with little resistance. Their steeply pitched gable roofs also provided space for a children's garret under the ridge.

Original colonial cottages from Sandwich to Provincetown were tiny with small rooms clustered around a chimney stack. They were cozy, warm, and practical dwellings. Their charm persists today, particularly in New England.

Their compactness maximized living space by minimizing hallways. Their rectangular shape was easily fabricated. The typical Cape Cod was a "half house," characterized by a simple central doorway with the basic medieval English hall. That great hall could be a single large room or divided essentially into a front vestibule, parlor, rear keeping room, borning room, and buttery. Stairs led upstairs to a sleeping attic.

Variations of this basic half house were generally simple expansions of the design. The three-quarter Cape Cod simply added one room opposite the parlor with one extra front window. This was generally a downstairs bedroom that could be entered from the front vestibule or keeping room. Its fireplace was located off the central chimney, like others in the house.

The full Cape Cod house simply doubled the half house. It resembles the popular Cape Cod cottage that survives today. While 17th-Century Cape Cods had gabled roofs with central

Design T62682, Pg. 144

11. The Half House
A simple Cape Cod cottage.

Design T62661, Pg. 147

12. Three-Quarter House
One extra room and window added.

Design T62644, Pg. 146

13. Bowed Full-Size Cape
Double the size of simple half house.

chimneys, some later variations included bowed roofs and two corner fireplaces off one chimney, like Fig. 13.

Dutch Heritage

Dutch settled the Hudson River Valley, west end of Long Island, and Northern New Jersey and controlled it until 1664 as New Netherlands.

The early Dutch were traders. Dutch architecture in Early America shows craftsmanship and pride in tradition. The Dutch built occasionally with stone, but preferably with brick which they prized.

The Dutch never built exterior chimneys, but employed double stacks within walls – often double stacks. When Dutch masons and craftsmen entered the Georgian period, their ideas melded with prevalent English styling.

14. Double Dutch Chimneys
Double Georgian chimney stacks put heat in all four corners of this Georgian rendition for a fireplace in virtually every room.

Design T61858, Pg. 78

Fig. 7 – Our rendition of George Washington's 1777-78 winter headquarters in Valley Forge (pictured at far left) is an Early American version of the gabled house. The stone exterior recalls the Pennsylvania farmhouses of Valley Forge in Colonial times. This is a home for all seasons. Windows are accented by patrician jabots.
Fig. 8 – The design at left, center, is a good example of Southern Colonial Architecture. This elegant pillared house with gable roof is typical of estates in

the Deep South between 1820 and 1860. This antebellum manor includes the Greek temple look that swept much of the old South during the Greek Revival in Early America. A portico with columns suggested that owners were cultured and civilized by classical standards. In these days, the Greek temple became the highest architectural ideal for a generation of Americans.
Fig. 9 – Pictured at near left is our adaptation of an eclectic New England Federal built in 1807. It incorporated

forms of architecture common during both the 17th and 18th Centuries. The Deane-Barstow House of Southeastern Massachusetts featured narrow clapboard typical of 18th-Century New England and overhanging gables typical of the 17th-Century and English practice. The symmetrical Georgian facade includes classical pilaster and pedimented doorway with bracketed cornices at the eaves. A massive chimney is centered in the gable roof.

The Dutch Colonial Farmhouse

When most Americans today think of Dutch architecture, they really are thinking Flemish. What sticks in their minds is the charming Dutch Colonial Farmhouse with its bell-shaped gambrel roof and flaring eaves. Typically, this house was made of clapboard, shingle, or stone. People commonly believe that Dutch colonists brought this delightful swept design with them to the new world.

It's likely, most scholars feel, that the farmhouse design is not Dutch and not even colonial in its present Twentieth Century form. Gambrel roofs were rare in Holland. The questions continue, while happy inhabitants of this cozy farmhouse smile, snug in their homes.

The design evolved to its present form as a graceful, simple cottage only a hundred years ago. That's long after the Dutch colony here disbanded and New Netherlands became New York. Possibly, therefore, the Dutch Colonial Farmhouse is a truly American innovation.

Many scholars believe the basic design with flaring eaves is Flemish or even French in origin. In maritime Flanders, an area that's now southern Holland, western Belgium, and northern France, similar farmhouses were constructed with low walls built of clay mixed with lime and straw. To protect the clay walls from weather, flared eaves called "flying gutters" were added to project out two feet or longer.

Many native Flemings fled to Holland during Spanish occupation in the early 17th-Century. Dutch farm land was scarce, however, so many Flemish farmers emigrated to New Netherlands in America.

Many early Dutch in New Netherlands were traders or clustered in Dutch communities, but the Flemish were peasant farmers. The Flemish remain hard to trace in the United States, but some scholars estimate two-thirds of certain counties in New Netherlands were Flemish, particularly in northern New Jersey. Elsewhere in southern New Netherlands the Flemish mixed with Dutch, Walloons, and French in "Dutch" communities. The Flemish projecting curved eaves appeared on Long Island homes as early as the mid-17th Century. The Dutch Colonial Farmhouse remains popular in rural Long Island and New Jersey.

Besides flaring eaves, these Flemish farmhouses were marked by a graceful version of the gambrel roof. However, this was not used until the 18th Century. The graceful curve of the roof line and its overhang provided a shelter. In the late 18th Century, posts were added under the projection to create a full-width porch. The overhang of the original Flemish farmhouse was designed to shield fragile walls of clay, lime, and straw – a curious regional mixture. It's possible, therefore, to compare the American Dutch Colonial's stone and wood components as abundant substitutes for the building materials of Flanders. The American stone houses often were plastered and whitewashed. Certainly that visual impact reminds one of Flemish homes, if indeed the forerunner.

Another clue lies in the mortar between the stones. Curiously, the American version used a mortar mixture of clay, lime, and straw. That mixture is identical to the wall material of Flemish houses. Most American mortar is harder.

Whether an American invention or a faithful import, the Dutch Colonial or Flemish farmhouse has not remained untouched as a pure art form in this country. The flaring Flemish eave can be seen in Bergen County, New Jersey, on French Huguenot houses.

The added porch may reflect French Colonial influence, or it may have come from the West Indies where the Dutch traded in the late 19th Century. Regional examples abound in French Louisiana, Missouri, and the Carolinas.

With all these changes and more than a century of local popularity, perhaps the so-called Dutch Colonial farmhouse should be considered an American creation, after all.

Design T62633, Pg. 111

16. A German Farmhouse

This is a Georgian with a German accent from Pennsylvania Dutch country. The comfortable Georgian farms arrived with English settlers. This illustration recalls the 1805 home of Johannes and Anne Hersche of Lancaster County. Hersche built this large house with front porch, using bricks made from the area's rich clay soil. The home was considered extravagant by his Mennonite Church, whose members almost expelled him. Elsewhere in Lancaster County, the Dutch country displays many roofs steeply pitched in the German medieval style.

Design T62680, Pg. 61

15. Dutch Colonial Farmhouse

The popular, cozy Dutch Colonial Farmhouse may have been Flemish or French in origin and evolved in recent centuries here in America. Its bell-shaped low gambrel roof, flying eaves, and posted porch make it a favorite – particularly in the Dutch counties of New England.

The German Legacy

German craftsmanship is evident in much Early American architecture, although German workmanship and exquisite detailing was meshed in the Georgian period into more prevalent English styles of design.

German and Dutch Mennonites arrived in Pennsylvania in 1683, and by the 18th Century Pennsylvania received the largest population of German descent of any state. German styling in many Pennsylvania religious communities remains an architectural statement today.

Some confusion over ancestry persists with Germanic immigrants, due to confusion over the words "Deutschland," meaning Germany, and "Deutsch," meaning German. Also, many Germanic peoples were lumped together in common consideration before emergence of strong German states.

Many of the Germans who emigrated to America were Quakers, Amish, and Mennonites who kept old-world customs. This is apparent in many buildings in settlements throughout Pennsylvania.

The German immigrants often built in stone and generally repeated the patterns of architecture most familiar to them back in the old country.

One major contribution of early German builders in Pennsylvania was an unsupported hood over the front door.

One of their settlements was the German Quaker Germantown near Philadelphia (part of present Philadelphia). What perhaps moved German settlers outward was the climate in outlying Lancaster, Berks, York, Dauphin, Bucks, and Lehigh Valley. The soil and dense forest may have reminded them of the old country. Back home, land had been scarce, and German farmers there lived close to one another in close-knit communities. They left home daily to work in outlying farms. They emigrated to America because of scarce land, harsh taxes, and religious oppression. Here in America they found plenty of land and freedom, but the once-necessary concept of close communities remained.

German preservation of old world traditions in Pennsylvania included German medieval architecture. This is true of many German houses in Maryland, Wisconsin, North Carolina, and Texas, as well. Much of present Pennsylvania reflects this medieval German architecture with roofs steeply pitched, blended with more elegant classical forms.

Readily available English materials, such as windows, were incorporated into German houses. The German builders made good use of rich red clay soil in Pennsylvania for brickmaking.

German farmers in America were constant builders who settled into a farm community to raise a family. Slowly they added to their homesteads, which likely grew over time.

The French Connection

French immigrants, mostly Huguenots facing religious persecution, began settling in southern colonies in the 17th Century. For the most part, they built simple homes to mirror peasant cottages in the old world.

The pattern for these homes is rooted in the early Mediterranean. The originals were distinguished by a steep gabled roof that broke near the peak and sloped easily over front and rear "galleries" or porches. The roof line broke farther down at the facade. The French farmhouse in America became a sort of cozy cottage and soon graced colonies all the way from the Carolinas to Maryland.

In Louisiana, the first French houses were one-story homes surrounded by a gallery or porch and hip roof. The framing was curious. Walls were made of posts sunk into the ground and positioned together, similar to log cabins, except that logs were laid vertically in the French homes. This sort of framing was called "poteau-en-terre", or posts in earth, by the French. Unfortunately, the posts rotted in the ground, so houses thereafter employed stone foundations. Builders raised these houses even higher above ground with piers in regions prone to floods. This, then, became the Louisiana plantation style. Such raised cottages became a popular French style in the South, regardless of flood conditions. Such raised cottages appeared in New Orleans in the early 18th Century. Framing of the revised French cottages resembled English style, rather than earlier French posts-in-ground fashion.

17. French Farmhouse

French immigrants built elegant raised cottages with broad porches the French called galleries. They evolved from simple dwellings from the Carolinas to Maryland. This design recalls a Chesapeake Bay home built around 1650. Characteristic of Tidewater design, its French profile includes five dormers.

Design T62650, Pg. 178

18. The Charleston "Single House"

Elegant Charleston Single Houses evolved from earlier French plantation houses with central block and attached porches. They were called Single Houses, because originally they were a single room deep. These tall, slender townhouses became popular in Charleston, South Carolina, in the 18th and 19th Centuries. They can be seen in profusion in Charleston to this day. The facade of these stately Southern homes did not face the street. Rather, the narrow end of the townhouse was accessible to the street from stairs and double-tiered colated porches which the French first had called "galleries" and then called "piazzas". The upper piazza typically overlooked a splendid front courtyard or garden. The French country farmhouse had been transformed from cozy raised cottage to elegant townhouse with stately columns and even pedimented gable in some cases. In hot summer days and muggy long nights, gentle sea breezes would blow across the piazza porches of these Southern homes.

Design T62660, Pg. 88

19. Louisiana Plantation House

French raised cottages popular in the early South included French "galleries" or porches to catch summer breezes on hot, sultry days. Purpose of the raised elevation was originally to protect against floods. The elevated cottage features six Doric columns in this typical design, as well as four single-windowed dormers. Often, as in the illustration, the house had paneled double French doors and tall chimneys. The classic French design remains functional and stately.

Design T62686, Pg. 175

The Georgian Period

The Georgian Period of architecture in colonial America was a time of formal style and elegance from approximately 1700 until 1780 when Georgian melted with subtle changes into Late Georgian or Federal. Pretentious Georgian mansions were marked by exquisite detailing, regular geometric shapes, ornament, formal symmetry, and often size. Regional variations created a wide variety of Georgian architecture. Basically, Georgian in the South included brick and occasionally stone construction, while New England Georgian occurred slightly later with mainly wood construction.

Georgian was the dominant style in its time for the landed gentry who could afford its grandeur. Roots of colonial Georgian are traced all the way to the Italian Renaissance and its emphasis on classical detailing. That early style resurfaced in England in the mid-17th Century where it dominated the architectural scene from approximately 1650 to 1750 under such masters as Christopher Wren. It reached the shores of colonial America approximately 1700 at a time of new prosperity. New American commerce was thriving with plantations in the South and seaports in the North, and the prosperous welcomed the pretentious Georgian design as a statement of their wealth and elegant lifestyle. Many early Georgian homes were built from patterns and carpentry books shipped from Europe.

While the basic Georgian house was a simple two-story or one-story box with symmetrical windows and doors and two rooms deep, many sub-types existed. These include Georgians with side-gabled roof in the North, gambrel roof mainly in the North, and hipped roof in the South. Another sub-style was the Georgian with centered gable in which triangular gable pediment was centered on the front facade. The Georgian townhouse was another sub-style. This is an urban house with narrow facade.

The front door was a major feature in Georgian architecture. Often the door was flanked with plain or fluted pilasters of full height or raised on pedestals. Later versions involved columns with pediments or cornices above the door. Ornaments over the door included curved molding topped by a row of small dentil blocks and molded cornice. Simple triangular pediment over the door was most common.

Design T62683, Pg. 66

20. Georgian with Pediment Gable

This dignified Georgian design echoes Woodlawn, the gracious abode that George Washington built near Mount Vernon for his niece, as well as Tulip Hill, a stately manor in Ann Arundel County, Maryland. Its Georgian facade features slender-column portico and round window that adorns the pediment.

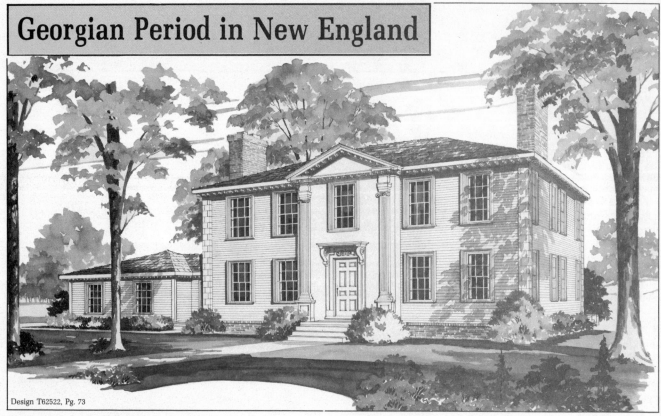

Design T62522, Pg. 73

21. New England Georgian

This stately design is based on the Lady Pepperrell House built approximately 1760 on a hill overlooking Portsmouth Harbor in Kittery Point, Maine. It is typical of New England Georgian design. The house captures the simple elegance of the period. It employs the frame construction characteristic of New England Georgian homes, rather than the brick construction used predominantly in the South. Exquisite detailing indoors and outdoors recreates the simple grace of the period. A set of short steps leads to a projected pavilion that is distinguished from the clapboard walls by its smooth boards that simulate masonry. A grand entrance is framed by applied Ionic pilasters that are elevated on

pedestals. Denticulated moldings and paneled wainscoting decorate the spacious two story interior.

Evolution of Georgian styling progressed slowly from 16th Century Renaissance Italy to 18th Century England. There it took the name of three of England's ruling kings, all named King George.

When transported to the American colonies, Georgian architecture's classical elegance suited the taste of a new emerging elite class. Georgian architecture was the predominant style for homes for the wealthy from the Carolinas to Maine by the middle of the 18th Century, with regional variations.

22. Cape Cod Georgian

This design recalls the Julia Wood House built approximately 1790 in Falmouth, Mass. and is typical of many Georgian two-story homes built in Cape Cod. Earlier two-story houses on the Cape employed a central chimney, tiny entry porch, and gabled roof. With Georgian and Federal style influences, later Cape Cod clapboard houses featured chimneys set either between front and rear rooms or at end elevations of the house. A hipped roof replaced the gable roof to relieve the boxlike proportions of the house. A center hall with elegant stairs replaced the cramped entry porch. Such homes generally had a balustraded roof deck where wives of captains looked to sea for signs of returning ships. Often they searched in vain, so the deck became known as a widow's walk.

Design T62690, Pg. 80

Design T62283, Pg. 84

23. Late Georgian Styling

Our illustration recalls the transition from Georgian architecture into the Late Georgian Period with greater emphasis on brick permanence and crisp lines to replace the florid carvings and sweeping curves of Early Georgian detailing. A hallmark of the new styles was the two-story projecting portico. The emerging style continued Georgian use of classical symmetry.

The simple two-story symmetrical box that was early Georgian architecture went through a Late Georgian period of transition from approximately 1760 to 1780 into the Federal Period. Late Georgian architecture made heavy use of classical details – notably doorways surrounded by pilasters or columns, surmounted by cornice or pediment, and semi-circular fanlight over doors. Use of columns and pilasters became more lavish, and so did use of classical detailing in the cornice. More elaborate houses would feature a projected entrance pavillion with a pedimented gable on top. After the Revolutionary War, many designers would reject a lot of the classical decoration of Late Georgian, but retain its basic Greco-Roman symmetry.

Design T62667, Pg. 71

24. 18th-Century Tidewater Virginia

This design, patterned after historic Semple House in Williamsburg, Virginia, is reminiscent of 18th Century Tidewater Virginia homes. Classic renaissance innovations were added to Georgian styling. The configuration featured a pedimented center section flanked by lower wings, typical in much Palladian design transported from Europe to the colonies. This classical form was derived from the classical architecture of ancient Rome, as interpreted by 16th Century Italian Renaissance architect Andrea Palladio. His styling was revived in England in the Early 18th Century. The imposing gable of the design dramatized the entire structure and gave the center section the jutting prominence of an ancient temple. Cornice treatments of the gable reappear at roof lines on all elevations and porch.

The Federal Period

Many people today still confuse Georgian and Federal styles of architecture. It's basically correct to say that Federal style emerged from the Georgian Period as a sedate late Georgian style more concerned with classical correctness and understatement than Georgian concern for classical form and overstatement.

It's also generally correct to associate Federal styling with the northern colonies, although it appears in brick late Georgian homes of the South. And it's correct to associate it with Palladian style which introduced a stripped-down classical look to Georgian after Christopher Wren architected a re-building of London after the Great Fire. At any rate, the Federal Style dominated Colonial architecture from approximately 1780 to 1830. The Federal Period also is sometimes referred to as the Adam Period, after transitional designer Robert Adams.

Particularly in the North, post-Revolutionary designers and builders rejected much of the classical decoration of Georgian architecture, particularly its heavy ornamentation in the later years of Greek and Roman influence. The new Federal look, however, kept the basic Roman symmetry found in Georgian design. Doorways kept their pilasters and columns for the most part. Doorways often were topped with flat entablature. Elliptical fanlights above doorways also were popular. Frames around windows were employed. Corners were unmarked by quoins or ornamental pilasters. Hipped roofs became more common. These hipped roofs were occasionally rimmed by a balustrade. Flat boarding was sometimes used on the exterior for a more classical effect.

By the time that Georgian architecture caught on in the seaports of the North, Georgian ornate grandeur had pretty well played itself out. That was fine, perhaps, for the God-fearing, practical New Englanders, who appreciated classical symmetry and grand homes, but not particularly pretentious splendor. Their resulting compromise of styles may be described as New England eclectic.

A desire for classical quality and correctness continued. White smoothness of flush-boarded walls or painted brick or stucco demonstrate this understatement, as does the bare simplicity of painted plaster walls.

The Federal house often featured a giant portico and almost always employed a certain doorway of narrow flanking side lights and embracing elliptical fanlight. This is the so-called Federal doorway. The Federal house also typically featured a curved or polygon-shaped bay on an exterior wall and balustrade or parapet over eaves (rather than high on the roof). Often such homes included fragile carved wood or molded plaster ornaments, inspired by Robert Adams, a devotee of Pompeii decorated walls.

The box shape of Georgian homes was expanded in the Federal period in many instances to include wings, from temple-form house shape.

Of course, there are variations. While hipped-roof houses were frequent in New England, there existed many side-gabled houses, and center gabled houses with triangular pediments centered on the front facade. Hipped roof houses of the period could be two-story or three-story buildings. Many Federal townhouses became so-called row houses in urban areas.

25. Massachusetts Palladian Manor

This elegant Massachusetts manor recalls the late 18th-Century Alexander Field House in Longmeadow. It demonstrates early New England regard for simple order and symmetry with Classical implementation of Palladian detailing. An elevated doorway is defined by pilasters and pediment, topped by a second-story Palladian window. The window is capped by a pediment that projects from the hipped roof. Clapboard covered most New England homes of the Late Georgian period.

Design T62639, Pg. 72

Design T62184, Pg. 90

26. The Greek Temple House

The Greek temple was the highest architectural ideal for many wealthy Americans from 1820 until the Civil War. Variations include everything from modest farmhouses in Maine to luxurious plantations in Mississippi. Hallmark of the dignified style is the classic white portico. Our illustra-tion shows symmetrical entry facade with a projecting central pavilion. Giant portico with fluted columns rise two stories to support a pedimented gable. Flat pilasters are used on external corners in same composite classical order as the portico columns. Entry facade details are repeated in the rear.

The Greek Revival Period

Colonial interest in classical Greek and Roman arts as well as English design trends led to a Greek Revival Period in American architecture. Focus on the Golden Age was prompted initially by archeological discoveries in the late 18th Century. It started with excavation of two lost Roman cities buried by eruption of Vesuvius in AD 79. Herculaneum was discovered in 1719, followed by Pompeii in 1748. Around the world people heard new stories about how people of these once glorious Roman cities had lived. Books on Greek classicism followed. Detailed documentation of the 5th Century B.C. structures of the Acropolis in Athens soon was incorporated into builders' handbooks and the textbooks of influential architects. Knowledge of classical architecture was also spread by new museums and the advent of photography. The Greek temple became the highest architectural ideal for Americans from 1820 to approximately 1860.

In truth, much of the American so-called Greek Revival in architecture employs Roman styling, particularly the heavy unfluted Roman columns. While the era might well be defined as a Greco-Roman revival, the concept was classical idealism best exemplified by Greek thinking. In America, what's meant to be elegant often becomes a bit pompous. It's best to remember that early Americans were enterprising imitators with a brash mind of their own. Greek Revival architects pretty much decided for themselves which classic order of many in both Greek and Roman design they chose to follow, often mixing and matching.

The typical Early American house of the Greek Revival period was a two-story or three-story symmetrical building that was essentially a copy of a Greek temple with columns, architraves, friezes, and cornices. Windows were small and hidden, since they were not truly a part of Greek temple architecture. Of course, the style has continued in modern America in design of public buildings.

Exterior walls of Greek Revival Period structures were clapboard, flush-board, stucco, stone, or even brick – but they were invariably white. Interior walls were smooth plaster. Trim was rich yet refined, with moldings adapted from classical orders. Ceiling trim often enhanced the elegance. The general tone of such period architecture was that of tranquility and order.

Southern Colonial architecture of the period absorbed the Greek Revival and adapted it to post-Georgian styling. Often the Doric or Ionic pillars were abbreviated to form entry porches or full-width porches supported by square or round columns only half the height of a two-story house.

Roof lines could be gabled or hipped roof with low pitch. A cornice line on the main roof and porch roof often was accentuated with a wide band of trim to represent classic entablature.

Columns can be distinguished by their capitals on top and their bases. Doric columns employ plain capitals, while Ionic columns employ capitals with scrolled spirals. Less frequent Corinthian capitals are shaped somewhat like inverted bells with leaves.

The Greek Revival employed round columns, never square. The thick Greek Doric fluted column with no base is most prominent, although thinner fluted Roman Dorics with base and unfluted Roman Tuscans with base also are found in Early American houses.

Greco-Roman Styling

27. 1820-1865 Revival Home

This Southern Colonial home illustrates how early America adapted both Greek and Roman classical styling with imposing columns and porticoes in forming porches. The broad Roman Tuscan columns are unfluted, yet impart a clean grace with sense of importance with their Ionic capitals at the tops. Interest in classical design grew in England, but reached the colonies sixty years later. Here it flourished as a classical form under American whims from approximately 1820 until the Civil War. Our illustration recalls the orderly pillared and pedimented manors built in America commonly during those forty years.

Design T62663, Pg. 174

American Traditional

Design T62694, Pg. 128

28. Northeast Country Vernacular

This design, patterned after the Bedford, New York, homestead of former Secretary of Foreign Affairs John Jay, typifies farmhouse styling of much American Traditional architecture. Notice the use of slender columns, typical of much Pennsylvania farm country, as well. The columns and railing form a comfortable farmhouse porch. John Jay was born in 1745 and inherited site for his home from his father, a wealthy New York merchant of French Huguenot descent. The modest yet comfortable two-story house features sienna shutters. An orderly symmetry of design has been maintained.

TWO-STORY
SALT BOXES, GARRISONS & MEDIEVAL VARIATIONS

The basic Medieval house in Early America saw addition of a lean-to wing across the rear elevation. This wing often enclosed a kitchen, flanked by a bedroom for child care and a pantry. The rear roof swept down from the ridge over the wing, giving the house a salt box configuration.

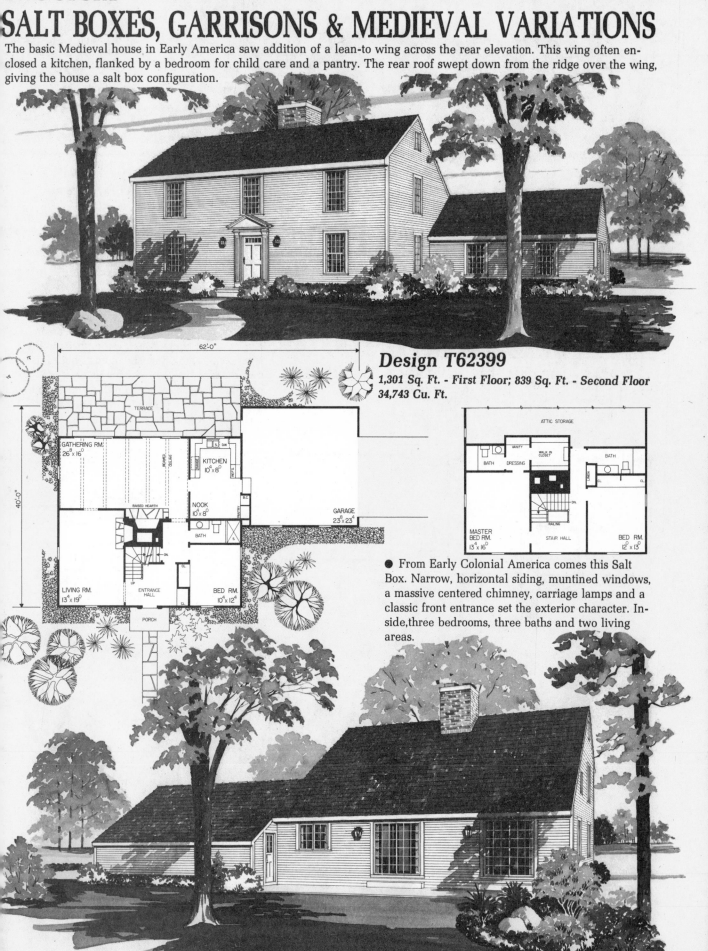

Design T62399
1,301 Sq. Ft. - First Floor; 839 Sq. Ft. - Second Floor
34,743 Cu. Ft.

62'-0"

40'-0"

TERRACE

GATHERING RM.
26'8" x 16'0"

KITCHEN
10'4" x 8'0"

NOOK
10'4" x 8'0"

BATH

GARAGE
23'5" x 23'4"

LIVING RM.
13'4" x 19'0"

ENTRANCE HALL

BED RM.
10'4" x 12'4"

PORCH

ATTIC STORAGE

BATH

VANITY

WALK IN CLOSET

DRESSING

BATH

MASTER BED RM.
13'4" x 16'0"

STAIR HALL

BED RM.
12'2" x 13'0"

● From Early Colonial America comes this Salt Box. Narrow, horizontal siding, muntined windows, a massive centered chimney, carriage lamps and a classic front entrance set the exterior character. Inside, three bedrooms, three baths and two living areas.

Design T62101
1,338 Sq. Ft. - First Floor
1,114 Sq. Ft. - Second Floor; 39,617 Cu. Ft.

● This is a modified version of one of America's most famous Colonial dwellings, the Parson Capen of Topsfield, Mass. Dating back to the 17th-Century, the English colonists built this medieval adaptation reproducing its bracketed second floor overhang, pendant drops at the corners, massive pilastered chimney and narrow clapboards. The floor plan, of course, has been updated to cater to today's living requirements.

Design T62651

1,404 Sq. Ft. - First Floor
1,323 Sq. Ft. - Second Floor; 45,203 Cu. Ft.

● This design is a replica of the medieval style of the housing in early New England. It is a Garrison with clapboards and sash windows highlighting the exterior. The inside has livability galore. The dramatic front entry features a curved staircase to the second floor which is open and overlooks the entry. Privacy will be enjoyed in the end-living room.

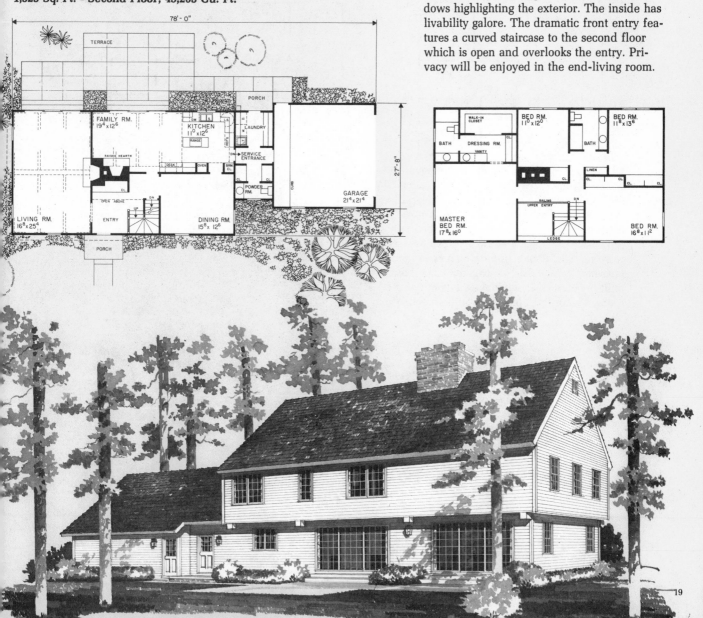

Design T62654
1,152 Sq. Ft. - First Floor
844 Sq. Ft. - Second Floor; 31,845 Cu. Ft.

ROOF

BEDROOM
11⁴ x 10⁰

ATTIC STORAGE   ATTIC STORAGE

CL.   CL.   LIN.   BATH

SHELVES   LINEN   DN

MASTER
BEDROOM
13⁸ x 17⁰   BATH   BEDROOM
10⁰ x 11⁴

CL.

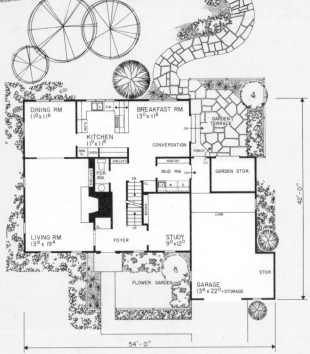

DINING RM.
11⁰ x 11⁸   BREAKFAST RM.
13⁰ x 11⁸   GARDEN TERRACE

D.W.   DN

KITCHEN
11⁰ x 11⁸   CONVERSATION

OVEN   PORCH

BRM. CL.   PANTRY   DN

SHELVES   MUD RM.   DN   GARDEN STOR.

PDR. RM.   BOOKS

DN

W D   CURB

LIVING RM.
13⁸ x 19⁴   FOYER   STUDY
9⁰ x 12⁰

CL.   UP

STOR.

FLOWER GARDEN

GARAGE
13⁸ x 22⁰+STORAGE

54' - 0"   42' - 0"

● This is certainly an authentic traditional salt-box. It features a symmetrical design with a center fireplace, a wide, paneled doorway and multi-paned, double-hung windows. Tucked behind the one-car garage is a garden shed which provides work and storage space. The breakfast room features French doors which open onto a flagstone terrace. The U-shaped kitchen has built-in counters which make efficient use of space. The upstairs plan houses three bedrooms.

Design T62616 1,415 Sq. Ft. - First Floor
1,106 Sq. Ft. - Second Floor; 36,880 Cu. Ft.

● Unlike the majority of the Salt Boxes of Colonial New England, this design has a distinguishing feature: a saw-tooth-shaped side wing that shares the same rear roofline as the house to which it was appended. History is exquisitely detailed in this exterior yet its floor plan has been planned to serve today's family conveniently.

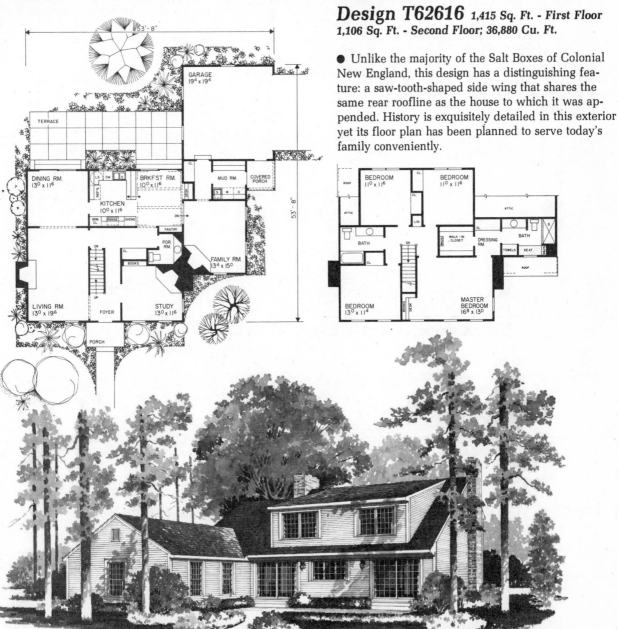

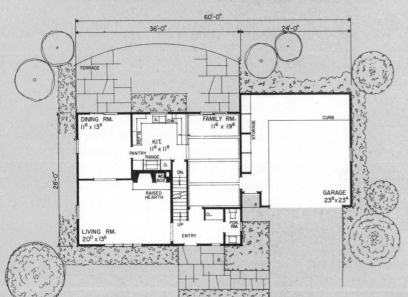

A Garrison type adaptation that projects all the romance of yesteryear. The narrow horizontal siding, the wide corner boards, the window detailing, the overhanging second floor and the massive, centered chimney help set this home apart.

Design T61849 1,008 Sq. Ft. - First Floor
1,080 Sq. Ft. - Second Floor; 31,153 Cu. Ft.

Design T62253 1,503 Sq. Ft. - First Floor; 1,291 Sq. Ft. - Second Floor; 44,260 Cu. Ft.

● The overhanging second floor sets the character of this Early American design. Study the features, both inside and out.

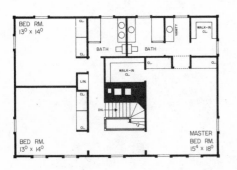

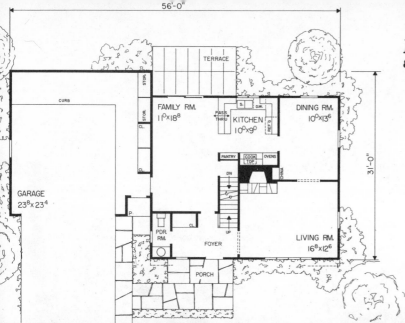

Design T61719 864 Sq. Ft. - First Floor
896 Sq. Ft. - Second Floor; 26,024 Cu. Ft.

● What an appealing low-cost Colonial adaptation. Most of the livability features generally found in the largest of homes are present to cater to family needs.

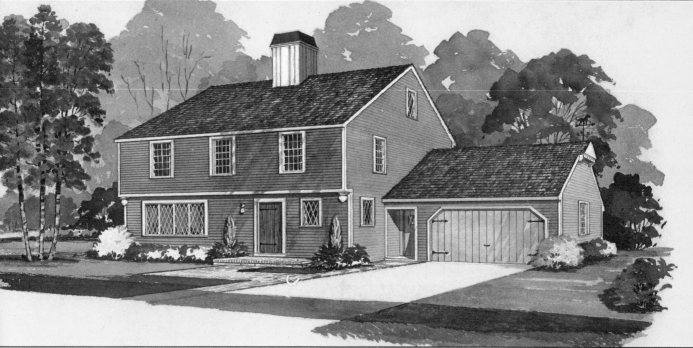

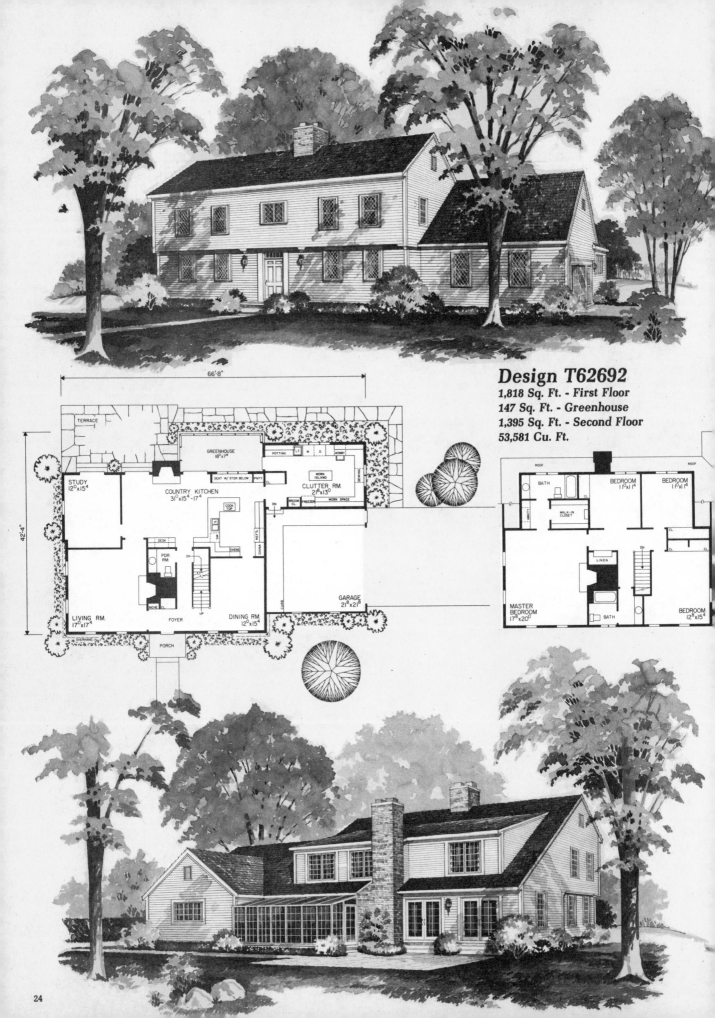

Design T62692

1,818 Sq. Ft. - First Floor
147 Sq. Ft. - Greenhouse
1,395 Sq. Ft. - Second Floor
53,581 Cu. Ft.

66'-8"

42'-4"

TERRACE

GREENHOUSE
18⁰x7⁸

SEAT w/ STOR BELOW

POTTING   LT   D

PNTY   CL

HOBBY

STUDY
12⁰x15⁴

COUNTRY KITCHEN
31⁰x15⁴-17⁴

WORK
ISLAND

CLUTTER RM.
21⁸x13⁰

COOK
TOP

DN

BROOM
CL

FREEZER

WORK SPACE

REF'G.

CHINA

DESK

OVENS

PDR.
RM.

DN

UP

NICHE   CL

LIVING RM.
17⁰x17⁴

FOYER

DINING RM.
12⁰x15⁴

CURB

GARAGE
21⁸x21⁸

OVERHANG

PORCH

ROOF   ROOF

BATH

BEDROOM
11⁰x11⁴

BEDROOM
11⁰x11⁴

VANITY

WALK-IN
CLOSET

CL

CL

CL

LINEN

DN

CL

MASTER
BEDROOM
17⁸x20⁰

BATH

BEDROOM
12⁸x15⁴

24

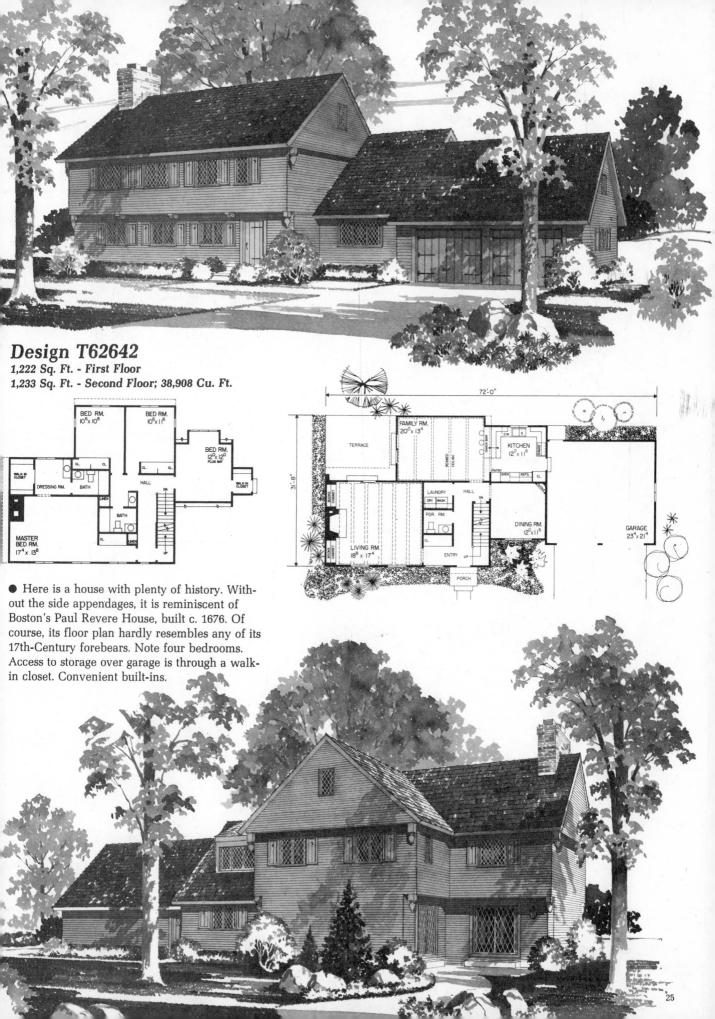

Design T62642

1,222 Sq. Ft. - First Floor
1,233 Sq. Ft. - Second Floor; 38,908 Cu. Ft.

BED RM.
10⁶ x 10⁸

BED RM.
10⁶ x 11⁶

BED RM.
12⁰ x 12⁰
PLUS BAY

WALK-IN
CLOSET

DRESSING RM.

BATH

CL.

CL.

HALL

DN

WALK-IN
CLOSET

LINEN

BATH

CL.

LINEN

UP

MASTER
BED RM.
17⁴ x 13⁸

CL.

● Here is a house with plenty of history. Without the side appendages, it is reminiscent of Boston's Paul Revere House, built c. 1676. Of course, its floor plan hardly resembles any of its 17th-Century forebears. Note four bedrooms. Access to storage over garage is through a walk-in closet. Convenient built-ins.

72'-0"

TERRACE

FAMILY RM.
20⁰ x 13⁴

BEAMED CEILING

SNACK BAR

DW   S

KITCHEN
12⁰ x 11⁶

RANGE

31'-8"

BOOK CABINET

PANTRY

OVEN   REFG.   CL.

BROOM

HALL

LAUNDRY

DRY   WASH

PDR. RM.

DN

DINING RM.
12⁰ x 11⁶

GARAGE
23⁴ x 21⁴

BOOK CABINET

LIVING RM.
18⁸ x 17⁴

CL.

ENTRY

UP

PORCH

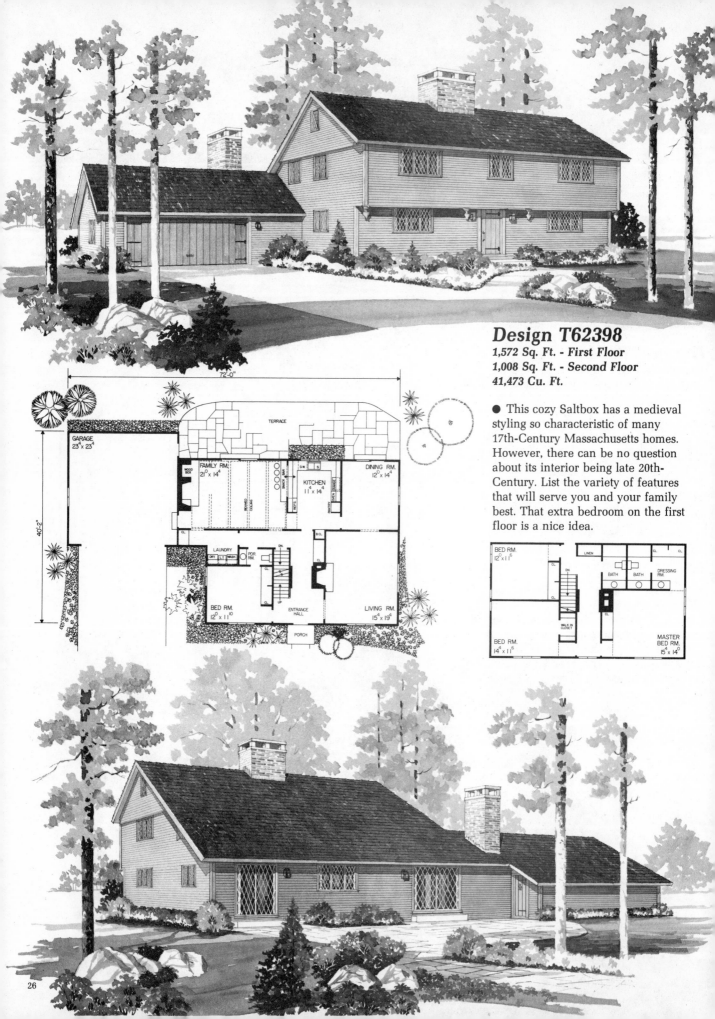

Design T62398

1,572 Sq. Ft. - First Floor
1,008 Sq. Ft. - Second Floor
41,473 Cu. Ft.

● This cozy Saltbox has a medieval styling so characteristic of many 17th-Century Massachusetts homes. However, there can be no question about its interior being late 20th-Century. List the variety of features that will serve you and your family best. That extra bedroom on the first floor is a nice idea.

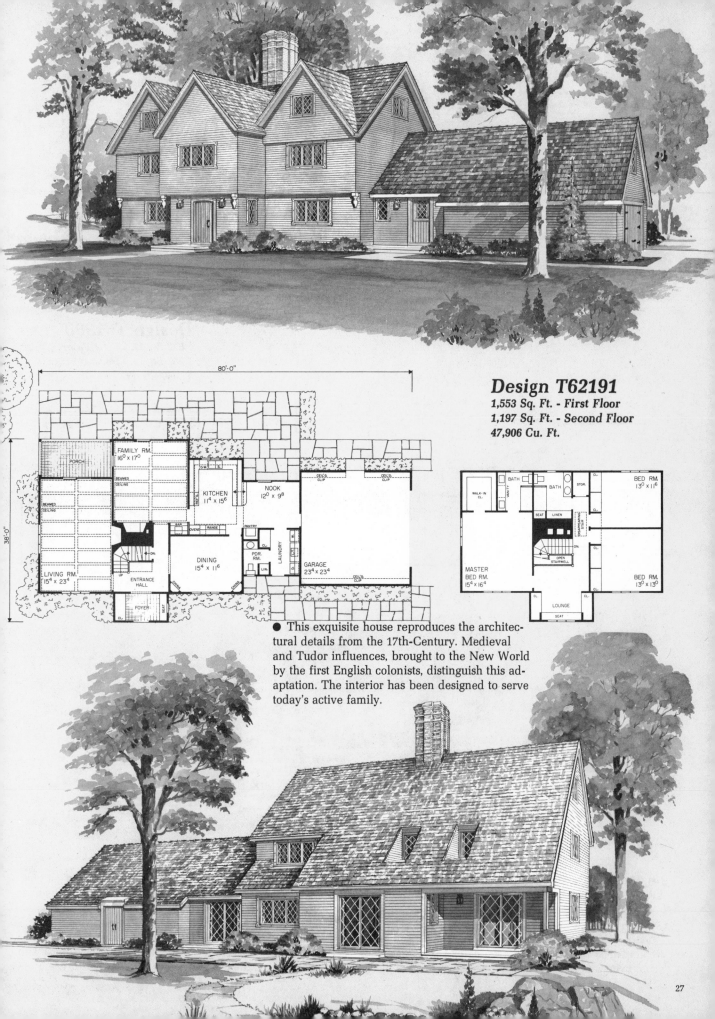

Design T62191

1,553 Sq. Ft. - First Floor
1,197 Sq. Ft. - Second Floor
47,906 Cu. Ft.

● This exquisite house reproduces the architectural details from the 17th-Century. Medieval and Tudor influences, brought to the New World by the first English colonists, distinguish this adaptation. The interior has been designed to serve today's active family.

First Floor

80'-0"
38'-0"

PORCH

FAMILY RM.
16⁰ x 17⁰
BEAMED CEILING

KITCHEN
11⁴ x 15⁶

NOOK
12⁰ x 9⁸

CEIL'G CLIP

CEIL'G CLIP

BEAMED CEILING

LIVING RM.
15⁴ x 23⁴

DINING
15⁴ x 11⁶

PANTRY

PDR. RM.

LAUNDRY

GARAGE
23⁴ x 23⁴

CEIL'G CLIP

ENTRANCE HALL

UP

FOYER

CL.

SEAT

Second Floor

WALK-IN CL.

BATH

BATH

STOR.

CL.

BED RM.
13⁰ x 11⁶

VANITY

SEAT

LINEN

MASTER BED RM.
15⁴ x 16⁴

OPEN STAIRWELL

DN.

CL.

BED RM.
13⁰ x 13⁰

LOUNGE

SEAT

CL.

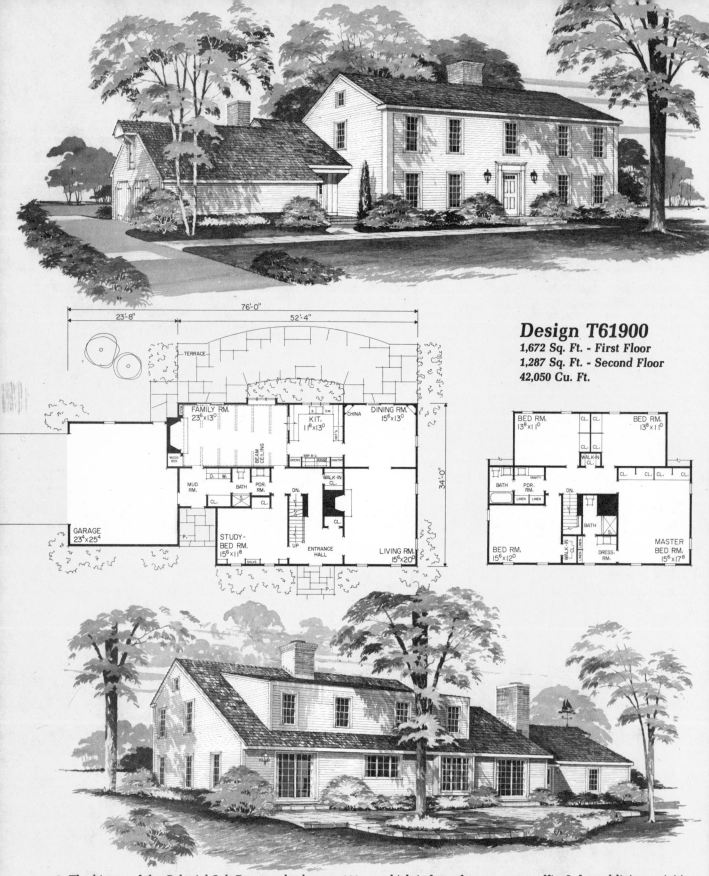

Design T61900

1,672 Sq. Ft. - First Floor
1,287 Sq. Ft. - Second Floor
42,050 Cu. Ft.

● The history of the Colonial Salt Box goes back some 200 years. This unusually authentic adaptation captures all the warmth and charm of the early days both inside as well as outside. To reflect today's living patterns, an up-dating of the floor plan was inevitable. The result is a room arrangement which will serve the active family wonderfully. Formal living and dining take place at one end of the house which is free of cross-room traffic. Informal living activities will center around the family room and expand through sliding glass doors to the terrace. The mud room area is strategically located and includes the laundry and a full bath. An extra study/bedroom supplements four bedrooms upstairs, all thoughtfully isolated from household noise and activity. Count the closets and the other storage areas.

Design T62731 1,039 Sq. Ft. - First Floor; 973 Sq. Ft - Second Floor; 29,740 Cu. Ft.

Windows highlight house with extras!

● The multi-paned windows with shutters of this two-story highlight the exterior delightfully. Inside the livability is ideal. Formal and informal areas are sure to serve your family with ease. Note efficient U-shaped kitchen with handy first-floor laundry. Sleeping facilities on second floor.

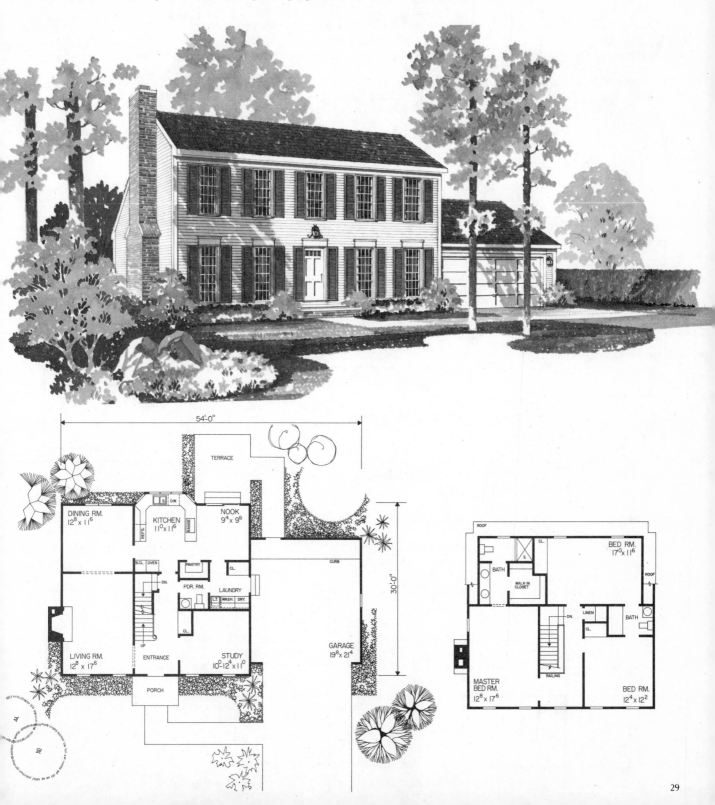

Design T62625
1,640 Sq. Ft. - First Floor
1,072 Sq. Ft. - Second Floor; 39,360 Cu. Ft.

● A 19th Century Farmhouse! So it might seem. But one with contemporary features . . . like the U-shaped kitchen with a built-in desk and appliances as well as a separate dining nook. Or the 20' by 13' family room. There, a beamed ceiling and raised-hearth fireplace add traditional warmth to a modern convention.

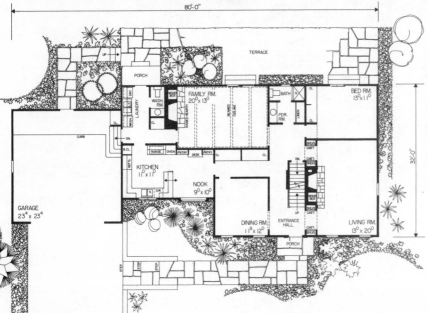

Design T61814 1,471 Sq. Ft. - First Floor
1,052 Sq. Ft. - Second Floor; 35,700 Cu. Ft.

● A Salt Box design that has all of the usual traditional exterior features. The interior shows what up-to-date floor planning can do inside the charm of yesteryear's exterior. A central entrance hall routes traffic directly to all major areas. The work area can be made to capture that cozy country kitchen atmosphere.

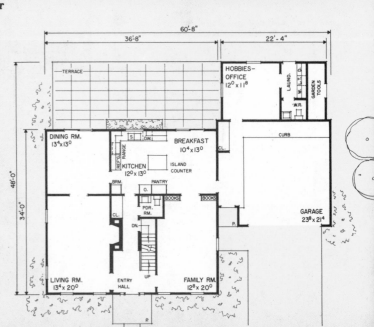

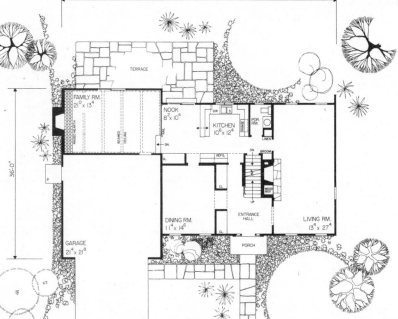

Design T62623
1,368 Sq. Ft. - First Floor
1,046 Sq. Ft. - Second Floor; 35,130 Cu. Ft.

● Take note of this four bedroom Salt Box design. Enter through the large entrance hall to enjoy this home. Imagine a living room 13 x 27 feet. Plus a family room. Both having a fireplace. Also, sliding glass doors in both the family room and nook leading to the rear terrace.

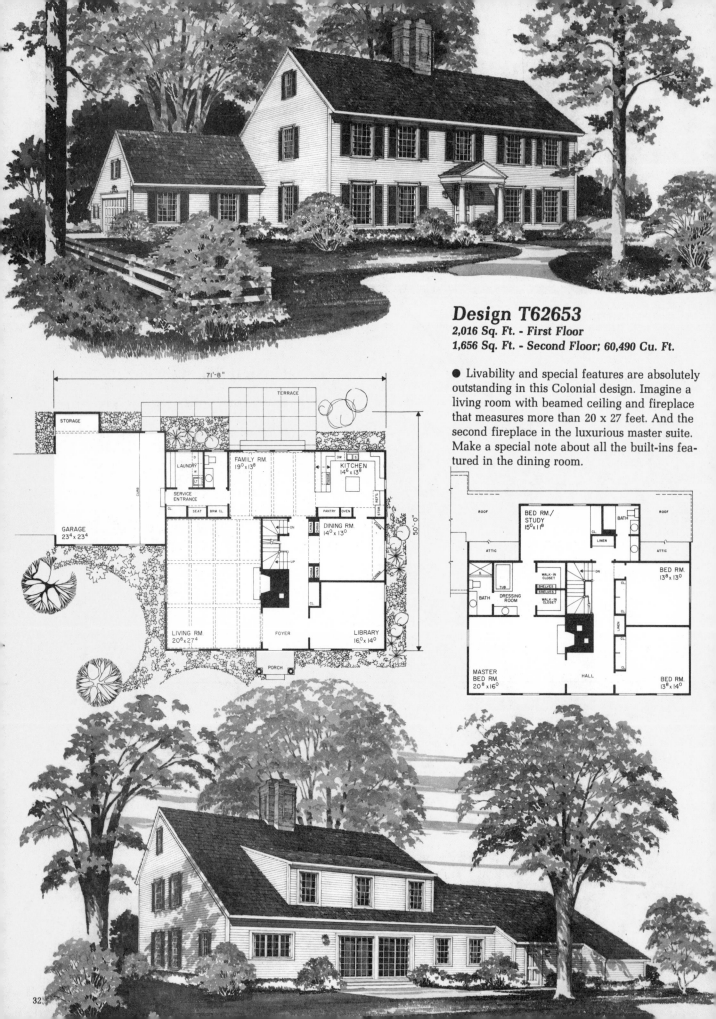

Design T62653

2,016 Sq. Ft. - First Floor
1,656 Sq. Ft. - Second Floor; 60,490 Cu. Ft.

● Livability and special features are absolutely
outstanding in this Colonial design. Imagine a
living room with beamed ceiling and fireplace
that measures more than 20 x 27 feet. And the
second fireplace in the luxurious master suite.
Make a special note about all the built-ins featured in the dining room.

First Floor Plan labels:

71'-8"

STORAGE

TERRACE

LAUNDRY

FAMILY RM.
19⁰ x 13⁸

KITCHEN
14⁶ x 13⁸

SERVICE
ENTRANCE

CL SEAT BRM CL

PANTRY OVEN

STOR.

REF'S.

GARAGE
23⁴ x 23⁴

50'-0"

DN

UP

CHINA

DINING RM.
14⁰ x 13⁰

CL

LIVING RM.
20⁸ x 27⁴

FOYER

LIBRARY
16⁰ x 14⁰

PORCH

Second Floor Plan labels:

ROOF

BED RM./
STUDY
15⁰ x 11⁸

BATH

ROOF

ATTIC

CL

LINEN

ATTIC

BATH

TUB

DRESSING
ROOM

WALK-IN
CLOSET

SHELVES

SHELVES

WALK-IN
CLOSET

DN

BED RM.
13⁸ x 13⁰

CL

CL

LINEN

CL

MASTER
BED RM.
20⁸ x 16⁰

HALL

BED RM.
13⁸ x 14⁰

Design T62666 *988 Sq. Ft. - First Floor*
1,147 Sq. Ft. - Second Floor; 35,490 Cu. Ft.

● A spacious country-kitchen highlights the interior of this two-story. Its features include an island work center, fireplace, beamed ceiling and sliding glass doors leading to the rear terrace. A washroom and a side door are only steps away. A second fireplace is in the large living room. It, too, has sliding glass doors in the rear.

Design T62733
1,177 Sq. Ft. - First Floor; 1,003 Sq. Ft. - Second Floor; 32,040 Cu. Ft.

● This is definitely a four bedroom Colonial with charm galore. The kitchen features an island range and other built-ins. All will enjoy the sunken family room with fireplace, which has sliding glass doors leading to the terrace. Also a basement for recreational activities with laundry remaining on first floor for extra convenience.

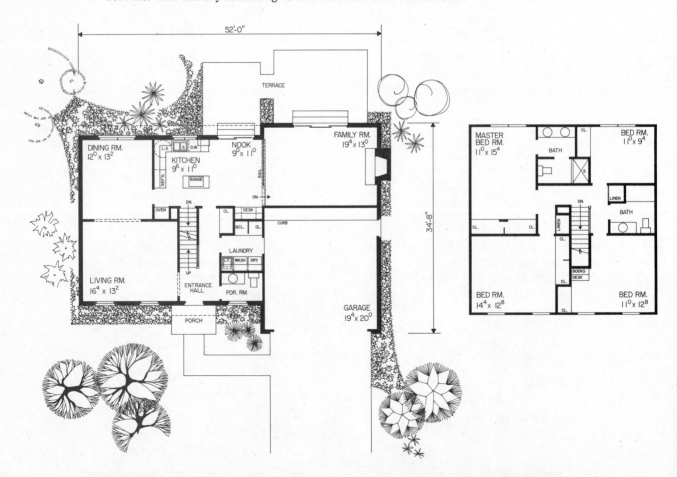

Design T62211
1,214 Sq. Ft. - First Floor; 1,146 Sq. Ft. - Second Floor: 32,752 Cu. Ft.

● The appeal of this Colonial home will be virtually everlasting. It will improve with age and service the growing family well. Imagine your family living here. There are four bedrooms, 2½ baths, plus plenty of first floor living space.

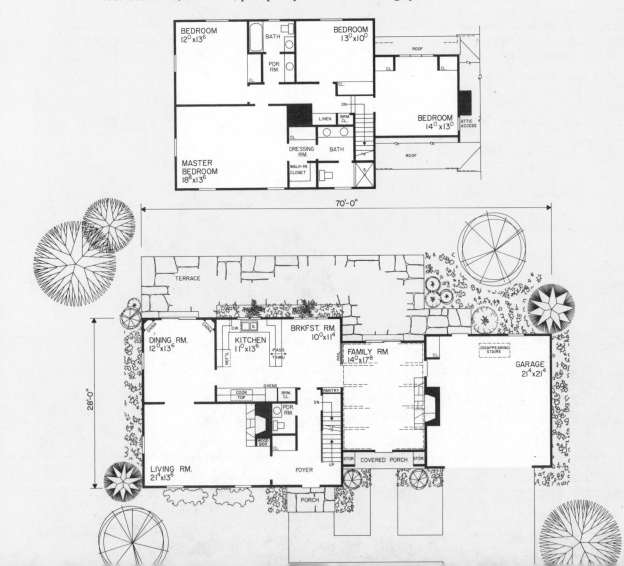

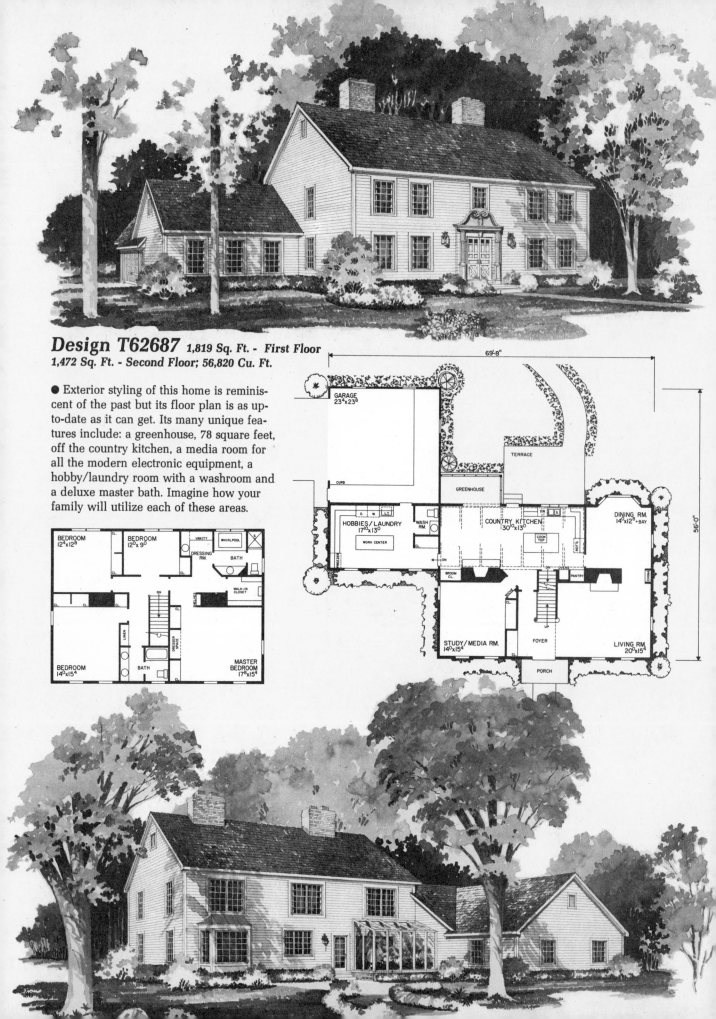

Design T62687
1,819 Sq. Ft. - First Floor
1,472 Sq. Ft. - Second Floor; 56,820 Cu. Ft.

● Exterior styling of this home is reminiscent of the past but its floor plan is as up-to-date as it can get. Its many unique features include: a greenhouse, 78 square feet, off the country kitchen, a media room for all the modern electronic equipment, a hobby/laundry room with a washroom and a deluxe master bath. Imagine how your family will utilize each of these areas.

Design T62521

1,272 Sq. Ft. - First Floor
1,139 Sq. Ft. - Second Floor; 37,262 Cu. Ft.

● Here is a house to remind one of the weather-beaten facades of Nantucket. The active family plan is as up-to-date as tomorrow. Along with formal and informal areas on the first floor, there is a music alcove. If a music alcove is not needed, this area would make an ideal intimate sitting area.

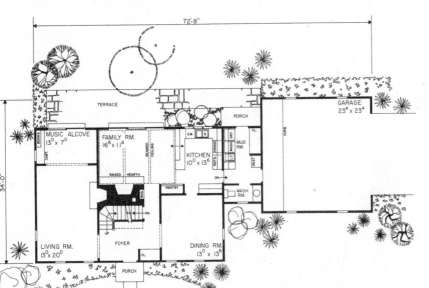

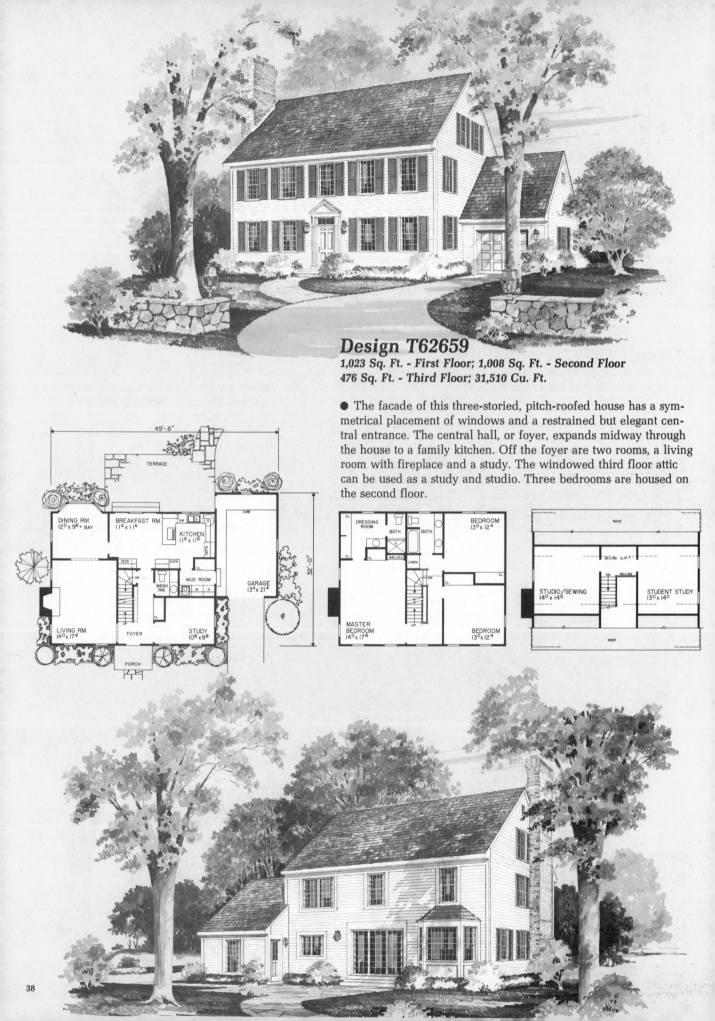

Design T62659

1,023 Sq. Ft. - First Floor; 1,008 Sq. Ft. - Second Floor
476 Sq. Ft. - Third Floor; 31,510 Cu. Ft.

● The facade of this three-storied, pitch-roofed house has a symmetrical placement of windows and a restrained but elegant central entrance. The central hall, or foyer, expands midway through the house to a family kitchen. Off the foyer are two rooms, a living room with fireplace and a study. The windowed third floor attic can be used as a study and studio. Three bedrooms are housed on the second floor.

Design T62649
1,501 Sq. Ft. - First Floor
1,280 Sq. Ft. - Second Floor; 43,537 Cu. Ft.

● This design's front exterior is highlighted by four pedimented nine-over-nine windows, five second-story eyebrow windows and a massive central chimney. Note the spacious kitchen of the interior. It is large in size and features an island range, pantry and broom closets, breakfast room with sliding glass doors to the rear porch and an adjacent laundry room which has access to the garage.

Design T62641

1,672 Sq. Ft. - First Floor
1,248 Sq. Ft. - Second Floor; 45,306 Cu. Ft.

● This Georgian adaptation is from the early 18th-Century and has plenty of historical background. The classical details are sedately stated. The plan promises up-to-date livability. The size of your site need not be large, either.

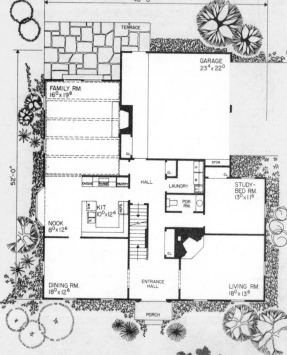

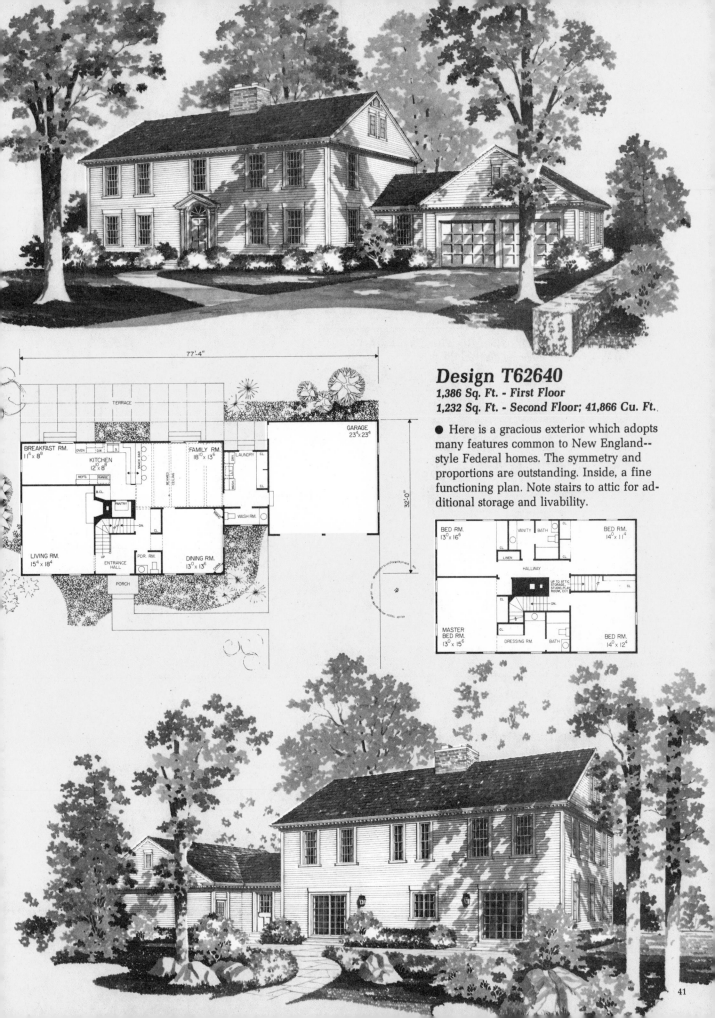

TERRACE

77'-4"

BREAKFAST RM.
11⁶ x 8⁸

KITCHEN
12⁰ x 8⁸

OVEN DW S

SNACK BAR

REFG. RANGE

B. CL.

PANTRY

DN.

UP

LIVING RM.
15⁴ x 18⁴

ENTRANCE HALL

PDR. RM.

PORCH

FAMILY RM.
18¹⁰ x 13⁶

BEAMED CEILING

LAUNDRY CL

WASH. D.

CL

WASH RM.

DINING RM.
13⁰ x 13⁶

CL

GARAGE
23⁴ x 23⁴

32'-0"

Design T62640

1,386 Sq. Ft. - First Floor
1,232 Sq. Ft. - Second Floor; 41,866 Cu. Ft.

● Here is a gracious exterior which adopts many features common to New England-- style Federal homes. The symmetry and proportions are outstanding. Inside, a fine functioning plan. Note stairs to attic for additional storage and livability.

BED RM.
13⁰ x 16⁶

VANITY BATH CL

LINEN

CL

BED RM.
14⁰ x 11⁴

CL

HALLWAY

UP TO ATTIC STORAGE, STUDIO, PLAY ROOM, ETC.

DN.

CL

MASTER BED RM.
13⁰ x 15⁶

CL

DRESSING RM.

BATH

BED RM.
14⁰ x 12⁴

Design T62840 1,529 Sq. Ft. - First Floor; 1,344 Sq. Ft. - Second Floor; 44,504 Cu. Ft.

● This traditional two-story home is super-insulated. The kitchen area has pass-thrus to a formal dining room and family room. All sleeping facilities – four bedrooms and two baths, are located on the second floor.

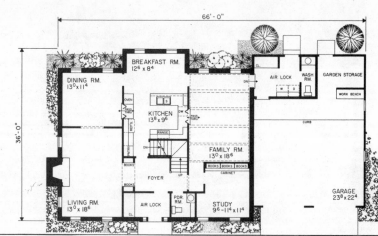

Design T62610 1,505 Sq. Ft. - First Floor; 1,344 Sq. Ft. - Second Floor; 45,028 Cu. Ft.

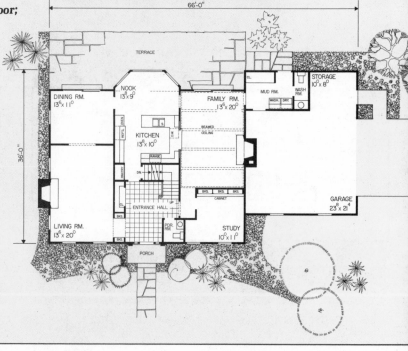

● This full two-story traditional features inviting front entrance detail, narrow horizontal siding, appealing corner boards, and two massive chimneys. The entrance hall is large with a powder room nearby. The kitchen has a pass-thru to the family room.

Design T62538 1,503 Sq. Ft. - First Floor; 1,095 Sq. Ft. - Second Floor; 44,321 Cu. Ft.

● This Salt Box is charming, indeed. The entry is open to the second floor balcony. For living areas, there is a study plus living and family rooms.

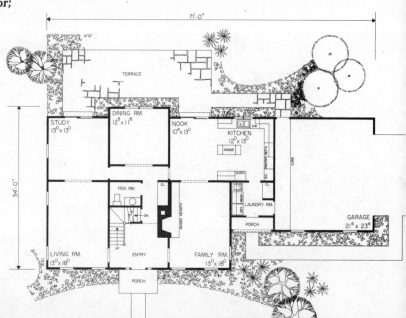

42

43

Design T62870 900 Sq. Ft. - First Floor
467 Sq. Ft. - Second Floor Left Suite
493 Sq. Ft. - Second Floor Right Suite; 35,970 Cu. Ft.

● This colonial home was designed to provide comfortable living space for two families. The first floor is the common living area, with all of the necessary living areas; the second floor has two two-bedroom-one-bath suites. Built-ins are featured in the smaller bedroom.

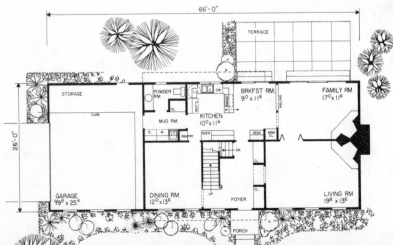

Design T62799 1,196 Sq. Ft. - First Floor
780 Sq. Ft. - Second Floor; 35,080 Cu. Ft.

● This two-story traditional design's facade with its narrow clapboards, punctuated by tall multi-paned windows, appears deceptively expansive. Yet the entire length of the house, including the garage, is 66 feet.

TWO-STORY
GAMBREL ROOF VARIATIONS

Gambrels punctuate the charm of the Early Colonial period with pleasing proportion and fine detailing. Although linked to the Dutch, the Gambrel Roof actually was introduced in America by the English and the Swedes who first built it in Pennsylvania. The French probably originated it.

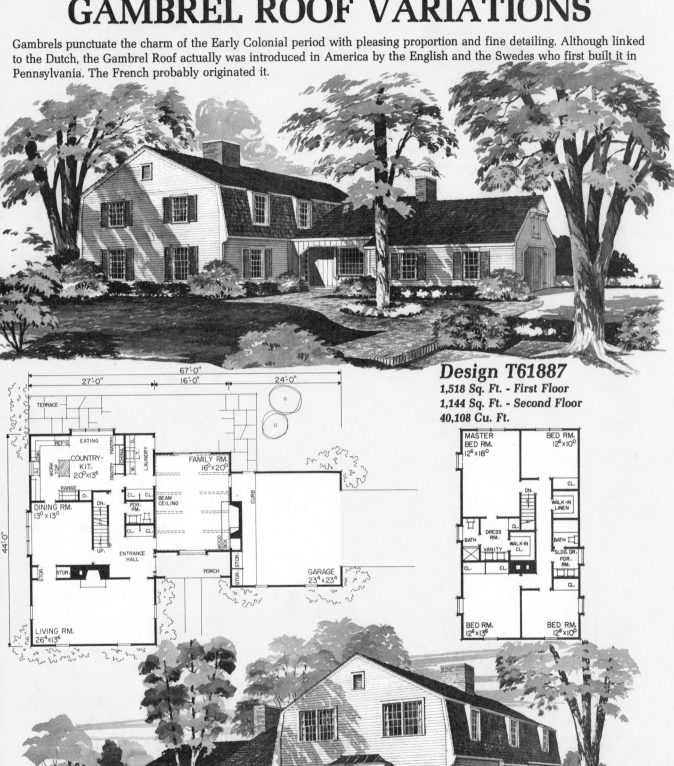

Design T61887
1,518 Sq. Ft. - First Floor
1,144 Sq. Ft. - Second Floor
40,108 Cu. Ft.

● This Gambrel roof Colonial is steeped in history. And well it should be, for its pleasing proportions are a delight to the eye. The various roof planes, the window treatment, and the rambling nature of the entire house revive a picture of rural New England.

The covered porch protects the front door which opens into a spacious entrance hall. Traffic then flows in an orderly fashion to the end living room, the separate dining room, the cozy family room, and to the spacious country-kitchen. There is a first floor

laundry, plenty of coat closets, and a handy powder room. Two fireplaces enliven the decor of the living areas. Upstairs there is an exceptional master bedroom layout, and abundant storage. Note the walk-in closets.

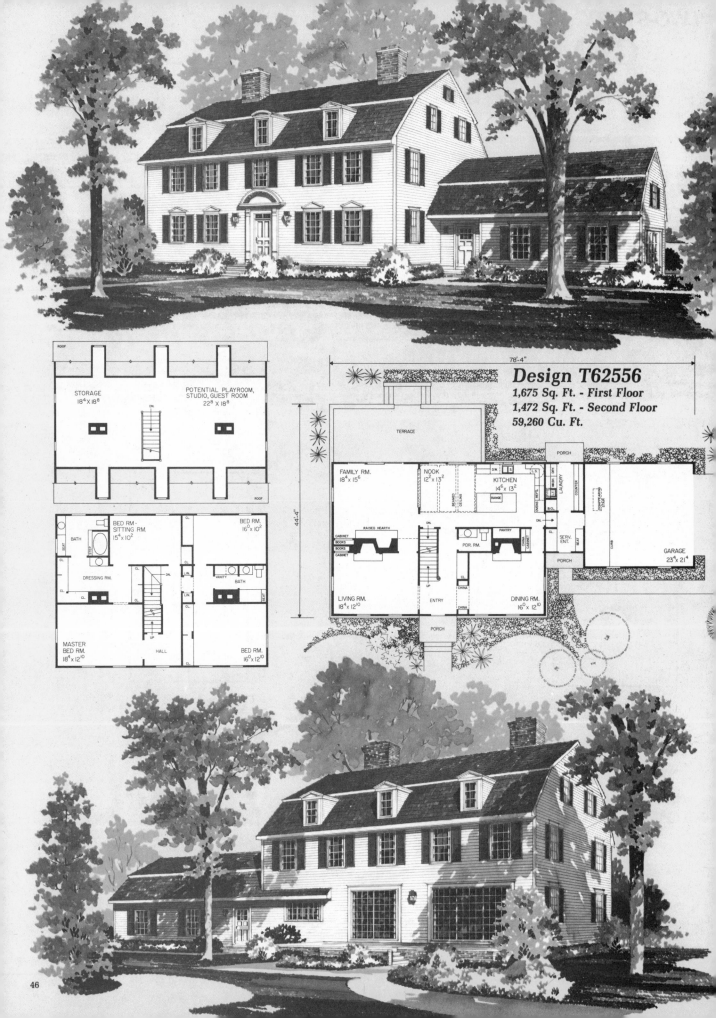

ROOF

STORAGE
18⁴ x 18⁸

POTENTIAL PLAYROOM,
STUDIO, GUEST ROOM
22⁸ x 18⁸

DN.

ROOF

BATH

BED RM.-
SITTING RM.
15⁴ x 10²

BED RM.
16⁰ x 10²

CL

CL

CL

DRESSING RM.

DN.

VANITY

BATH

CL

LIN.

CL

LIN.

CL

SEAT

DN.

UP

MASTER
BED RM.
18⁴ x 12¹⁰

HALL

BED RM.
16⁰ x 12¹⁰

78'-4"

Design T62556

1,675 Sq. Ft. - First Floor
1,472 Sq. Ft. - Second Floor
59,260 Cu. Ft.

TERRACE

44'-4"

PORCH

FAMILY RM.
18⁴ x 15⁶

NOOK
12² x 13²

KITCHEN
14⁶ x 13²

D.W.

RANGE

OVENS

REFG.

L.S.

WASH.

DRY.

LAUNDRY

B.CL.

COUNTER

SERV.
ENT.

SEAT

GARAGE
23⁴ x 21⁴

CABINET
BOOKS
BOOKS
CABINET

RAISED HEARTH

DN.

PDR. RM.

PANTRY

CHINA
CABINET

DN.

CL

PORCH

LIVING RM.
18⁴ x 12¹⁰

UP

ENTRY

CHINA

CHINA

DINING RM.
16⁰ x 12¹⁰

PORCH

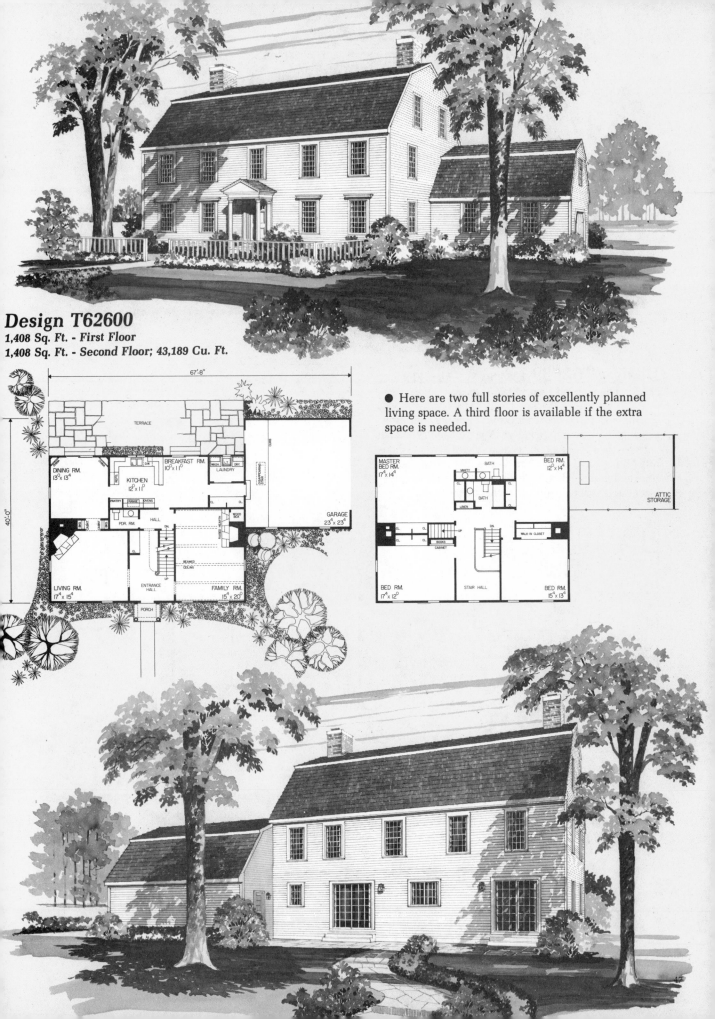

Design T62600
1,408 Sq. Ft. - First Floor
1,408 Sq. Ft. - Second Floor; 43,189 Cu. Ft.

● Here are two full stories of excellently planned living space. A third floor is available if the extra space is needed.

67'-8"

40'-0"

TERRACE

DINING RM.
13⁰ x 13⁴

KITCHEN
12' x 11⁰

BREAKFAST RM.
10⁰ x 11⁰

LAUNDRY

WASH. DRY.

PANTRY RANGE OVENS

PDR. RM.

HALL

WOOD BOX

RAISED HEARTH

GARAGE
23⁴ x 23⁴

LIVING RM.
17⁴ x 15⁴

ENTRANCE HALL

BEAMED CEILING

FAMILY RM.
15' x 20⁰

PORCH

MASTER BED RM.
17' x 14⁴

VANITY

BATH

BATH

LINEN

BED RM.
12⁰ x 14⁴

ATTIC STORAGE

BOOKS
CABINET

UP

DN

WALK IN CLOSET

BED RM.
17⁴ x 12⁰

STAIR HALL

BED RM.
15⁴ x 13⁴

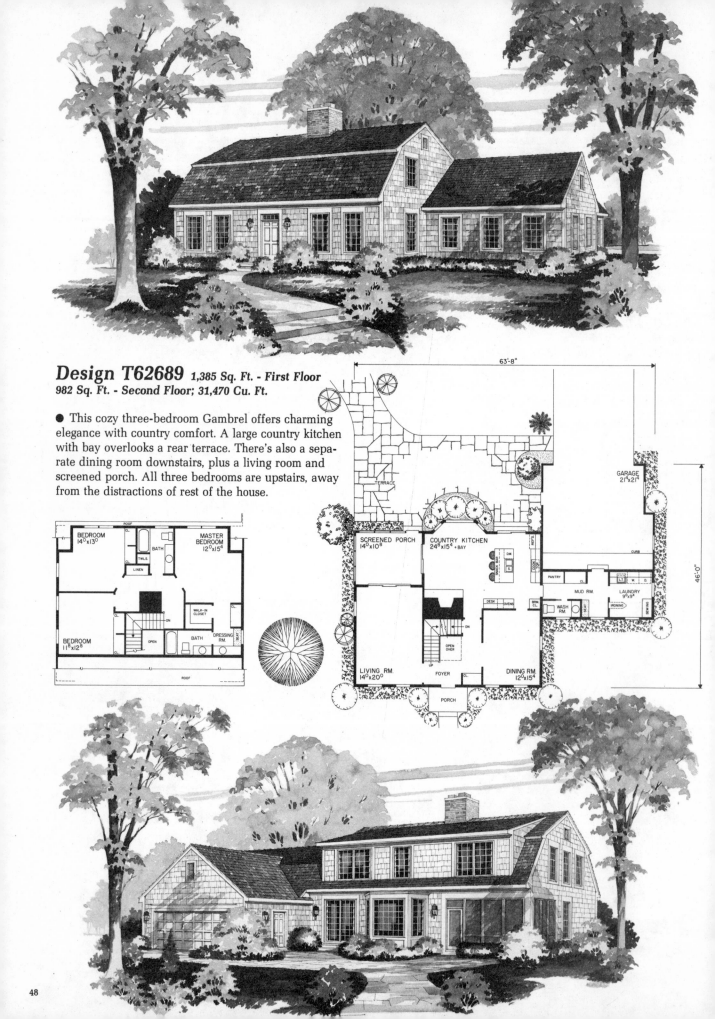

Design T62689 1,385 Sq. Ft. - First Floor
982 Sq. Ft. - Second Floor; 31,470 Cu. Ft.

● This cozy three-bedroom Gambrel offers charming elegance with country comfort. A large country kitchen with bay overlooks a rear terrace. There's also a separate dining room downstairs, plus a living room and screened porch. All three bedrooms are upstairs, away from the distractions of rest of the house.

BEDROOM 14⁰x13⁰

MASTER BEDROOM 12⁰x15⁴

BATH

TWLS.

LINEN

BEDROOM 11⁶x12⁸

WALK-IN CLOSET

BATH

DRESSING RM.

OPEN

DN

CL

CL

CL

SEAT

ROOF

ROOF

63'-8"

TERRACE

SCREENED PORCH 14⁰x10⁸

COUNTRY KITCHEN 24⁸x15⁴ + BAY

GARAGE 21⁴x21⁴

CURB

PANTRY

MUD RM.

LAUNDRY 9⁰x9⁴

WASH RM.

SEAT

IRONING

SEWING

DESK

OVENS

DW

REF'G.

LT.

W.

D.

DN

OPEN OVER

UP

LIVING RM. 14⁰x20⁰

FOYER

DINING RM. 12⁰x15⁴

PORCH

46'-0"

Design T62652
1,728 Sq. Ft. - First Floor
1,335 Sq. Ft. - Second Floor; 47,760 Cu. Ft.

● This two-story Gambrel has features that will delight all.
Note the corner fireplace in the living room and the second
fireplace in the large breakfast room which has sliding glass
doors to the terrace.

Floor plan labels (first floor)

- TERRACE
- 69'-8"
- 40'-0"
- BREAKFAST RM. 13⁸ x 12⁶
- KITCHEN 12⁰ x 13⁶
- DW
- RANGE
- COVERED PORCH
- LAUNDRY RM.
- D
- W
- LT
- REFG.
- GARAGE 21⁴ x 21⁴
- SERVICE ENTRANCE
- CURB
- CL.
- RAISED HEARTH
- DESK OVEN PANTRY
- POWDER RM.
- CL.
- DN
- UP
- ENTRY
- FAMILY RM. 16⁴ x 21⁶
- RM.

Floor plan labels (second floor)

- BATH
- BATH
- S
- BED RM. 14⁰ x 12⁶
- SHELVES
- WALK-IN CLOSET
- DRESSING ROOM
- WALK-IN CLOSET
- WALK-IN CLOSET
- DN
- CL.
- LINEN
- MASTER BED RM. 22⁸ x 15⁶
- BED RM. 14⁰ x 15⁶
- CL.

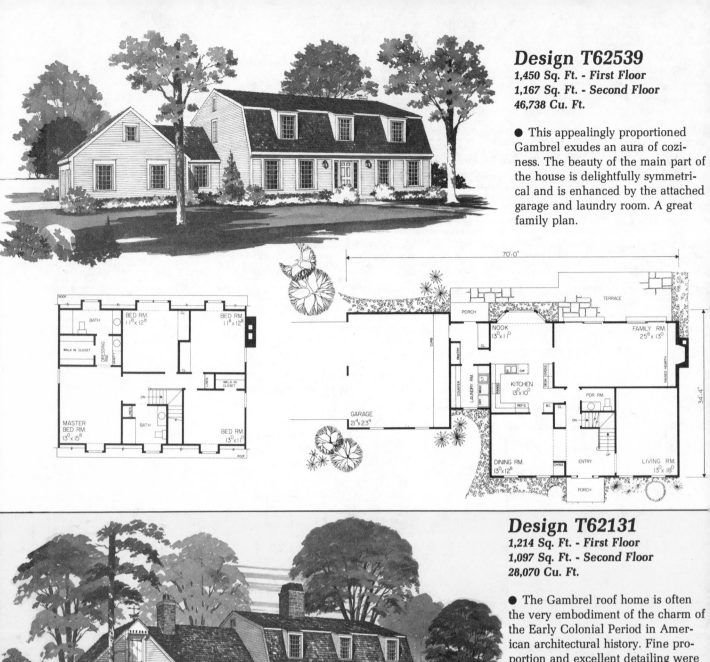

Design T62539
1,450 Sq. Ft. - First Floor
1,167 Sq. Ft. - Second Floor
46,738 Cu. Ft.

● This appealingly proportioned Gambrel exudes an aura of coziness. The beauty of the main part of the house is delightfully symmetrical and is enhanced by the attached garage and laundry room. A great family plan.

Design T62131
1,214 Sq. Ft. - First Floor
1,097 Sq. Ft. - Second Floor
28,070 Cu. Ft.

● The Gambrel roof home is often the very embodiment of the charm of the Early Colonial Period in American architectural history. Fine proportion and excellent detailing were the hallmarks of the era. Study the interior.

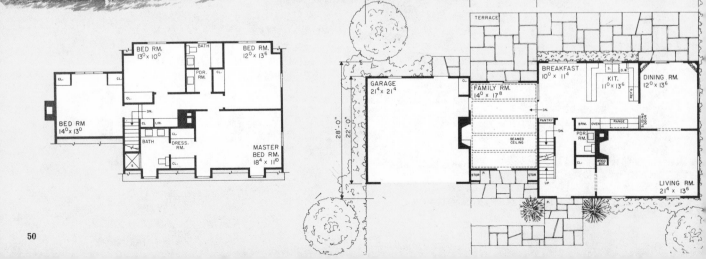

Design T61986

896 Sq. Ft. - First Floor
1,148 Sq. Ft. - Second Floor
28,840 Cu. Ft.

● This Gambrel roof design spells charm wherever it may be situated - far out in the country, or on a busy thoroughfare. Compact and economical to build, it will be easy on the budget. There's a full basement, too.

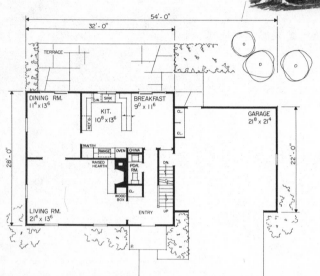

Design T62617

1,223 Sq. Ft. - First Floor
1,018 Sq. Ft. - Second Floor
30,784 Cu. Ft.

● Another Gambrel roof version just loaded with charm. Notice the delightful symmetry of the window treatment. Inside, the large family will enjoy all the features that assure convenient living. The end-living room will have excellent privacy.

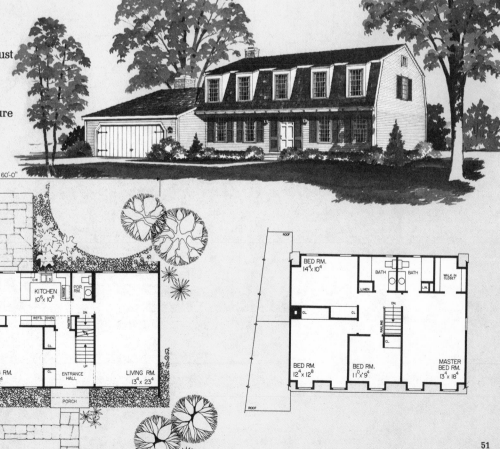

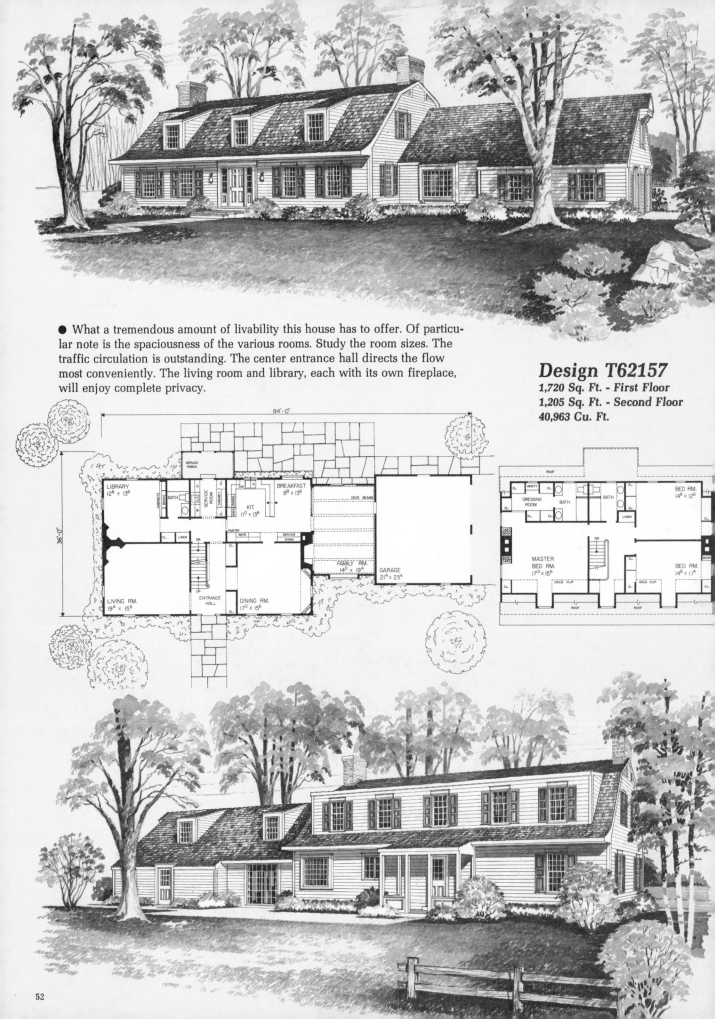

● What a tremendous amount of livability this house has to offer. Of particular note is the spaciousness of the various rooms. Study the room sizes. The traffic circulation is outstanding. The center entrance hall directs the flow most conveniently. The living room and library, each with its own fireplace, will enjoy complete privacy.

Design T62157
1,720 Sq. Ft. - First Floor
1,205 Sq. Ft. - Second Floor
40,963 Cu. Ft.

Design T62320 1,856 Sq. Ft. - First Floor; 1,171 Sq. Ft. - Second Floor; 46,699 Cu. Ft.

● A charming Colonial adaptation with a Gambrel roof front exterior and a Salt Box rear. The focal point of family activities will be the spacious family kitchen with its beamed ceiling and fireplace. Blueprints include details for both three and four bedroom options. In addition to the family kitchen, note the family room with beamed ceiling and fireplace. Don't miss the study with built-in bookshelves and cabinets.

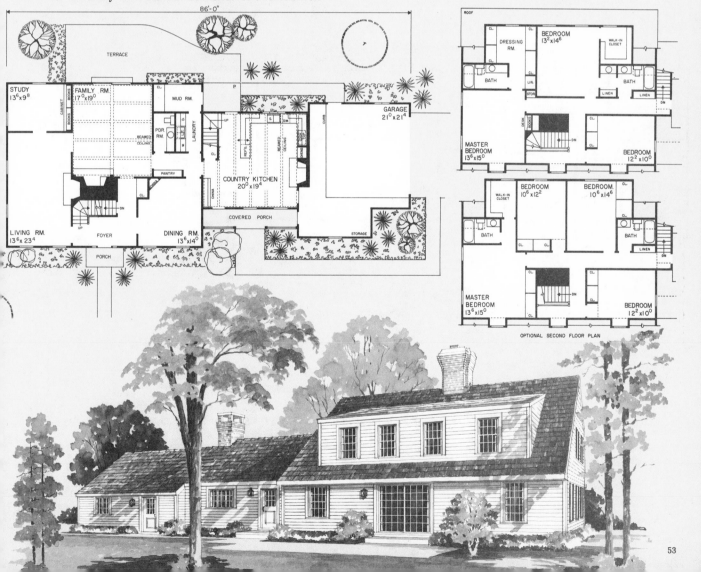

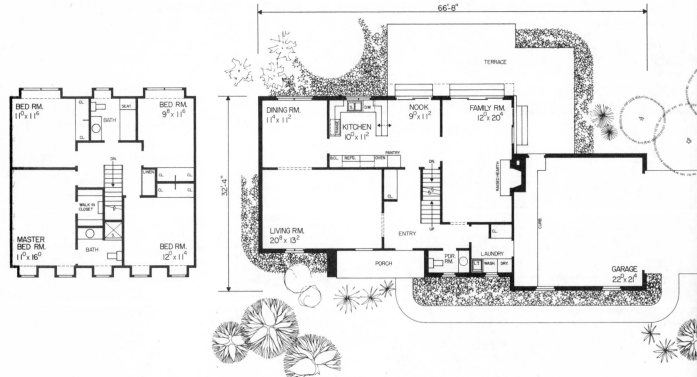

Design T62751 *1,202 Sq. Ft. - First Floor; 964 Sq. Ft. - Second Floor; 33,830 Cu. Ft.*

● This Gambrel-roof version of a Colonial home is sure to serve your family efficiently. The U-shaped kitchen with pass-thru to breakfast nook will be very convenient to the busy homemaker. There are also many built-ins to help ease kitchen duties. The nook and family room have sliding glass doors to the terrace. Notice that all four bedrooms are located on the second floor, away from the rest of household activity.

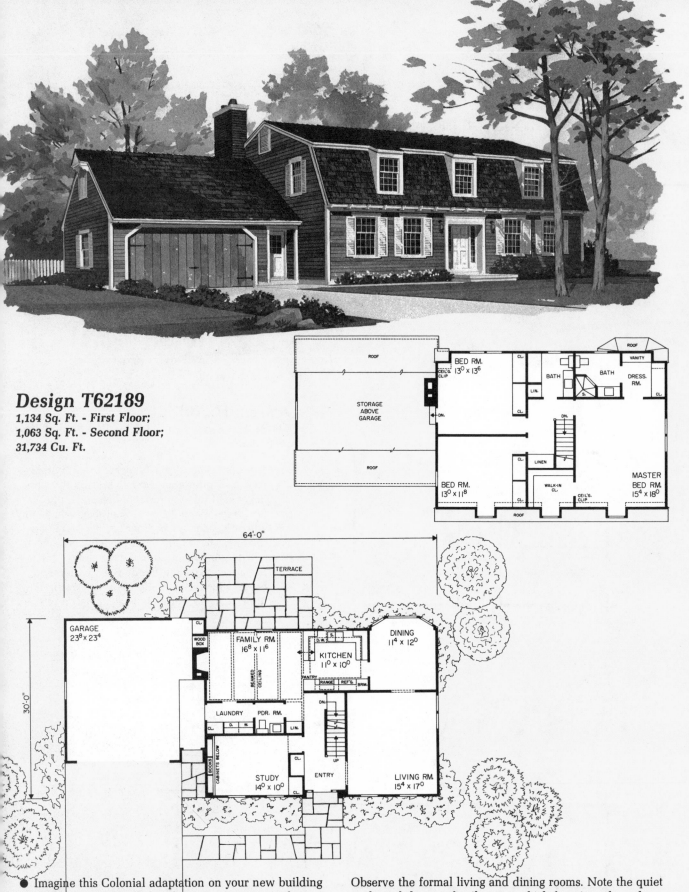

Design T62189

1,134 Sq. Ft. - First Floor;
1,063 Sq. Ft. - Second Floor;
31,734 Cu. Ft.

ROOF

STORAGE ABOVE GARAGE

ROOF

BED RM.
13⁰ x 13⁶

CEIL'G. CLIP

CL.

DN.

LIN.

BATH

BATH

VANITY

DRESS. RM.

CL.

DN.

CL.

CL.

LINEN

WALK-IN CL.

CEIL'G. CLIP

ROOF

BED RM.
13⁰ x 11⁸

MASTER BED RM.
15⁴ x 18⁰

64'-0"

30'-0"

TERRACE

GARAGE
23⁸ x 23⁴

CL.

WOOD BOX

FAMILY RM.
16⁸ x 11⁶

BEAMED CEILING

KITCHEN
11⁰ x 10⁰

S.

PANTRY

RANGE | REF'G. | BRM.

DINING
11⁴ x 12⁰

DN.

LAUNDRY

CL. | D. | W.

PDR. RM.

LIN.

BOOKS | CABINETS BELOW

CL.

DN.

UP

ENTRY

STUDY
14⁰ x 10⁰

CL.

LIVING RM.
15⁴ x 17⁰

● Imagine this Colonial adaptation on your new building site! The symmetry and the pleasing proportion make it a wonderful addition to the local scene. The recessed entrances add an extra measure of appeal. Inside there is a superabundance of features. While each family member will probably have his own favorite set of highlights, all will surely agree that the living patterns will be just great.

Observe the formal living and dining rooms. Note the quiet study and the rear family room which functions through sliding glass doors with the outdoor terrace. Don't miss the efficient kitchen, the separate laundry, and extra powder room. The second floor is not to be overlooked. Particularly the master bedroom. Bedrooms are upstairs, screened from household activity. Further, there is a full basement.

Design T62897

1,648 Sq. Ft. - First Floor; 1,140 Sq. Ft. - Second Floor
33,655 Cu. Ft.

● Second-story dormers pierce the gambrel roof for comfortable window seats in the sleeping area of this comfortable home. An upper family room and all three bedrooms – including a luxurious master bedroom suite, are located upstairs. There's plenty of livability downstairs with a living room, formal dining room, breakfast area, study, and family room with raised hearth. Good zoning allows smooth traffic flow throughout the house.

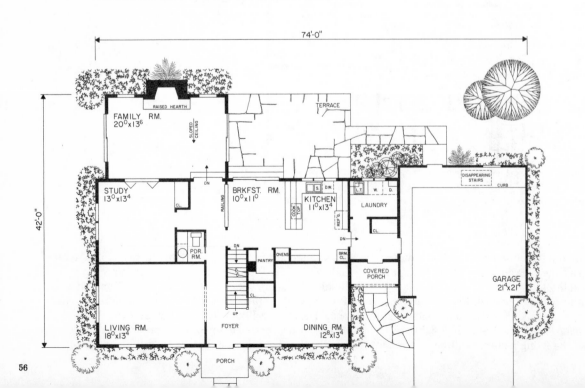

Design T62891
1,405 Sq. Ft. - First Floor
1,226 Sq. Ft. - Second Floor; 39,122 Cu. Ft.

● Here is a charming two-story house with a Gambrel roof that is very appealing. Entering this home, you will find a large dining room to the right which precedes an efficient kitchen. The adjacent breakfast room makes serving meals easy. The nice sized living room has a fireplace as does the family room. A wet bar and sliding glass doors are also in the family room. A powder room and laundry are on the first floor, too. Upstairs, you will find two bedrooms, a bath and a master bedroom suite with walk-in closet, tub and shower. Note that the second floor hall is open to the first floor.

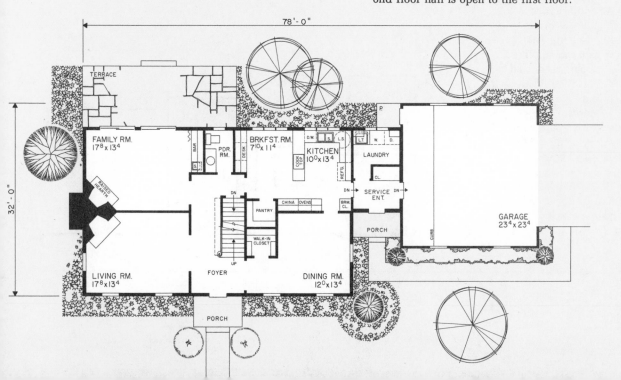

Design T61777

1,142 Sq. Ft. - First Floor
1,010 Sq. Ft. - Second Floor
28,095 Cu. Ft.

● This charming four-bedroom home with Gambrel roof offers plenty of comfort for today's family. Distinctions in its design include an attached family room unit and two-car garage. Our design obviously is patterned after an authentic Early American favorite. The main floor also includes an efficient kitchen, large breakfast room, and a dining room. A spacious living room features a raised-hearth fireplace for cozy gatherings. All four bedrooms are located upstairs, a zoning feature that allows quiet and isolation from traffic patterns of the rest of the household. The master bedroom includes its own bath, dressing room, and three dormer windows that pierce the Gambrel roof line. The fourth bedroom at one end of the house would convert into a very comfortable study. Notice also how the wide vertical siding of this house contrasts delightfully with the narrow horizontal siding. This home is a charmer!

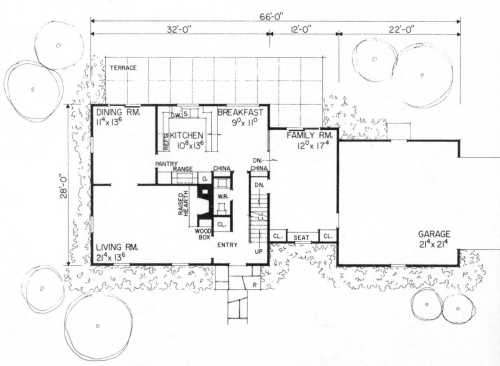

Design T62531 *1353 Sq. Ft. First Floor*
1,208 Sq. Ft. - Second Floor; 33,225 Cu. Ft.

● This design has its roots in the early history of New England. While its exterior is decidedly and purposely dated, the interior reflects an impressive 20th-Century floor plan. All of the elements are present to guarantee outstanding living patterns for today's large, active family. The convenient kitchen includes a nook, in addition to a dining room. There's a spacious living room with fireplace in front, in addition to a family room with beamed ceiling and fireplace in the rear. Four bedrooms, including a master bedroom suite, are located upstairs. Note the charming dormer windows cut into the roof line.

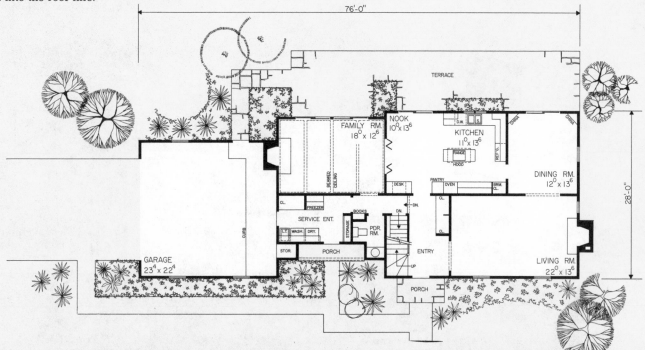

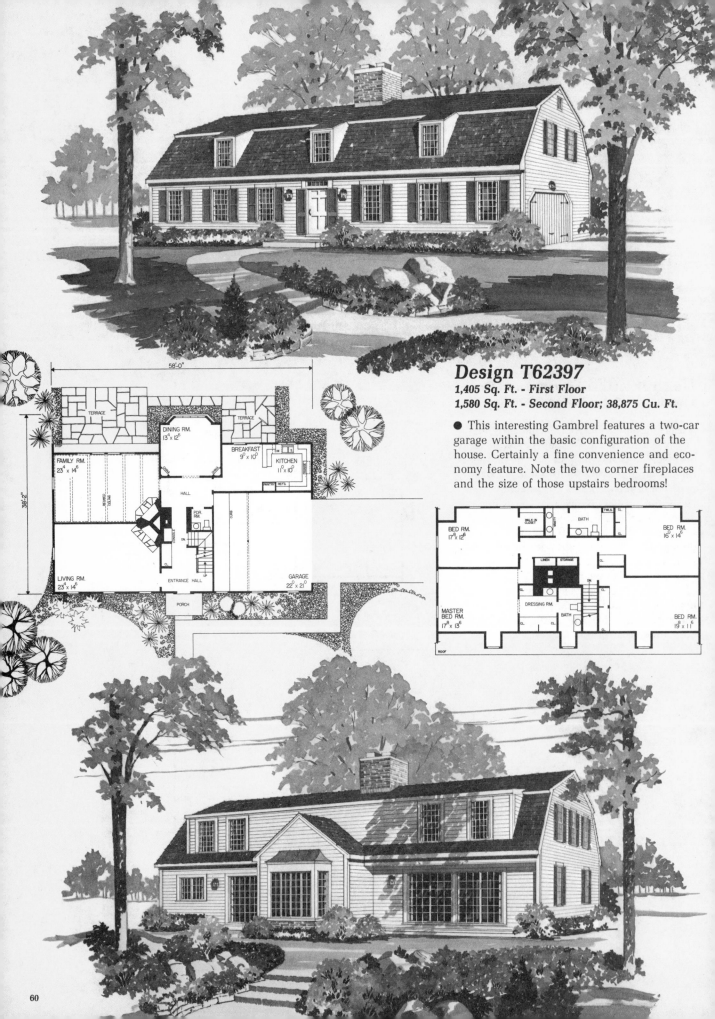

Design T62397
1,405 Sq. Ft. - First Floor
1,580 Sq. Ft. - Second Floor; 38,875 Cu. Ft.

● This interesting Gambrel features a two-car garage within the basic configuration of the house. Certainly a fine convenience and economy feature. Note the two corner fireplaces and the size of those upstairs bedrooms!

58'-0"

38'-2"

TERRACE

DINING RM.
13'⁴ x 12'⁶

TERRACE

FAMILY RM.
23'⁴ x 14'⁶

BREAKFAST
9'² x 10'⁰

KITCHEN
11'⁰ x 10'⁰

PANTRY REFG.

HALL

FOR. RM.

LIVING RM.
23'⁴ x 14'⁶

DN

UP

CL

ENTRANCE HALL

GARAGE
22' x 21'⁰

PORCH

BED RM.
17'⁶ x 12'⁶

WALK-IN CLOSET

PANTRY

BATH

TWLS CL

BED RM.
15'⁰ x 14'⁰

LINEN STORAGE

CL

MASTER BED RM.
17'⁸ x 13'⁶

DRESSING RM.

DN

BATH

BED RM.
19'⁸ x 11'⁰

CL

CL

ROOF

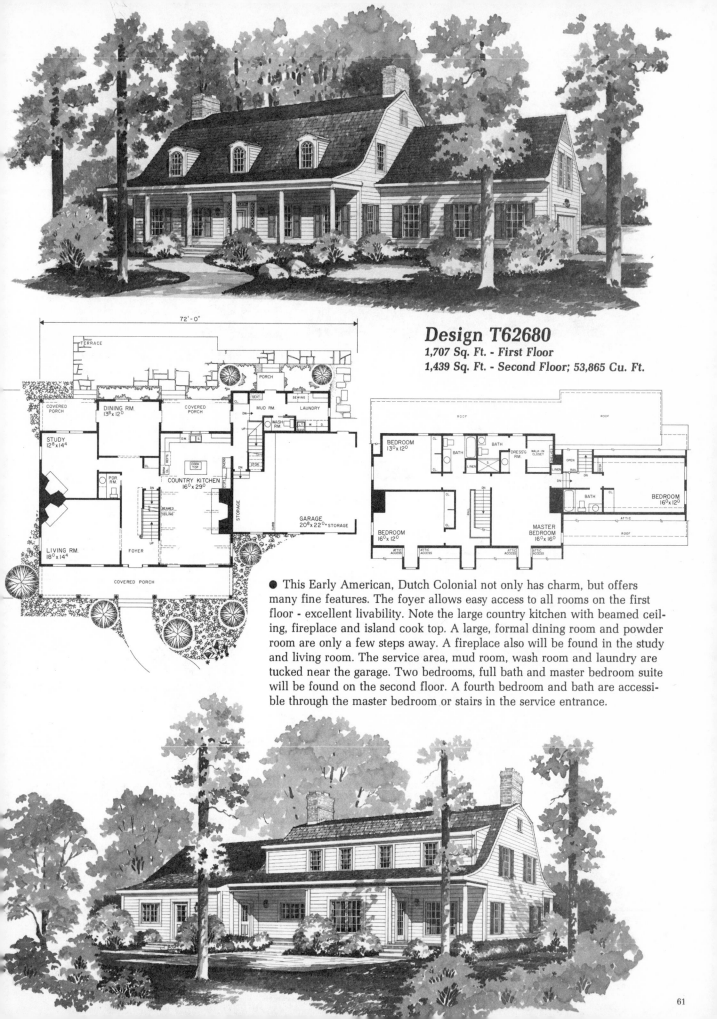

Design T62680
1,707 Sq. Ft. - First Floor
1,439 Sq. Ft. - Second Floor; 53,865 Cu. Ft.

● This Early American, Dutch Colonial not only has charm, but offers many fine features. The foyer allows easy access to all rooms on the first floor - excellent livability. Note the large country kitchen with beamed ceiling, fireplace and island cook top. A large, formal dining room and powder room are only a few steps away. A fireplace also will be found in the study and living room. The service area, mud room, wash room and laundry are tucked near the garage. Two bedrooms, full bath and master bedroom suite will be found on the second floor. A fourth bedroom and bath are accessible through the master bedroom or stairs in the service entrance.

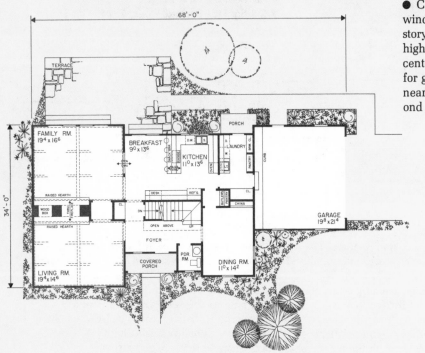

68'-0"

34'-0"

TERRACE

FAMILY RM.
19⁴ x 16⁶

BREAKFAST
9⁰ x 13⁶

PORCH

KITCHEN
11⁰ x 13⁶

LAUNDRY

RAISED HEARTH

WOOD BOX

RAISED HEARTH

DESK

REF'G.

CL.

CHINA

OPEN ABOVE

UP

DN

FOYER

LIVING RM.
19⁴ x 14⁶

COVERED PORCH

PDR. RM.

DINING RM.
11⁰ x 14²

GARAGE
19⁸ x 21⁴

● Clapboard siding and shuttered, multi-paned windows create the delightful detailing of this two-story gambrel. Beamed ceilings and a thru-fireplace highlight the living and family rooms. The work centers, kitchen and laundry, are clustered together for greater convenience. The formal dining room is nearby to make the serving of meals easy. The second floor houses all of the sleeping facilities.

BEDROOM
11⁸ x 13⁸

ROOF

ATTIC

BATH

CL.

ROOF

MASTER BEDROOM
15⁰ x 13⁶

ATTIC

STORAGE

CL.

CL.

ATTIC

CL.

LINEN

LINEN

OPEN

CL.

BATH

CL.

ROOF

BEDROOM
11⁸ x 11⁸

ROOF

ATTIC

Design T62632
1,460 Sq. Ft. - First Floor
912 Sq. Ft. - Second Floor; 39,205 Cu. Ft.

Design T62907 *1,546 Sq. Ft. - First Floor; 1,144 Sq. Ft. - Second Floor; 40,750 Cu. Ft.*

● This traditional L-shaped farmhouse is charming, indeed, with gambrel roof, dormer windows, and covered porch supported by slender columns and side rails. A spacious country kitchen with a bay provides a cozy gathering place for family and friends, as well as convenient place for food preparation with its central work island and size. There's a formal dining room also adjacent to the kitchen. A rear family room features its own fireplace, as does a large living room in the front. All four bedrooms are isolated upstairs, away from other household activity and noise. Included is a larger master bedroom suite with its own bath, dressing room, and abundant closet space. This is a comfortable home for the modern family who can appreciate the tradition and charm of the past.

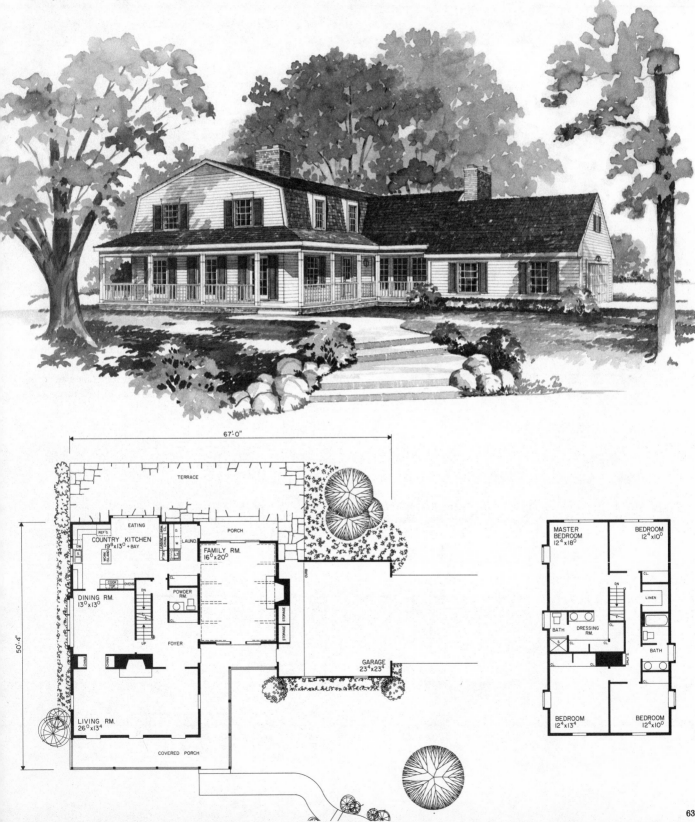

Design T62713
1,830 Sq. Ft. - First Floor
1,056 Sq. Ft. - Second Floor; 41,370 Cu. Ft.

● This home with its Gambrel roof and paned windows is sure to be a pleasure for the entire family. Along with the outside, the inside is a delight. The spacious family room creates an inviting atmosphere with sliding glass doors to the terrace, beamed ceiling and a raised hearth fireplace that includes a built-in wood box. A spectacular kitchen, too. Presenting a cooking island as well as a built-in oven, desk and storage pantry. A sunny breakfast nook, too, also with sliding glass doors leading to the terrace. A service entrance and laundry are adjacent. Note the size of the formal dining room and the fireplace in the living room. A first floor study/bedroom has a private terrace. Upstairs, there is the master suite and two more bedrooms and a bath.

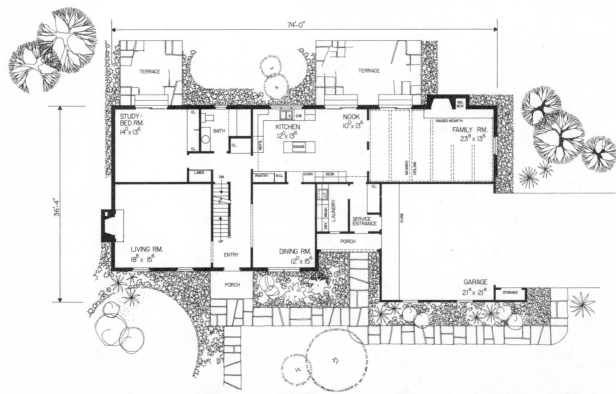

TWO-STORY
GEORGIAN ARCHITECTURE & FEDERAL VERSIONS

Quaker colonists in the late 17th-Century brought English Renaissance architecture that was Palladian, but stripped of excess in Continental design. It was stately, yet restrained with simple grace. Its facades were symmetrical, punctuated by classic details and double-hung windows. Its blossoming as an art form marked the ascension of George I in England — hence the name.

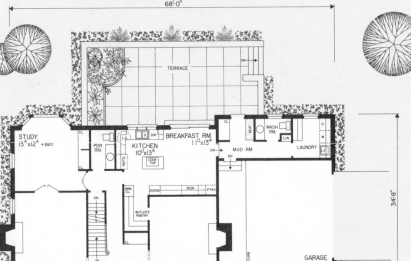

Design T62899
1,685 Sq. Ft. - First Floor
1,437 Sq. Ft. - Second Floor
59,135 Cu. Ft.

● This impressive Georgian home with massive twin chimneys and slender Roman Doric columns is authentic in its 18th-Century detailing. Inside, the home offers comfort and elegance with living room, study, large formal dining room, breakfast room, and even a butler's pantry. Smooth traffic flow is enhanced by a central foyer that opens to stairs leading to the second story. Downstairs there's also a mud room adjacent to the laundry. Upstairs is thoughtfully zoned, too, with a central bath to accommodate a master bedroom and three other bedrooms there.

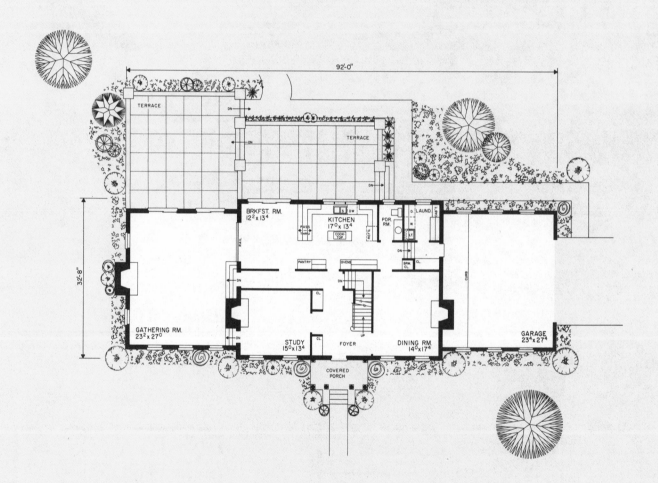

Design T62683 *2,126 Sq. Ft. - First Floor; 1,882 Sq. Ft. - Second Floor; 78,828 Cu.Ft.*

● This historical Georgian home has its roots in the 18th-Century. Dignified symmetry is a hallmark of both front and rear elevations. The full two-story center section is delightfully complimented by the 1½-story wings. Interior livability has been planned to serve today's active family. The elegant gathering room, three steps down from the rest of the house, has ample space for entertaining on a grand scale. It fills an entire wing and is dead-ended so that traffic does not pass through it. Guests and family alike will enjoy the two rooms flanking the foyer, the study and formal dining room. Each of these rooms will have a fireplace as its highlight. The breakfast room, kitchen, powder room and laundry are arranged for maximum efficiency. This area will always have that desired light and airy atmosphere with the sliding glass door and the triple window over the kitchen sink. The second floor houses the family bedrooms. Take special note of the spacious master bedroom suite. It has a deluxe bath, fireplace and sunken lounge with dressing room and walk-in closet. Surely an area to be appreciated.

Georgian Elegance from the Past

● A big, end living room featuring a fireplace and sliding glass doors is the focal point of this Georgian design. Adjacent is the formal dining room strategically located but a couple of steps from the efficient kitchen. Functioning closely with the kitchen is the family room.

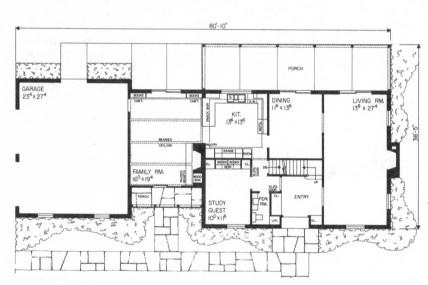

Design T62176
1,485 Sq. Ft. - First Floor
1,175 Sq. Ft. - Second Floor; 41,646 Cu. Ft.

Design T61767
1,510 Sq. Ft. - First Floor
1,406 Sq. Ft. - Second Floor
42,070 Cu. Ft.

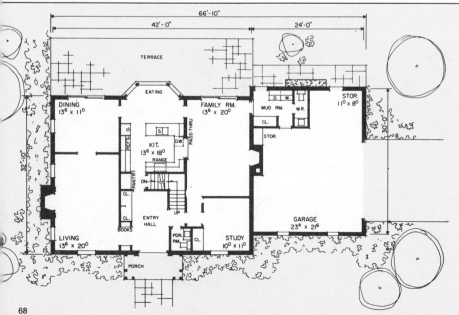

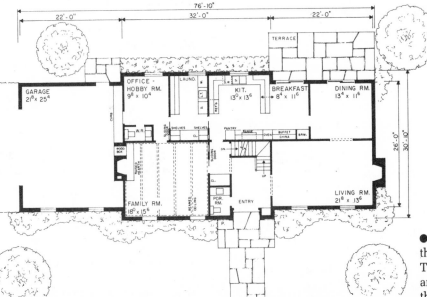

GARAGE
21⁸ x 25⁴

OFFICE -
HOBBY RM.
9⁸ x 10⁴

LAUND.

KIT.
13⁰ x 13⁶

BREAKFAST
8⁴ x 11⁶

DINING RM.
13⁴ x 11⁶

TERRACE

W.R.

SHELVES

SHELVES

PANTRY

RANGE

OVEN

BUFFET
CHINA

B.RM.

CL.

WOOD
BOX

SLIDING
DOORS

DN.

UP

CL.

PDR.
RM.

ENTRY

FAMILY RM.
18⁰ x 15⁶

LIVING RM.
21⁸ x 13⁶

22'-0" 32'-0" 22'-0"

76'-10"

26'-0"

30'-10"

Design T62139
1,581 Sq. Ft. - First Floor
991 Sq. Ft. - Second Floor
36,757 Cu. Ft.

BED RM.
11⁴ x 13⁶

CL.

BATH

CL.

BED RM.
9⁶ x 13⁶

PDR.
RM.

LIN.

LIN.

CL.

DN.

BOOKS

CL.

BATH

MASTER
BED RM.
11⁴ x 15⁶

DRESS.
RM.

BED RM.
12⁰ x 9⁸

● Four bedrooms and two baths make-up the second floor of this two-story design. The first floor has all of the living areas and work center. Note the convenience of the powder room at the entry.

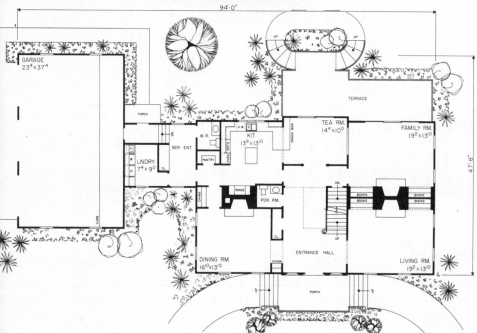

94'-0"

GARAGE
23⁴x37⁴

PORCH

W.R.

LNDRY.
7⁴ x 9⁰

SER. ENT.

KIT.
13⁹x13¹⁰

PANTRY

TEA RM.
14⁴x10⁰

TERRACE

FAMILY RM.
19²x13¹⁰

47'-8"

RANGE

PDR. RM.

CHINA

DINING RM.
16¹⁰x13¹⁰

CHINA

ENTRANCE HALL

BOOKS
BOOKS
BOOKS
BOOKS

LIVING RM.
19²x13¹⁰

PORCH

Design T62301

2,044 Sq. Ft. - First Floor
1,815 Sq. Ft. - Second Floor
69,925 Cu. Ft.

BED RM.
12²x13¹⁰

BATH

SITTING RM.
11⁸x10⁴

BATH

BE
12

LINEN

CL.

CL.

WALK-IN CL.

LINEN

CL.

BATH

WALK-IN CL.

BED RM.
19²x13¹⁰

BATH

DRESS'G.

MA
BE
19²

● Reminiscent of architecture with roots in the deep South, this finely detailed home is exquisite, indeed. Study the contemporary floor plan and the living patterns it offers.

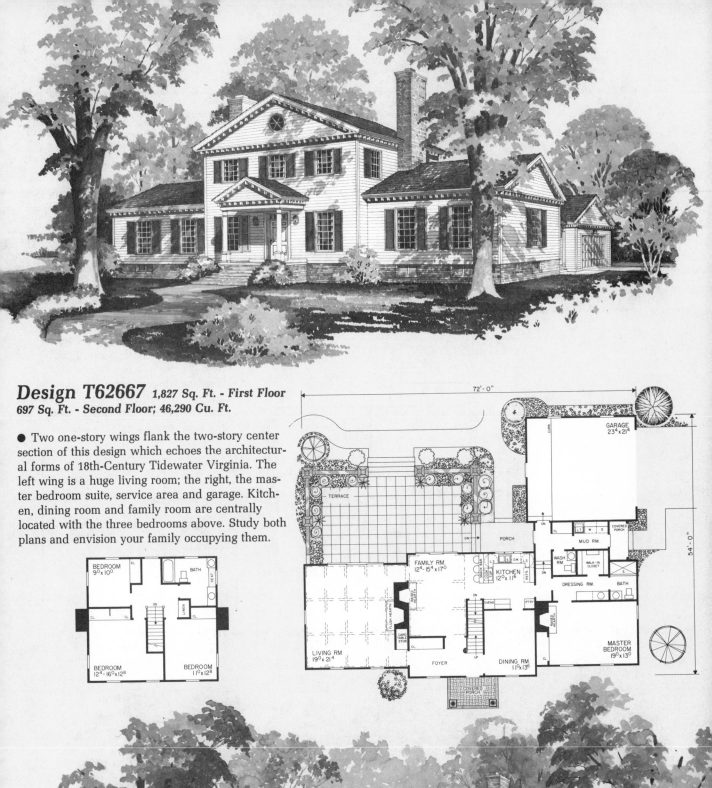

Design T62667 1,827 Sq. Ft. - First Floor
697 Sq. Ft. - Second Floor; 46,290 Cu. Ft.

● Two one-story wings flank the two-story center section of this design which echoes the architectural forms of 18th-Century Tidewater Virginia. The left wing is a huge living room; the right, the master bedroom suite, service area and garage. Kitchen, dining room and family room are centrally located with the three bedrooms above. Study both plans and envision your family occupying them.

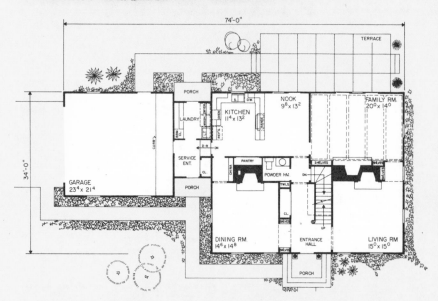

Here is a New England Georgian adaptation with an elevated doorway highlighted by pilasters and a pediment. It gives way to a second-story Palladian window, capped in turn by a pediment projecting from the hipped roof. The interior is decidedly up-to-date with even an upstairs lounge.

Design T62639 1,556 Sq. Ft. - First Floor; 1,428 Sq. Ft. - Second Floor; 46,115 Cu. Ft.

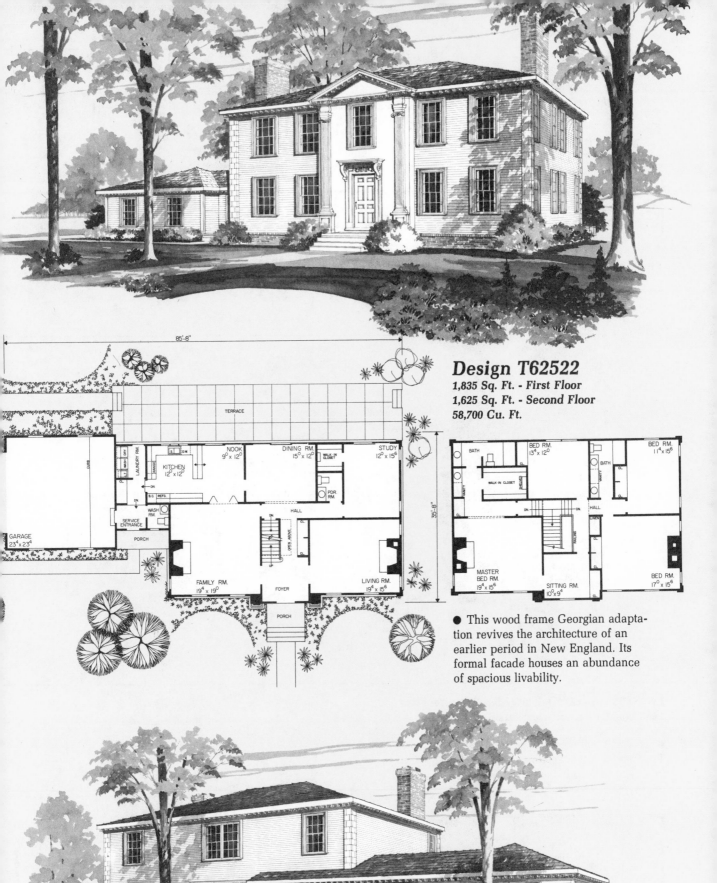

Design T62522
1,835 Sq. Ft. - First Floor
1,625 Sq. Ft. - Second Floor
58,700 Cu. Ft.

● This wood frame Georgian adaptation revives the architecture of an earlier period in New England. Its formal facade houses an abundance of spacious livability.

85'-8"

TERRACE

NOOK 9⁰ x 12⁰

DINING RM. 15⁰ x 12⁰

STUDY 12⁰ x 15⁶

LAUNDRY RM.

WASH DRY

KITCHEN 12⁰ x 12⁰

WALK-IN CLOSET

PDR. RM.

WASH RM.

SERVICE ENTRANCE

PORCH

GARAGE 23⁴ x 23⁴

HALL

FAMILY RM. 19⁴ x 19⁰

FOYER

LIVING RM. 19⁴ x 15⁶

PORCH

35'-8"

BATH

BED RM. 13⁴ x 12⁰

WALK-IN CLOSET

BED RM. 11⁴ x 15⁶

BATH

MASTER BED RM. 19⁴ x 15⁶

HALL

LINEN

SITTING RM. 10⁰ x 9⁴

BED RM. 17⁰ x 15⁶

Design T62188

1,440 Sq. Ft. - First Floor
1,280 Sq. Ft. - Second Floor
40,924 Cu. Ft.

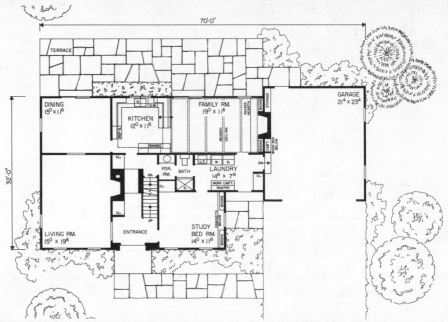

Design T61852

1,802 Sq. Ft. - First Floor
1,603 Sq. Ft. - Second Floor; 51,361 Cu. Ft.

● This is an impressive Georgian adaptation. The front entrance detailing, the window treatment and the masses of brick help put this house in a class of its own.

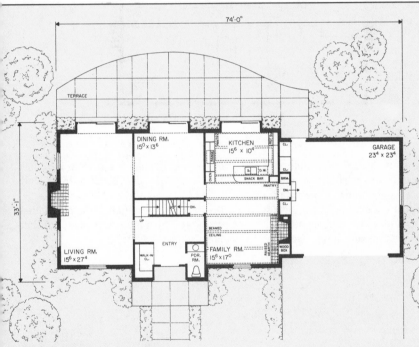

This stately home, whose roots go back to an earlier period in American architecture, will forever retain its aura of distinction. The spacious front entry effectively separates the formal and informal living zones. Four bedrooms on second floor.

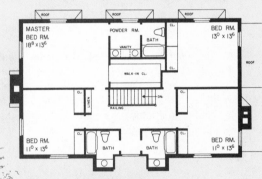

Design T62250

1,442 Sq. Ft. - First Floor
1,404 Sq. Ft. - Second Floor; 46,326 Cu. Ft.

Design T62192

1,884 Sq. Ft. - First Floor
1,521 Sq. Ft. - Second Floor
58,380 Cu. Ft.

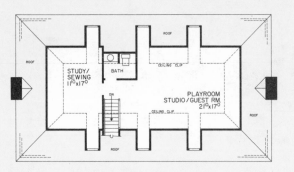

● This is surely a fine adaptation from the 18th-Century when formality and elegance were by-words. The authentic detailing of this design centers around the fine proportions, the dentils, the window symmetry, the front door and entranceway, the massive chimneys and the masonry work. The rear elevation retains all the grandeur exemplary of exquisite architecture. The appeal of this outstanding home does not end with its exterior elevations. Consider the formal living room with its corner fireplace. Also, the library with its wall of bookshelves and cabinets. Further, the dining room highlights corner china cabinets. This plan offers plenty of livability with classic style.

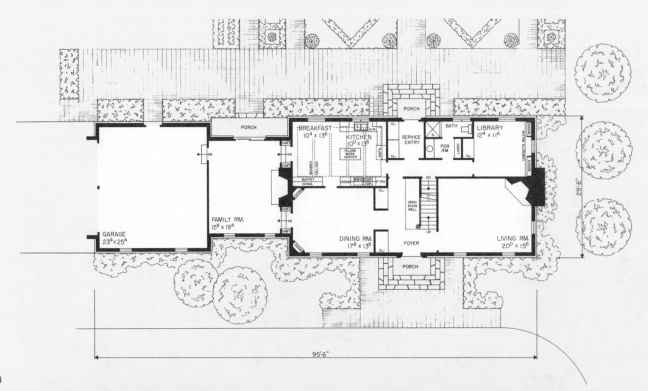

Formal and elegant with 18th-Century detailing . . .

MASTER BED RM. 15⁶ x 18⁸
VANITY
DRESS. RM.
BATH
BED RM. 12⁰ x 13⁶
CL.
CL.
BOOKS
STOR. LINEN STOR.
S.
BOOKS
CL.
CL.
CL.
DN. UP
CL.
CL.
WALK IN CL.
CL.
DN.
STUDIO- MAID'S RM. 19⁴ x 12⁰
BATH
LIN.
CL.
BED RM. 15⁶ x 12⁰
VANITY
BATH
BED RM. 15⁶ x 14⁰

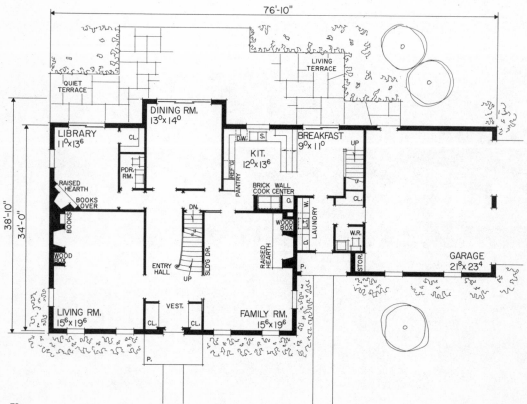

76'-10"
38'-10"
34'-0"

QUIET TERRACE
LIVING TERRACE
LIBRARY 11⁰ x 13⁶
CL.
DINING RM. 13⁰ x 14⁰
DW. S.
BREAKFAST 9⁰ x 11⁰
UP
RAISED HEARTH
PDR. RM.
REF'G
PANTRY
KIT. 12⁰ x 13⁶
BOOKS OVER
BRICK WALL COOK CENTER
O.
CL.
BOOKS
DN.
WOOD BOX
W.
LAUNDRY
WOOD BOX
SLDG DR.
RAISED HEARTH
D. L.H.
W.R.
STOR.
P.
GARAGE 21⁸ x 23⁴
ENTRY HALL
UP
P.
LIVING RM. 15⁶ x 19⁶
VEST.
CL.
CL.
FAMILY RM. 15⁶ x 19⁶
P.

Design T61858

1,794 Sq. Ft. - First Floor
1,474 Sq. Ft. - Second Floor
424 Sq. Ft. - Studio
54,878 Cu. Ft.

● You'll never regret your choice of this Georgian design. Its stately facade seems to foretell all of the exceptional features to be found inside. From the delightful spacious front entry hall, to the studio or maid's room over the garage, this home is unique all along the way. Imagine four fireplaces three full baths, two extra washrooms, a family room, plus a quiet library. Don't miss the first floor laundry. Note the separate set of stairs to the studio, or maid's room. The center entrance leads to the vestibule and the wonderfully spacious entry hall. All the major areas are but a step or two from this formal hall. The kitchen is well-planned and strategically located between the separate dining room and the breakfast room. Sliding glass doors permit easy access to the functional rear terraces.

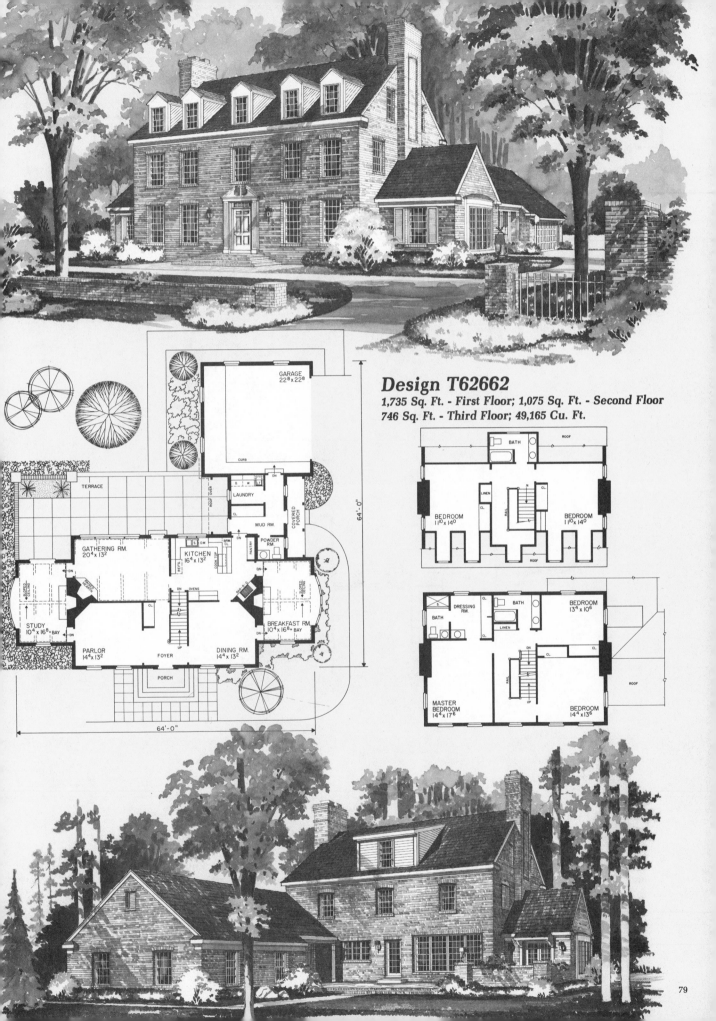

GARAGE
22⁸ x 22⁸

Design T62662
1,735 Sq. Ft. - First Floor; 1,075 Sq. Ft. - Second Floor
746 Sq. Ft. - Third Floor; 49,165 Cu. Ft.

CURB

64'-0"

TERRACE

LAUNDRY

ROOF OVER

COVERED PORCH

MUD RM.

POWDER RM.

GATHERING RM.
20⁴ x 13²

KITCHEN
16⁴ x 13²

COOK TOP

PANTRY

STUDY
10⁴ x 16⁸ BAY

PARLOR
14⁴ x 13²

FOYER

OVENS

DINING RM.
14⁴ x 13²

BREAKFAST RM.
10⁴ x 16⁸ BAY

PORCH

64'-0"

BATH

ROOF

BEDROOM
11¹⁰ x 14⁰

LINEN

CL.

CL.

BEDROOM
11¹⁰ x 14⁰

ROOF

BATH

DRESSING RM.

BATH

LINEN

CL.

BEDROOM
13⁴ x 10⁶

MASTER BEDROOM
14⁴ x 17⁶

CL.

BEDROOM
14⁴ x 13⁶

ROOF

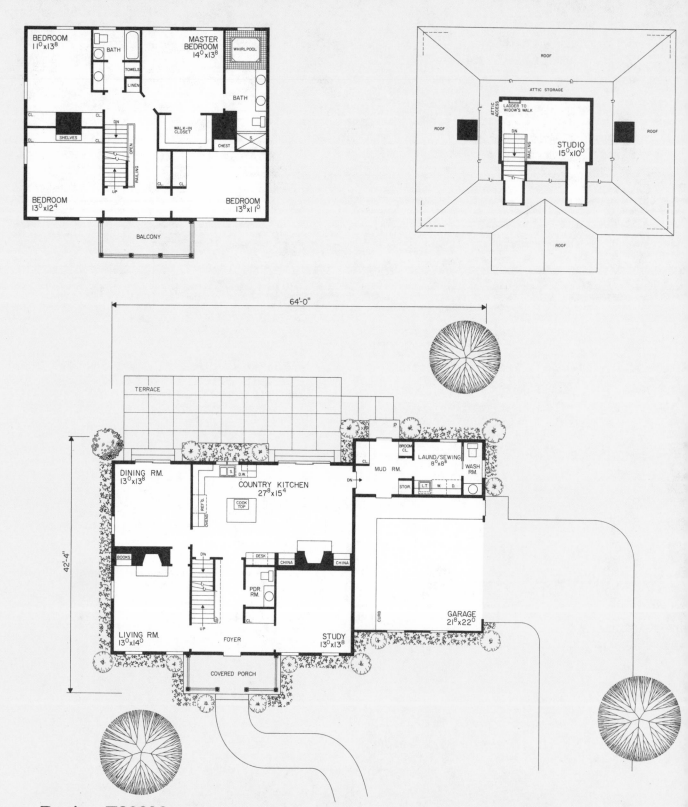

BEDROOM 11⁰x13⁸

BATH

TOWELS

LINEN

MASTER BEDROOM 14⁰x13⁸

WHIRLPOOL

BATH

CL

CL

SHELVES

DN

OPEN

RAILING

WALK-IN CLOSET

CHEST

S

CL

CL

UP

BEDROOM 13⁰x12⁴

CL

CL

BEDROOM 13⁸x11⁰

BALCONY

ROOF

ATTIC STORAGE

ROOF

ATTIC ACCESS

LADDER TO WIDOW'S WALK

DN

RAILING

STUDIO 15⁰x10⁰

ROOF

ROOF

ROOF

64'-0"

42'-4"

TERRACE

DINING RM. 13⁰x13⁸

S

D.W.

REF'S.

OVENS

COUNTRY KITCHEN 27⁸x15⁴

COOK TOP

CL

MUD RM.

STOR.

L.T.

W.

D.

DN

BROOM CL

LAUND/SEWING 8⁰x8⁸

WASH RM.

P

BOOKS

DN

DESK

CHINA

CHINA

PDR. RM.

CL

LIVING RM. 13⁰x14⁰

UP

FOYER

STUDY 13⁰x13⁸

CURB

GARAGE 21⁸x22⁰

COVERED PORCH

Design T62690 1,559 Sq. Ft. - First Floor; 1,344 Sq. Ft. - Second Floor; 176 Third Floor; 49,115 Cu. Ft.

● This classic design faithfully recalls the "captain's house" that graced many New England sea ports in the 18th and 19th Centuries. Such homes had a balustraded roof deck. From this vantage point, wives of captains could look to the sea for signs of their husbands' return. Often the search was in vain, so the perch became known as a "widow's walk." Now the deck can serve leisure activities such as sunbathing or rooftop entertaining. This design is totally updated on the inside for modern convenience and lifestyle. The house offers a third-floor studio, four bedrooms, and a comfortable country kitchen large enough for gatherings. There's also a dining room, living room, study, and mud room off the garage for dirty boots, a laundry or sewing room, and a master bedroom suite with its own whirlpool. There's a fireplace in the kitchen and another in the living room.

Design recalls 18th-Century captain's house

Design T62103 *1,374 Sq. Ft. - First Floor; 1,056 Sq. Ft. - Second Floor; 36,672 Cu. Ft.*

● This Federal version of Later Georgian architecture displays all the charm and styling of the period. Note the massive central chimney, stately front door, symmetrical design, and elegant proportions. The formal entry opens directly to stairs for easy upstairs access, or else to the downstairs living room or dining room. In addition to a formal dining room, this comfortable home also offers a downstairs breakfast area adjacent to the kitchen. And there's also a large family room in addition to the spacious living room. The rear view of the home is fully terraced, with easy access outdoors from all rooms that share the view – living room, family room, kitchen, and breakfast area. Beamed ceiling enhances the family room for a feeling of spaciousness, openness and security. Upstairs, all three bedrooms are carefully isolated from the traffic and noise of downstairs. The master bedroom enjoys a suite all its own. This classic design offers plenty of modern comfort for today's family!

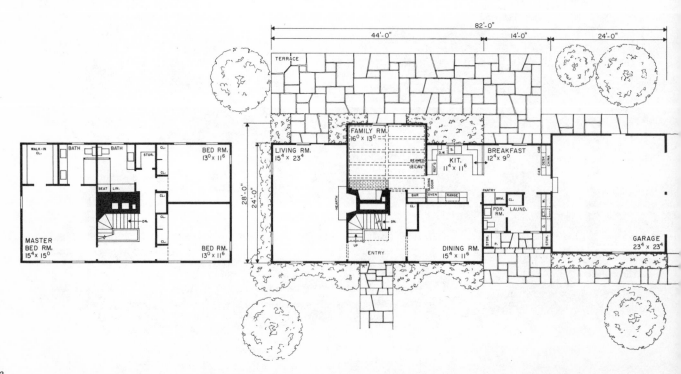

TWO-STORY
SOUTHERN COLONIAL HOMES

Greek revival architecture in America began approximately 1830 with rekindled interest in classical Greek and Roman art. The style uses classical columns with Greco-Roman pediments and cornice treatments, either standing free or against the wall (pilasters or half columns). Southern Colonials generally feature Greco-Roman ornamental details including frets, shell designs, and acanthus leaves. Design generally is symmetrical, with a center hall from front to back.

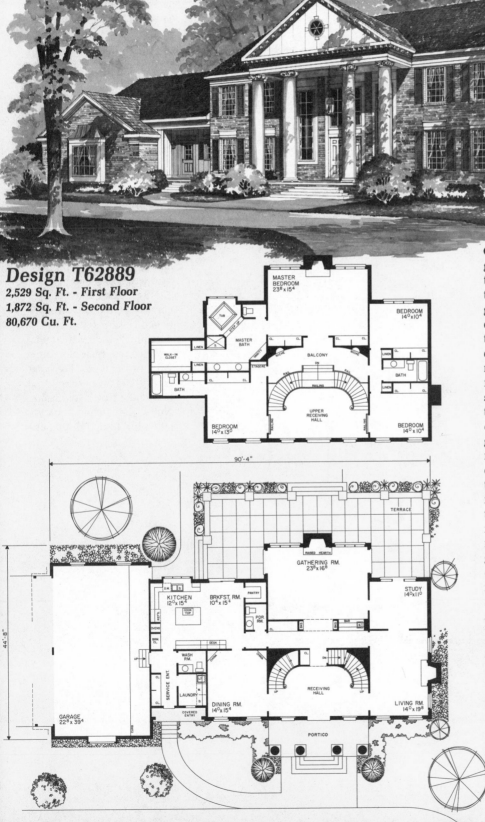

Design T62889
2,529 Sq. Ft. - First Floor
1,872 Sq. Ft. - Second Floor
80,670 Cu. Ft.

● This is truly classical, Georgian design at its best. Some of the exterior highlights of this two-story include the pediment gable with cornice work and dentils, the beautifully proportioned columns, the front door detailing and the window treatment. These are just some of the features which make this design so unique and appealing. Behind the facade of this design is an equally elegant interior. Imagine greeting your guests in the large receiving hall. It is graced by two curving staircases and opens to the formal living and dining rooms. Beyond the living room is the study. It has access to the rear terrace. Those large, informal occasions for family get-togethers or entertaining will be enjoyed in the spacious gathering room. It has a centered fireplace flanked by windows on each side, access to the terrace and a wet bar. Your appreciation for this room will be never-ending. The work center is efficient: the kitchen with island cook top, breakfast room, washroom, laundry and service entrance. The second floor also is outstanding. Three family bedrooms and two full baths are joined by the feature-filled master bedroom suite. Study this area carefully.

Stately, replete with details. . .

BED RM. 13⁶ x 14⁴
BATH
CL.
DRESS. RM.
WALK-IN CL.
BATH
WALK-IN CL.
CL.
CL.
CL.
CL. LIN.
DN.
CL. CL.
BED RM. 13⁶ x 14⁴
BED RM. 13⁸ x 10⁰
MASTER BED RM. 13⁶ x 19⁶
UPPER PORTICO
ROOF
ROOF
ROOF

Design T62283
1,559 Sq. Ft. - First Floor
1,404 Sq. Ft. - Second Floor
48,606 Cu. Ft.

● This elegant two-story home is reminiscent of the stately character of Federal architecture during an earlier period in our history. The home is replete with exquisite detailing. Features that make this design unique and appealing include cornice work, pediment gable, dentils, brick quoins at the corners, beautifully proportioned columns, front door detailing, window treatment, and massive twin chimneys. All four bedrooms are located upstairs away from other household traffic and noise. Notice the kitchen nook and adjoining formal dining area.

66'-10"
44'-10"
32'-10"

TERRACE
NOOK 13⁶ x 9⁰
DINING RM. 13⁶ x 11⁰
MUD RM. **W.R.** **STORAGE**
CL.
D. W.
BEAMED CEILING
REF'L. OVEN
KIT. 13⁶ x 10⁰
RANGE
BLDG. DOORS
FAMILY RM. 13⁶ x 20⁰
PANTRY
DN.
WALK-IN CL.
BOOKS **BOOKS**
CABINET
ENTRANCE HALL
UP
GARAGE 23⁴ x 21⁴
BOOKS
LIVING RM. 13⁶ x 20⁰
BOOKS
PDR. RM.
CL.
STUDY 10⁰ x 11⁰
PORTICO

● A Southern Colonial adaptation under 2,000 square feet. The two projecting, one-story wings are devoted to the living room and garage. The two-story portion houses three bedrooms, 2½ baths, study, laundry, dining room and kitchen with eating area.

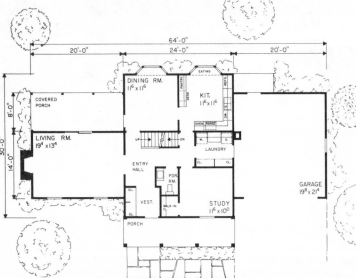

Design T62107
1,020 Sq. Ft. - First Floor
720 Sq. Ft. - Second Floor
25,245 Cu. Ft.

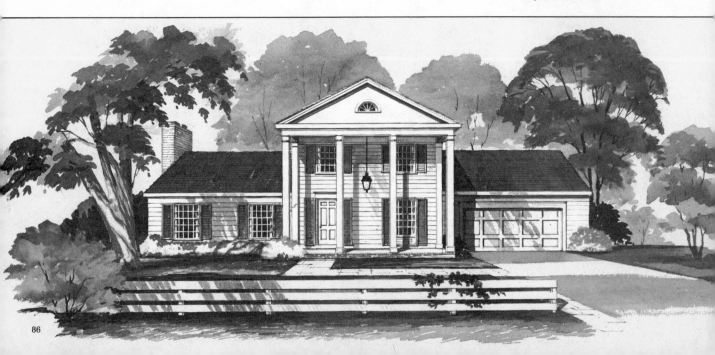

Design T61773
1,546 Sq. Ft. - First Floor
1,040 Sq. Ft. - Second Floor
33,755 Cu. Ft.

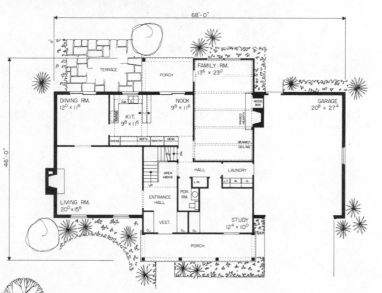

Design T61208
1,170 Sq. Ft. - First Floor
768 Sq. Ft. - Second Floor
26,451 Cu. Ft.

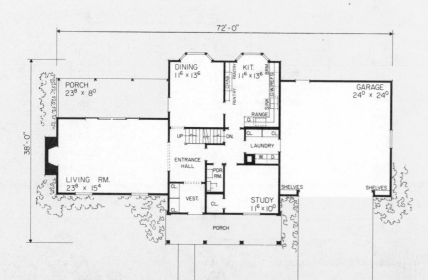

87

Design T62660

1,479 Sq. Ft. - First Floor
1,501 Sq. Ft. - Second Floor
912 Sq. Ft. - Third Floor
556 Sq. Ft. - Activities Room Area
57,440 Cu. Ft.

A Charleston Single House

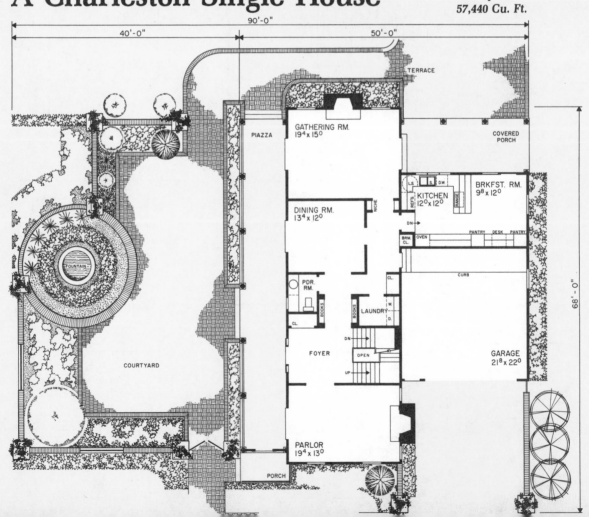

90'-0"
40'-0" 50'-0"

TERRACE

PIAZZA

GATHERING RM.
19⁴ x 15⁰

COVERED PORCH

KITCHEN
12⁰ x 12⁰

BRKFST. RM.
9⁸ x 12⁰

DINING RM.
13⁴ x 12⁰

NICHE

DN

PANTRY DESK PANTRY

BRM. CL. OVEN

FOUNTAIN

CURB

PDR. RM.

CL.

BOOKS BOOKS LAUNDRY

W. D.

CL.

COURTYARD

DN

OPEN

UP

FOYER

GARAGE
21⁸ x 22⁰

PARLOR
19⁴ x 13⁰

PORCH

68'-0"

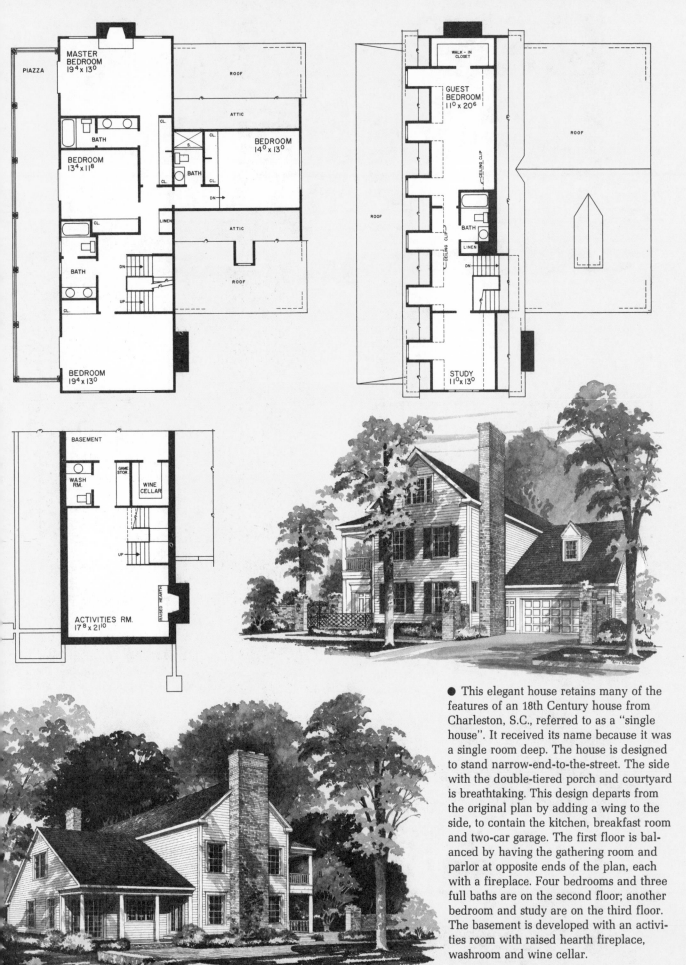

PIAZZA

MASTER
BEDROOM
19⁴ x 13⁰

ROOF

ATTIC

BATH

CL.

CL.

BATH

S.

CL.

BEDROOM
14⁰ x 13⁰

BEDROOM
13⁴ x 11⁸

CL.

DN

LINEN

ATTIC

BATH

DN

ROOF

CL.

UP

BEDROOM
19⁴ x 13⁰

WALK - IN
CLOSET

GUEST
BEDROOM
11⁰ x 20⁶

ROOF

ROOF

CEILING CLIP

BATH

CEILING CLIP

CEILING CLIP

LINEN

DN

STUDY
11⁰ x 13⁰

BASEMENT

GAME
STOR.

WASH
RM.

WINE
CELLAR

UP

RAISED HEARTH

ACTIVITIES RM.
17⁸ x 21¹⁰

● This elegant house retains many of the features of an 18th Century house from Charleston, S.C., referred to as a "single house". It received its name because it was a single room deep. The house is designed to stand narrow-end-to-the-street. The side with the double-tiered porch and courtyard is breathtaking. This design departs from the original plan by adding a wing to the side, to contain the kitchen, breakfast room and two-car garage. The first floor is balanced by having the gathering room and parlor at opposite ends of the plan, each with a fireplace. Four bedrooms and three full baths are on the second floor; another bedroom and study are on the third floor. The basement is developed with an activities room with raised hearth fireplace, washroom and wine cellar.

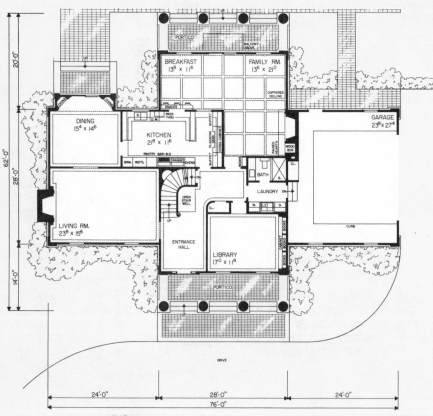

Design T62184

1,999 Sq. Ft. - First Floor
1,288 Sq. Ft. - Second Floor
58,441 Cu. Ft.

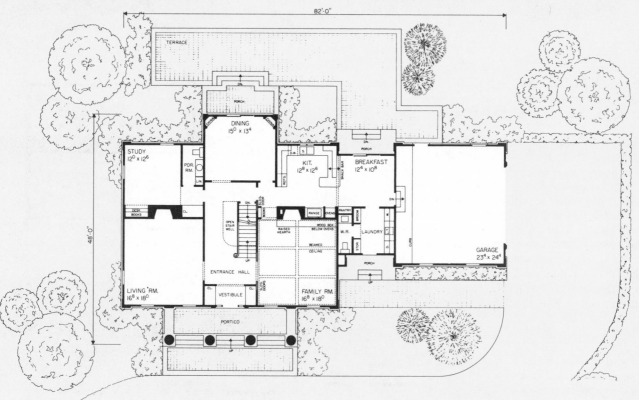

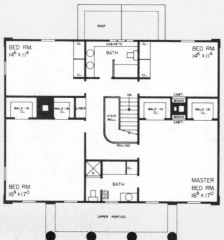

Design T62185 1,916 Sq. Ft. - First Floor
1,564 Sq. Ft. - Second Floor; 59,649 Cu. Ft.

● The elements of Greek Revival architecture when adapted to present day standards can be impressive, indeed. A study of this floor plan will reveal its similarity to that on the opposite page. There is a vestibule which leads to a wonderfully spacious entrance hall. The open stairwell is most dramatic. As it affords a view of the four bedroom, two bath second floor. The study and family room will be favorite spots for family relaxation. Both the dining and living rooms can be made to function as formally as you wish.

Design T62673

1,895 Sq. Ft. - First Floor
1,661 Sq. Ft. - Second Floor; 59,114 Cu. Ft.

● A two-story pillared entrance portico and tall multi-paned windows, flanking the double front doors, together accentuate the facade of this Southern Colonial design. This brick home is stately and classic in its exterior appeal. The three-car garage opens to the side so it does not disturb the street view. This is definitely a charming home that will stand strong for many years into the future. Not only is the exterior something to talk about, but so is the interior. Enter into the extremely spacious foyer and begin to discover what this home has to offer in the way of livability. Front, living and dining rooms are at each end of this foyer. The living room is complimented by a music room, or close it off and make it a bedroom. A full bath is nearby. The formal dining room will be easily served by the kitchen as will the breakfast room and snack bar. The family room is spacious and features a built-in wet bar which can be closed off by doors. An open, staircase leads to the second floor, four bedroom sleeping area.

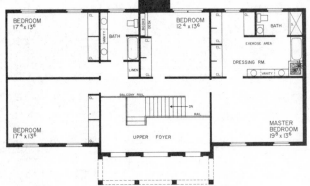

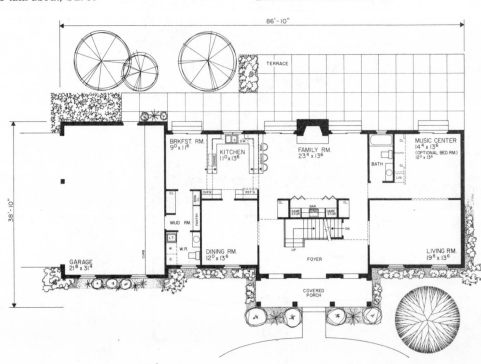

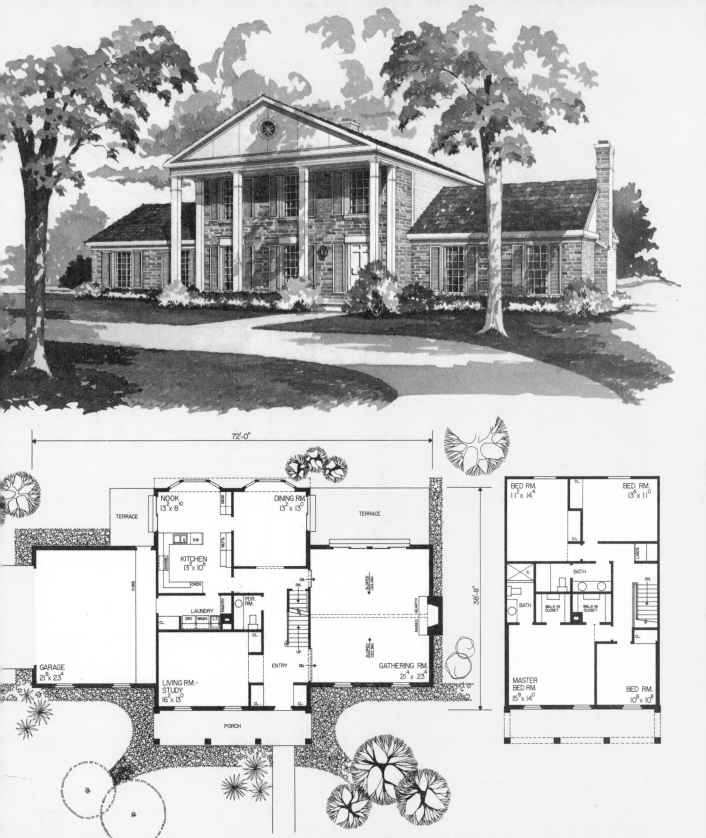

Design T62700
1,640 Sq. Ft. - First Floor; 1,129 Sq. Ft. - Second Floor; 42,200 Cu. Ft.

● Southern Colonial grace! And much more. An elegant gathering room, more than 21' by 23' large. . . with sloped ceilings and a raised-hearth fireplace. Plus two sets of sliding glass doors that open onto the terrace. Correctly appointed formal rooms! A living room with full length paned windows. And a formal dining room that features a large bay window. Plus a contemporary kitchen. A separate dining nook that includes another bay window. Charming and sunny! Around the corner, a first floor laundry offers more modern conveniences. Four large bedrooms! Including a master suite with two walk-in closets and private bath. This home offers all the conveniences that make life easy! And its eminently suited to a family with traditional tastes. List your favorite features.

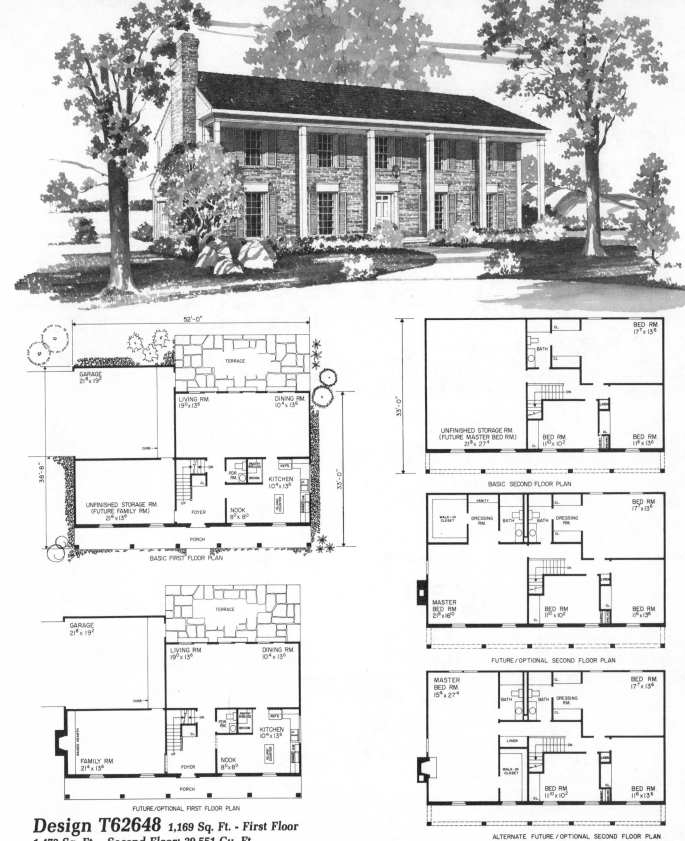

Design T62648 1,169 Sq. Ft. - First Floor
1,473 Sq. Ft. - Second Floor; 39,551 Cu. Ft.

● If you are looking for a house to fit your present family, but also need one when it is full grown, then this is the design for you. This house appears large, but until the two unfinished rooms (one upstairs and one on the first floor), are completed it is an eco-

nomical house. Later development of these rooms conserves initial construction expense. A major economy has been realized because the basic structural work is already standing. From the outside, onlookers will never know that there are unfinished rooms inside.

The exterior appeal is outstanding with its two-story pillars extending from the overhanging roof and its rows of windows which cover the length of the facade. The rear elevation features three sets of sliding glass doors.

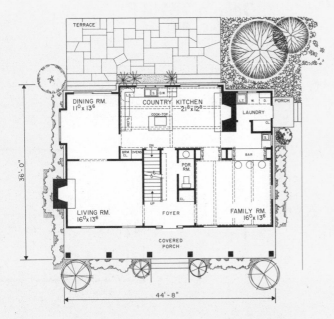

The exterior of this full two-story is highlighted by the covered porch and balcony. Many enjoyable hours will be spent at these outdoor areas. The interior is highlighted by a spacious country kitchen. Be sure to notice its island cook-top, fireplace and the beamed ceiling. A built-in bar is in the family room.

Design T62664
1,308 Sq. Ft. - First Floor
1,262 Sq. Ft. - Second Floor; 49,215 Cu. Ft.

Design T62627

845 Sq. Ft. - First Floor
896 Sq. Ft. - Second Floor; 28,685 Cu. Ft.

● This charming, economically built, home with its stately porch columns is reminiscent of the South. The efficient interior features bonus space over garage and in the third-floor attic.

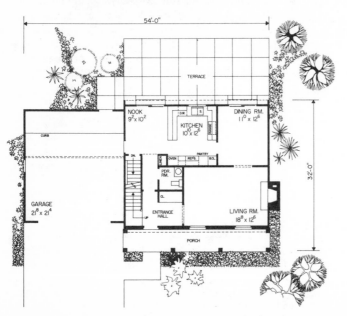

Design T61816 2,036 Sq. Ft. - First Floor

1,836 Sq. Ft. - Second Floor; 55,566 Cu. Ft.

● The influence of the Colonial South is delightfully apparent in this gracious design. The stately columns of the front porch set the stage for a memorable visit.

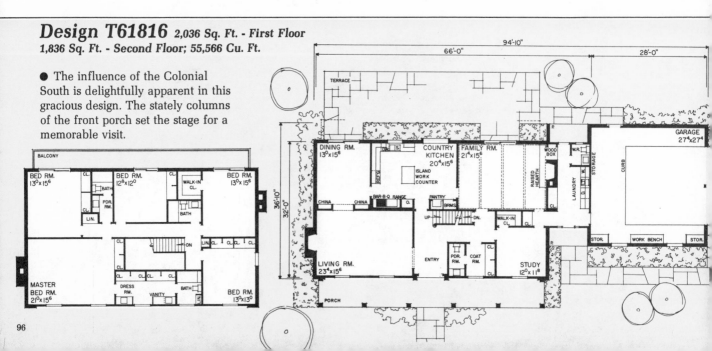

Design T62524

994 Sq. Ft. - First Floor
994 Sq. Ft. - Second Floor; 32,937 Cu. Ft.

● This small two-story with a modest investment, will result in an impressive exterior and an outstanding interior which will provide exceptional livability. Your list of features will be long.

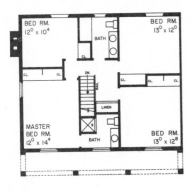

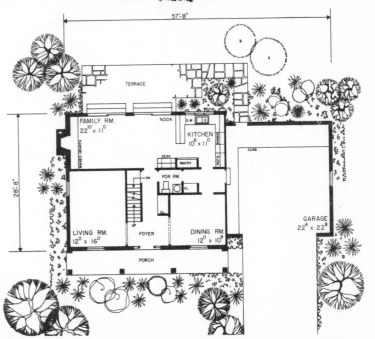

Design T62668 1,206 Sq. Ft. - First Floor
1,254 Sq. Ft. - Second Floor; 47,915 Cu. Ft.

● This elegant exterior houses a very livable plan. Every bit of space has been put to good use. The front country kitchen is a good place to begin. It is efficiently planned with its island cook top, built-ins and pass-thru to the dining room. The large great room will be the center of all family activities. Quiet times can be enjoyed in the front library. Study the second floor sleeping areas.

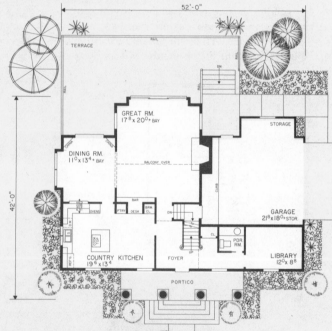

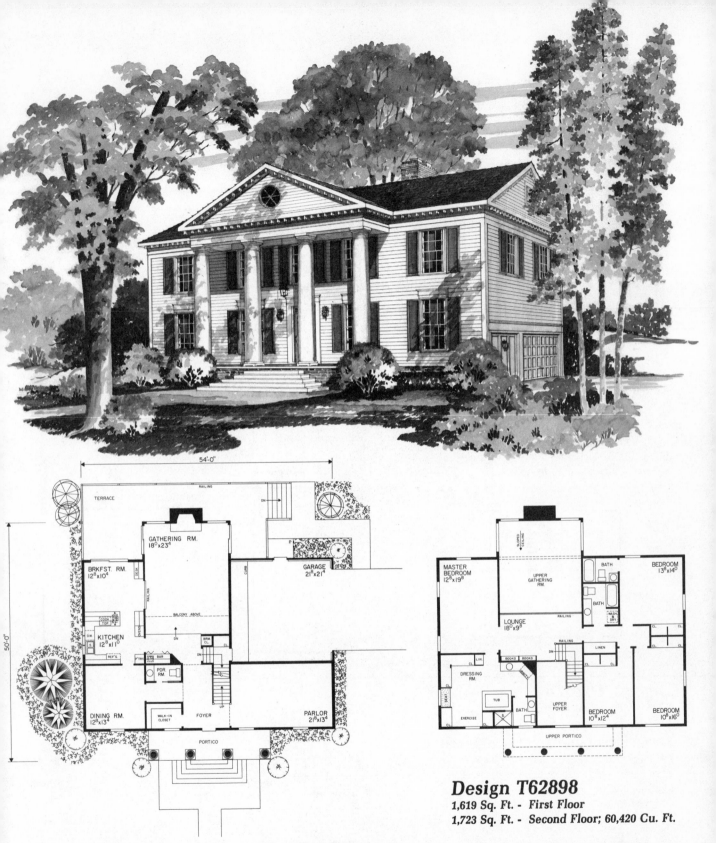

Design T62898
1,619 Sq. Ft. - First Floor
1,723 Sq. Ft. - Second Floor; 60,420 Cu. Ft.

● Four soaring Doric columns highlight the exterior of this Greek Revival dwelling. The elevation reflects a balanced design that incorporates four bedrooms and a two-car garage in one central unit. The stylish heart of this dwelling is a two-story gathering room. A balcony lounge on the second floor offers a quiet aerie overlooking this living area. Both of these areas will have sunlight streaming through the high windows. A second living area is the parlor. It could serve as the formal area whereas the gathering room could be considered informal. Entrance to all of these areas will be through the foyer. It has an adjacent powder room and spacious walk-in closet. The U-shaped kitchen will conveniently serve the breakfast and dining rooms. Second floor livability is outstanding. Study all of the features in the master bedroom: dressing room, tub and shower, large vanity and exercise area. Three more bedrooms, another has a private bath, which would make it an ideal guest room.

99

Design T62572

1,258 Sq. Ft. - First Floor
1,251 Sq. Ft. - Second Floor; 42,160 Cu. Ft.

● This home offers great livability. Four bedrooms and two baths (each with a vanity) upstairs. And the first floor has features galore. Note the barbecue in the kitchen. Two fireplaces for added charm.

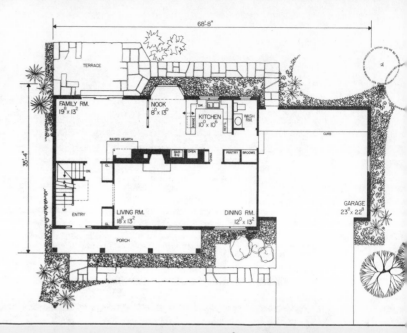

Design T62762

2,345 Sq. Ft. - First Floor
1,016 Sq. Ft. - Second Floor; 53,740 Cu. Ft.

● This home features a full apartment to the side to accommodate a live-in relative. The main house has all the features to ensure happiness for years to come. The three-car garage is sure to come in handy.

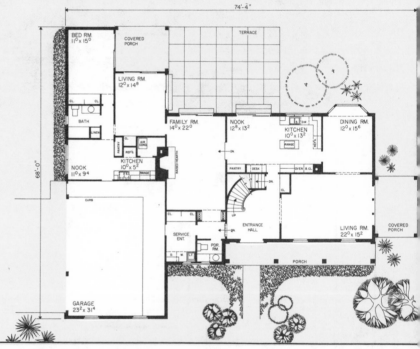

Design T62575

2,207 Sq. Ft. - First Floor
1,611 Sq. Ft. - Second Floor; 71,750 Cu. Ft.

● What a fine home this will make. Note the large entry with circular staircase. Three separate terraces. Lounge upstairs overlooking the gathering room. Extra storage space in three-car garage.

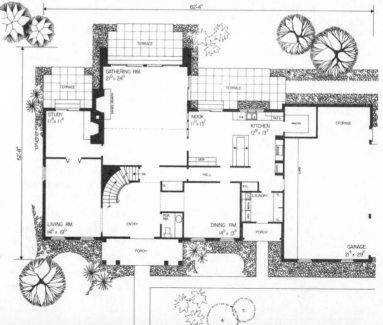

A Mount Vernon Reminiscence

● This magnificent manor's streetview illustrates a centralized mansion connected by curving galleries to matching wings. What a grand presentation this home will make! The origin of this house dates back to 1787 and George Washington's stately Mount Vernon. The underlying aesthetics for this design come from the rational balancing of porticoes, fenestration and chimneys. The rear elevation of this home also deserves mention. Six two-story columns, along with four sets of French doors, highlight this view. Study all of the intricate detailing that is featured all around these exteriors.

The flanking wings create a large formal courtyard where guests of today can park their cars. This home, designed from architecture of the past, is efficient and compact enough to fit many suburban lots. Its interior has been well planned and is ready to serve a family of any size.

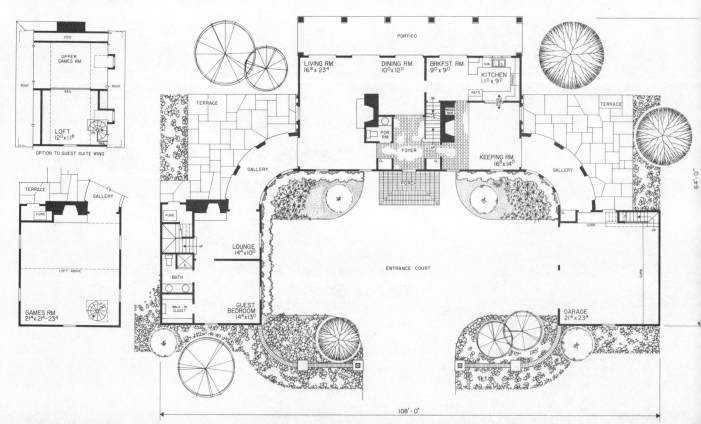

Design T62665 *1,152 Sq. Ft. - First Floor*
1,152 Sq. Ft. - Second Floor; 38,754 Cu. Ft. (Excludes Guest Suite and Galleries)

● The main, two-story section of this home houses the living areas. First - there is the large, tiled foyer with two closets and powder room. Then there is the living room which is the entire width of the house. This room has a fireplace and leads into the formal dining room. Three sets of double French doors lead to the rear portico from this formal area. The kitchen and breakfast room will function together. There is a pass-thru from the kitchen to the keeping room. All of the sleeping facilities, four bedrooms, are on the second floor. The gallery on the right leads to the garage; the one on the left, to a lounge and guest suite with studio above. The square and cubic footages quoted above do not include the guest suite or gallery areas. The first floor of the guest suite contains 688 sq. ft.; the second floor studio, 306 sq. ft. The optional plan shows a game room with a loft above having 162 sq. ft.

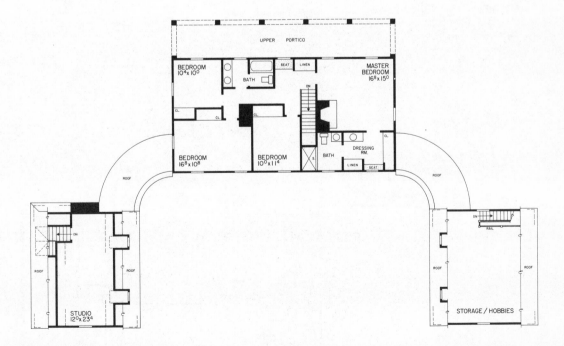

Design T62553

2,065 Sq. Ft. - First Floor
1,612 Sq. Ft. - Second Floor; 65,772 Cu. Ft.

● A stately Southern Colonial that could
hardly be more impressive, or offer more
pleasurable livability. The massive columns and the pediment gable are dramatic.
No less so, is the open ceiling of the large
gathering room. The second floor lounge
area looks down on this favorite family
living area. The two-story front entrance
has its special appeal, also. Observe the
quiet living room and its adjacent study.
The bedroom bath arrangement of the second floor is particularly noteworthy. The
oversized garage will accommodate
three cars.

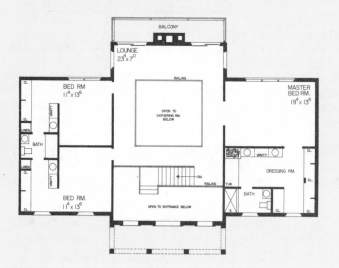

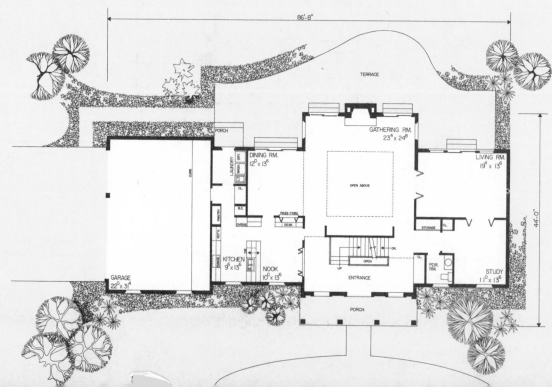

Design T62140 1,822 Sq. Ft. - First Floor; 1,638 Sq. Ft. - Second Floor; 52,107 Cu. Ft.

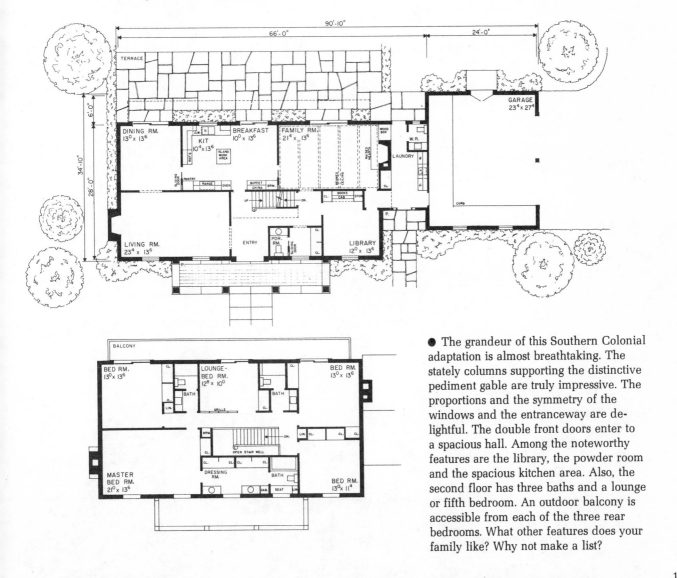

● The grandeur of this Southern Colonial adaptation is almost breathtaking. The stately columns supporting the distinctive pediment gable are truly impressive. The proportions and the symmetry of the windows and the entranceway are delightful. The double front doors enter to a spacious hall. Among the noteworthy features are the library, the powder room and the spacious kitchen area. Also, the second floor has three baths and a lounge or fifth bedroom. An outdoor balcony is accessible from each of the three rear bedrooms. What other features does your family like? Why not make a list?

Design T62839 1,565 Sq. Ft. - First Floor; 1,120 Sq. Ft. - Second Floor; 58,925 Cu. Ft.

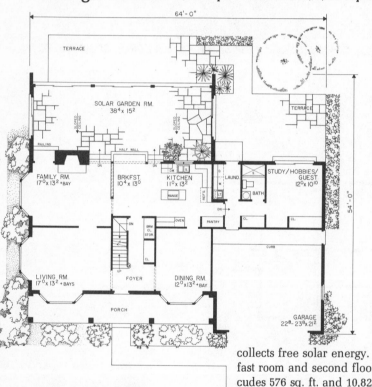

● Bay windows highlight the front and side exteriors of this three-bedroom Colonial. For energy efficiency, this design has an enclosed garden room that collects free solar energy. This area opens to the family room, breakfast room and second floor master suite. The solar garden room incudes 576 sq. ft. and 10,828 cu. ft. These figures are not included in the above total.

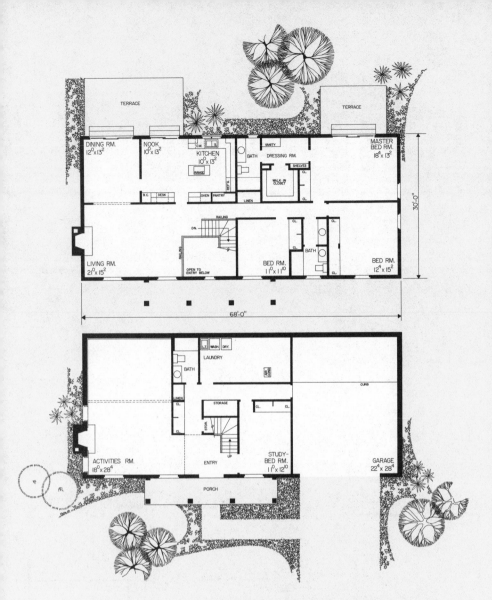

Design T62547
1,340 Sq. Ft. - First Floor
1,946 Sq. Ft. - Second Floor
40,166 Cu. Ft.

● Here are living patterns that are decidedly different for two-story living. In fact, since it is built into a sloping site, it may also be characterized as a bi-level adaptation. It is the exposure of the first floor in the front that creates that two story effect. With the activities room and the study (or fourth bedroom) there is significant livability on this level. Of course, upstairs there is the complete living unit. Its access to outdoor living is through sliding glass doors to the rear yard terraces. The master bedroom with all that space and storage, is outstanding. The living room is spacious and enjoys the open view of the high ceilinged entry. There are two fireplaces, three full baths and a fine laundry room. Note garage storage space.

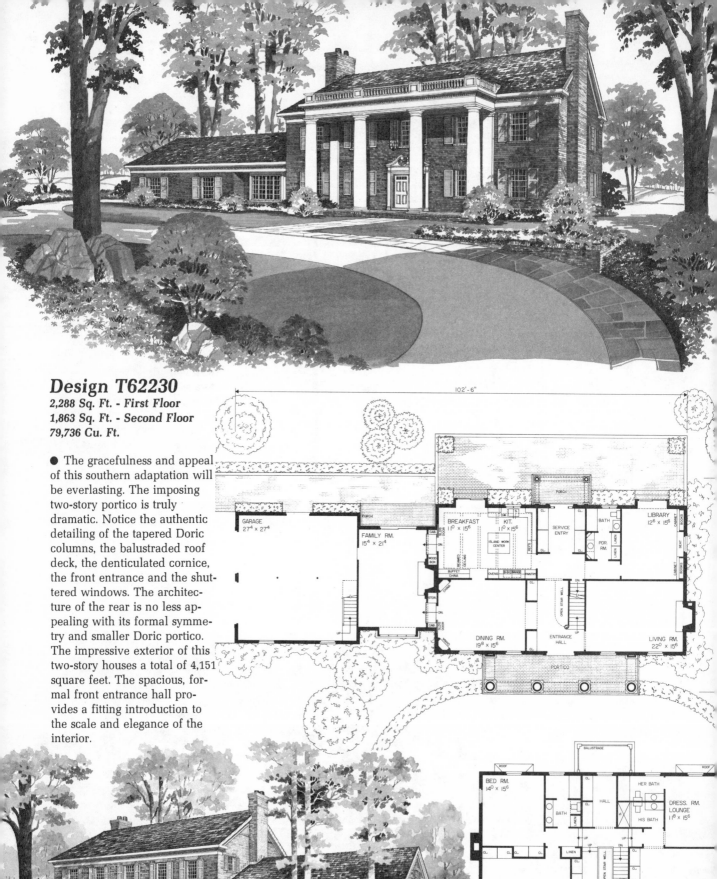

Design T62230

2,288 Sq. Ft. - First Floor
1,863 Sq. Ft. - Second Floor
79,736 Cu. Ft.

● The gracefulness and appeal of this southern adaptation will be everlasting. The imposing two-story portico is truly dramatic. Notice the authentic detailing of the tapered Doric columns, the balustraded roof deck, the denticulated cornice, the front entrance and the shuttered windows. The architecture of the rear is no less appealing with its formal symmetry and smaller Doric portico. The impressive exterior of this two-story houses a total of 4,151 square feet. The spacious, formal front entrance hall provides a fitting introduction to the scale and elegance of the interior.

108

TWO-STORY
EARLY AMERICAN FARMHOUSES

The Early American Farmhouse shows a simplicity in form and family comfort that make up its total design. It's often an all-wood house, but with regional variations sometimes in brick or stone. Livability is a hallmark of Farmhouse design. Many fine examples feature porches.

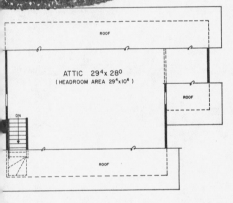

ATTIC 29⁴ x 28⁰
(HEADROOM AREA 29⁴ x 10⁶)

Design T62774
1,370 Sq. Ft. - First Floor
969 Sq. Ft. - Second Floor
38,305 Cu. Ft.

● Another Farmhouse adaptation with all the most up-to-date features expected in a new home. Beginning with the formal areas, this design offers pleasures for the entire family. There is the quiet corner living room which has an opening to the sizeable dining room. This room will enjoy plenty of natural light from the delightful bay window overlooking the rear yard. It is also conveniently located with the efficient U-shaped kitchen just a step away. The kitchen features many built-ins with pass-thru to the beamed ceiling nook. Sliding glass doors to the terrace are fine attractions in both the sunken family room and nook. The service entrance to the garage has a storage closet on each side, plus there is a secondary entrance through the laundry area. Recreational activities and hobbies can be pursued in the basement area. Four bedrooms, two baths upstairs.

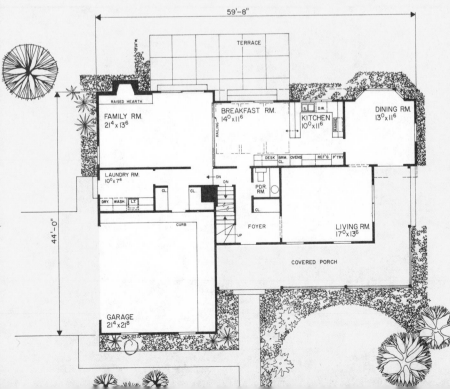

Design T62685 1,605 Sq. Ft. - First Floor
1,561 Sq. Ft. - Second Floor; 46,124 Cu. Ft.

● The stone exterior of this historical house recalls the Pennsylvania farmhouses of Valley Forge in Colonial times. Spaciously planned, the interior will easily serve the family of today. The country kitchen has been planned as an efficient hub of daily family life. Sleeping facilities are on the second floor. The master bedroom occupies its own tranquil zone.

Design T62633

1,338 Sq. Ft. - First Floor
1,200 Sq. Ft. - Second Floor
506 Sq. Ft. - Third Floor
44,525 Cu. Ft.

● This is certainly a pleasing Georgian. Its facade features an atypical porch with a roof supported by simple wooden posts. The garage wing has a sheltered service entry and brick facing which complements the design. Sliding glass doors link the terrace and family room, providing an indoor/outdoor area for entertaining as pictured in the rear elevation. The floor plan has been designed to serve the family efficiently. The stairway in the foyer leads to four second-floor bedrooms. The third floor is windowed and can be used as a studio and study.

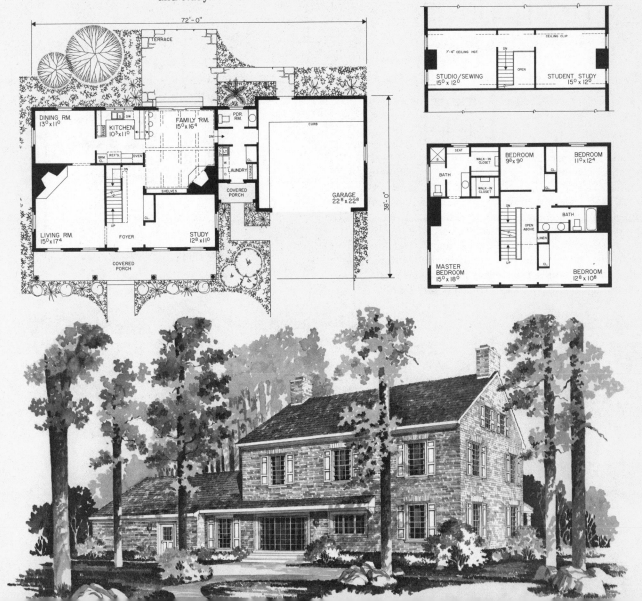

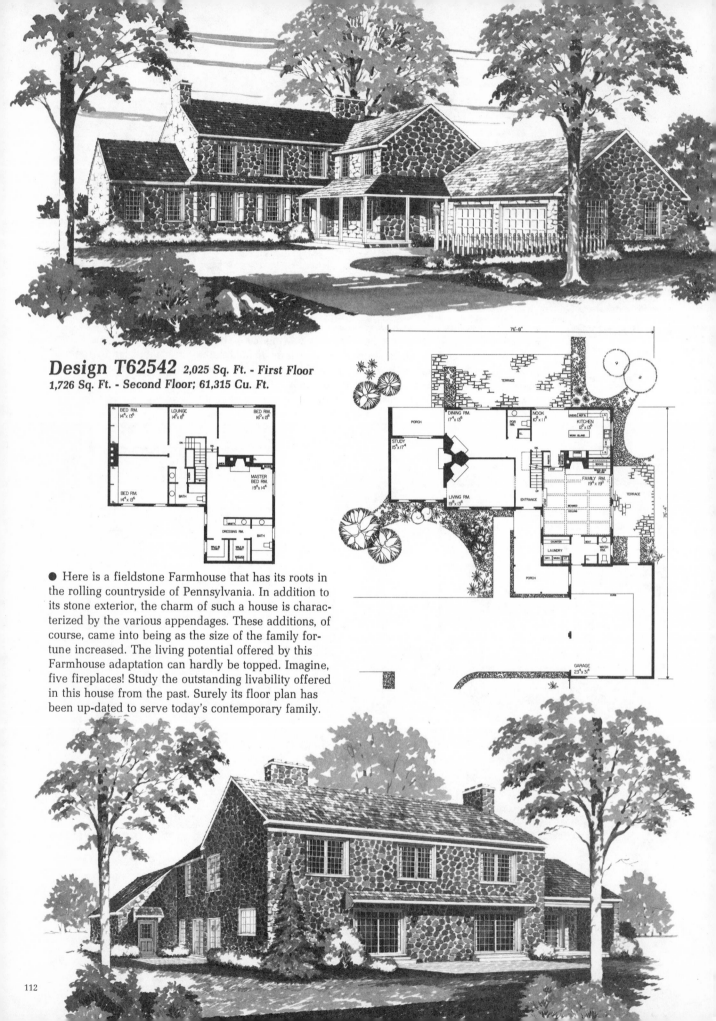

Design T62542 2,025 Sq. Ft. - First Floor
1,726 Sq. Ft. - Second Floor; 61,315 Cu. Ft.

● Here is a fieldstone Farmhouse that has its roots in the rolling countryside of Pennsylvania. In addition to its stone exterior, the charm of such a house is characterized by the various appendages. These additions, of course, came into being as the size of the family fortune increased. The living potential offered by this Farmhouse adaptation can hardly be topped. Imagine, five fireplaces! Study the outstanding livability offered in this house from the past. Surely its floor plan has been up-dated to serve today's contemporary family.

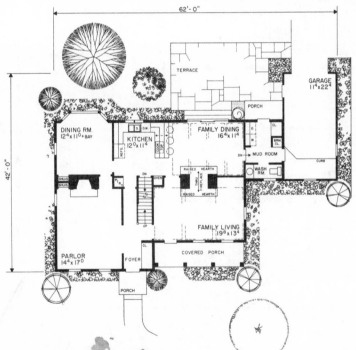

Design T62681 1,350 Sq. Ft. - First Floor
1,224 Sq. Ft. - Second Floor; 35,890 Cu. Ft.

● The charm of Early America is exemplified in this delightful design. Note the three areas which are highlighted by a fireplace. The three bedroom second floor is nicely planned. Make special note of the master bedroom's many fine features. Study the rest of this design's many fine qualities.

Design T61933

1,184 Sq. Ft. - First Floor
884 Sq. Ft. - Second Floor; 27,976 Cu. Ft.

● An attractive Farmhouse adaptation
with just loads of livability. The center
entrance routes traffic efficiently to all
areas. Note spacious end, living room
and its adjacent formal dining room. A
great family room, laundry, and four
bedroom second floor.

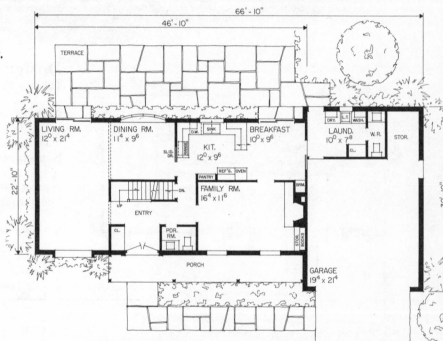

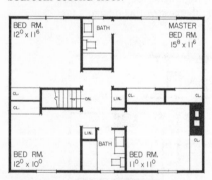

Design T62585

990 Sq. Ft. - First Floor
1,011 Sq. Ft. - Second Floor; 30,230 Cu. Ft.

● Here is an elegant version of the
front porch type house. Note the
overhanging second floor. An efficient and economical home for the
large family.

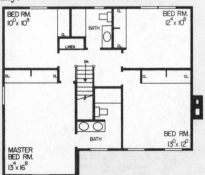

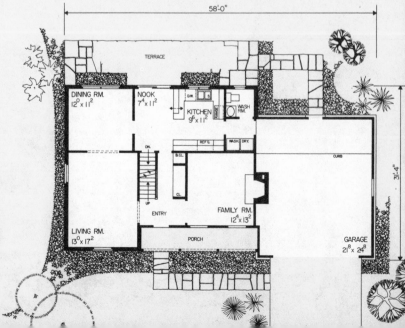

Design T61285

1,210 Sq. Ft. - First Floor
896 Sq. Ft. - Second Floor; 27,385 Cu. Ft.

● Designed for years of livability. And what great livability this two-story traditional has to offer. The spacious center entry hall routes traffic conveniently to all areas. The formal living room is big and features two windows overlooking the front yard.

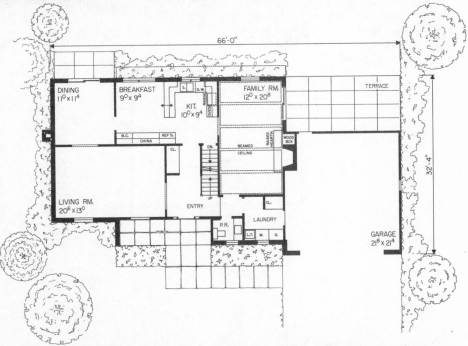

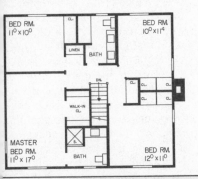

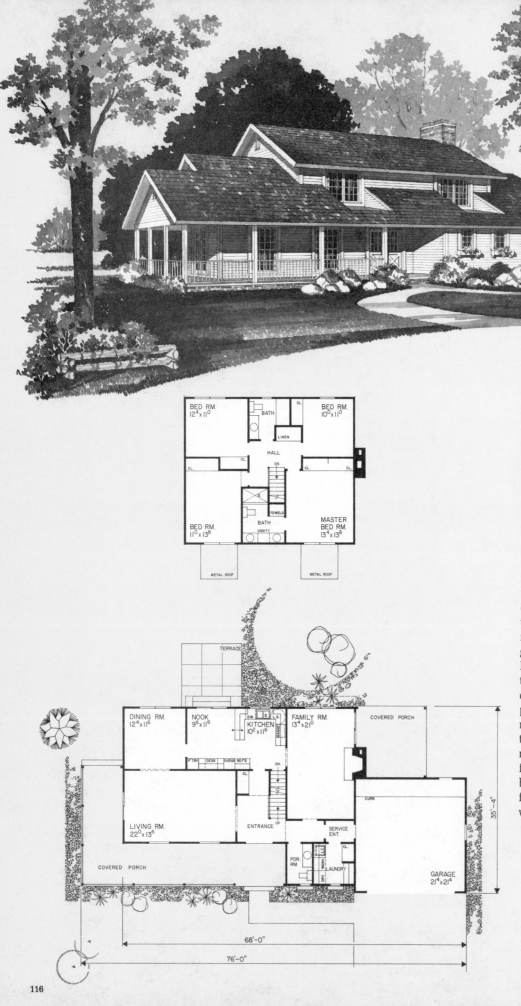

Design T62775

1,317 Sq. Ft. - First Floor
952 Sq. Ft. - Second Floor
47,795 Cu. Ft.

● This front porch Farmhouse adaptation is characteristic of the rolling hills of Pennsylvania. Warm summer evenings will be a delight when the outdoors can be enjoyed in such an impressive manner. You will also be impressed by the interior after the floor plan is reviewed. Double front doors lead the way into this interior. Both the formal and informal areas are outstandingly spacious. There are two eating areas: the formal dining room and the nook with sliding glass doors to a dining terrace. Many built-ins will be found in the nook-kitchen area; including a desk, pantry and more. Notice pass-thru counter. Make special note, there is a covered porch to the side of the family room for more outside enjoyment. Three family bedrooms, bath and master bedroom suite are on the second floor. Years of pleasurable living will be enjoyed in this home.

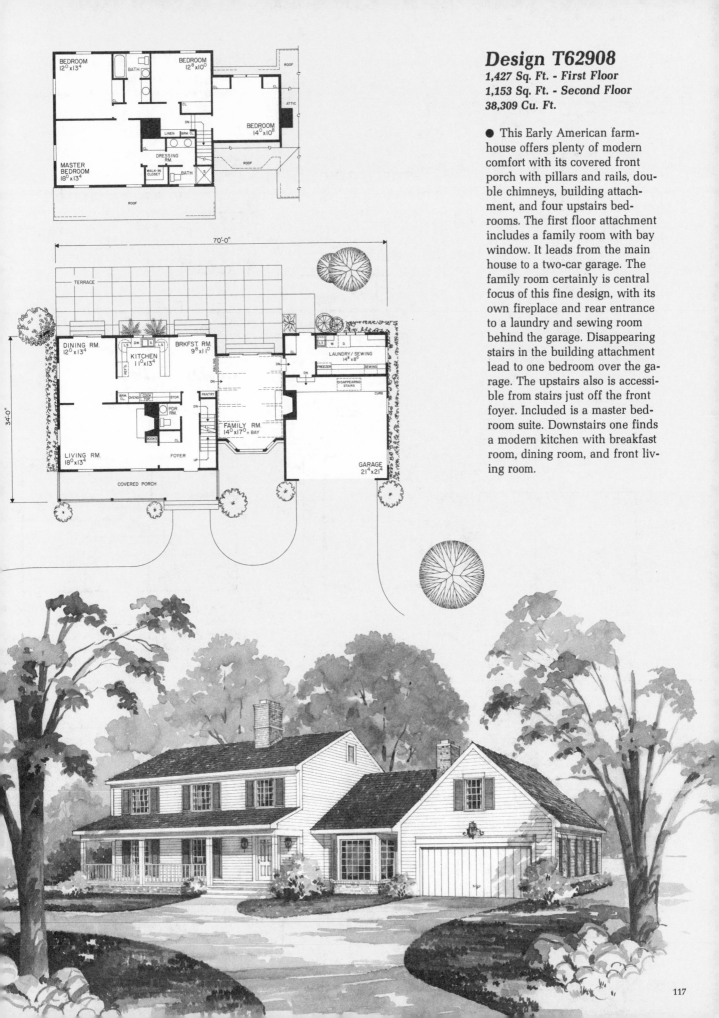

BEDROOM
12⁰x13⁴

BEDROOM
12⁸x10⁰

BEDROOM
14⁰x10⁶

ATTIC

ROOF

ROOF

BATH

CL

CL

CL

DN

LINEN

BRM. CL.

DRESSING RM.

MASTER BEDROOM
18⁰x13⁴

WALK-IN CLOSET

BATH

S

ROOF

70'-0"

34'-0"

TERRACE

DINING RM.
12⁰x13⁴

KITCHEN
11⁰x13⁴

REF'G.

LS   DW   LS

BRKFST RM.
9⁸x11⁰

LAUNDRY / SEWING
14⁸x8⁰

W.   D.

FREEZER   SEWING

CL

DISAPPEARING STAIRS

CURB

BRM. CL.

OVENS   COOK

STOR.

PANTRY

DN

DN

POR. RM.

BOOKS

CL

FAMILY RM.
14⁰x17⁰+ BAY

LIVING RM.
18⁰x13⁴

FOYER

UP

GARAGE
21⁴x21⁴

COVERED PORCH

Design T62908

1,427 Sq. Ft. - First Floor
1,153 Sq. Ft. - Second Floor
38,309 Cu. Ft.

● This Early American farmhouse offers plenty of modern
comfort with its covered front
porch with pillars and rails, double chimneys, building attachment, and four upstairs bedrooms. The first floor attachment
includes a family room with bay
window. It leads from the main
house to a two-car garage. The
family room certainly is central
focus of this fine design, with its
own fireplace and rear entrance
to a laundry and sewing room
behind the garage. Disappearing
stairs in the building attachment
lead to one bedroom over the garage. The upstairs also is accessible from stairs just off the front
foyer. Included is a master bedroom suite. Downstairs one finds
a modern kitchen with breakfast
room, dining room, and front living room.

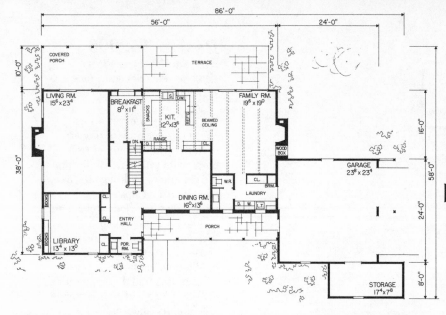

Design T61239
1,822 Sq. Ft. - First Floor
1,419 Sq. Ft. - Second Floor; 41,650 Cu. Ft.

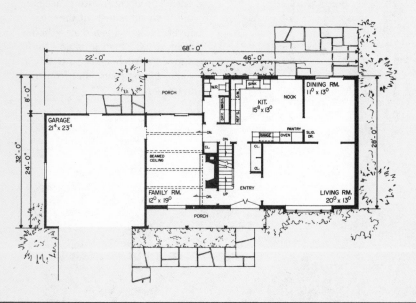

Design T61955
1,192 Sq. Ft. - First Floor
1,192 Sq. Ft. - Second Floor; 32,408 Cu. Ft.

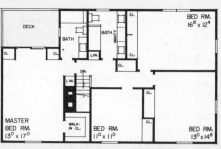

● Here is a design with all of the features a home owner would want most in a new house. It abound in exterior appeal and will be a neighborhood sho place. Picture yourself relaxing on the front, cove porch after a hard day of work.

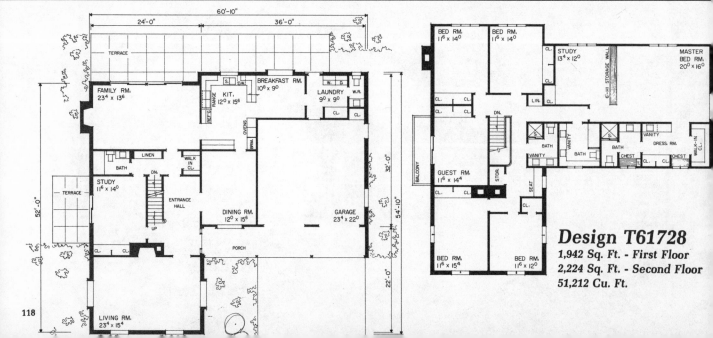

Design T61728
1,942 Sq. Ft. - First Floor
2,224 Sq. Ft. - Second Floor
51,212 Cu. Ft.

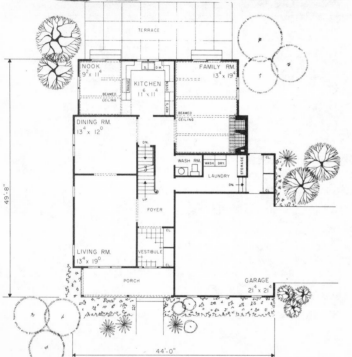

TERRACE

NOOK
9² x 11⁴

KITCHEN
11 x 11

BEAMED CEILING

DINING RM.
13⁴ x 12⁰

FAMILY RM.
13⁴ x 19⁴

BEAMED CEILING

WASH RM.

WASH. DRY.

LAUNDRY

STORAGE

DN.

DN.

UP

FOYER

LIVING RM.
13⁴ x 19⁰

VESTIBULE

CL

PORCH

GARAGE
21⁴ x 21⁴

49'-8"

44'-0"

Design T62333
1,411 Sq. Ft. - First Floor
1,152 Sq. Ft. - Second Floor
31,825 Cu. Ft.

DECK

MASTER
BED RM.
13⁴ x 17⁰

BED RM.
12² x 11⁸

CL

DN.

LINEN STORAGE

BATH

DRESSING

BED RM.
11⁴ x 11⁸

BED RM.
12² x 11⁸

CL

Design T62172
1,618 Sq. Ft. - First Floor
1,205 Sq. Ft. - Second Floor
42,667 Cu. Ft.

66'-6"

TERRACE

FAMILY RM.
26⁰ x 13⁴

RAISED HEARTH

BEAMED CEILING

KIT.
12⁸ x 13⁴

NOOK
10⁸ x 11⁸

W.R.

LNDRY.

DESK

CHINA

PNTRY.

RANGE OVEN

CL

CHINA

34'-10"

UP

DN.

FOYER

PDR. RM.

DINING RM.
11⁰ x 13⁸

PORCH

CURB

LIVING RM.
13⁴ x 19⁸

GARAGE
23⁴ x 21⁴

BATH

DRESS.
RM.

BED RM.
11⁰ x 10⁰

BED RM.
12⁰ x 13¹¹

CL

CL

CL

RAILING

DN.

LINEN

CL

MASTER
BED RM.
13⁹ x 17⁴

BATH

BED RM.
13⁰ x 13⁶

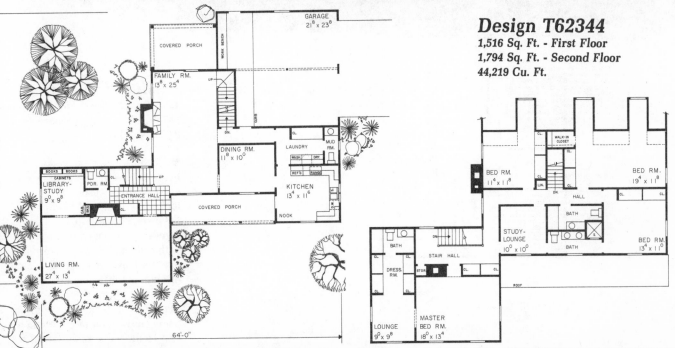

GARAGE
21⁸ x 23⁸

COVERED PORCH

WORK BENCH

FAMILY RM.
13⁸ x 25⁴

UP

DN.

DINING RM.
11⁸ x 10⁰

LAUNDRY

WASH. DRY.

MUD RM.

CL.

REFG RANGE

KITCHEN
13⁴ x 11⁶

NOOK

COVERED PORCH

BOOKS BOOKS

CABINETS

LIBRARY-STUDY
9⁰ x 9⁸

PDR. RM.

UP

ENTRANCE HALL

CL.

CAB SINK

LIVING RM.
27⁴ x 13⁴

64'-0"

Design T62344
1,516 Sq. Ft. - First Floor
1,794 Sq. Ft. - Second Floor
44,219 Cu. Ft.

WALK-IN CLOSET

CL.

BED RM.
11⁴ x 11⁸

LIN.

DN.

HALL

BED RM.
19⁴ x 11⁸

CL.

CL.

BATH

STUDY-LOUNGE
10⁰ x 10⁰

BATH

BED RM.
13⁴ x 11⁰

ROOF

BATH

DN.

STAIR HALL

CL.

CL.

DRESS. RM.

STOR

CL.

CL.

LOUNGE
9⁰ x 9⁸

MASTER BED RM.
18⁰ x 13⁴

BED RM.
11⁰x 11⁶

BATH

SEAT

BED RM.
9⁸x 11⁶

CL.

DN.

LINEN

CL.

CL.

WALK IN
CLOSET

S.

MASTER
BED RM.
11⁴x 17⁶

BATH

BED RM.
12⁰x 12¹⁰

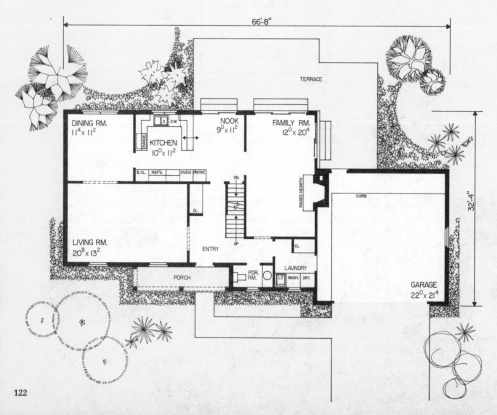

66'-8"

TERRACE

DINING RM.
11⁴x 11²

KITCHEN
10⁰x 11²

RANGE   S.   D.W.

NOOK
9⁰x 11²

FAMILY RM.
12⁰x 20⁴

B.CL. REF'G. OVEN PNTRY.

DN.

RAISED HEARTH

CURB

CL.

LIVING RM.
20⁸x 13²

ENTRY

UP

CL.

32'-4"

PORCH

PDR.
RM.

LT

LAUNDRY

WASH. DRY.

GARAGE
22⁰x 21⁴

Design T62752

1,209 Sq. Ft. - First Floor
960 Sq. Ft. - Second Floor
34,725 Cu. Ft.

● This impressive two-story
home is sure to catch the eye of
even the most casual of on--
lookers. The extended one-story
wing adds great appeal to the
exterior. The covered porch
with pillars also is a charming
feature. Now take a walk
through the efficient floor plan.
The living/dining room is L-
shaped with the dining room
being convenient to the kitchen.
The U-shaped kitchen has a
pass-thru to the breakfast nook
plus has many built-ins to help
ease kitchen duties. The nook,
along with the family room, has
sliding glass doors to the terrace. Also on the first floor is a
powder room and laundry. The
second floor houses the three
family bedrooms, bath and the
master bedroom suite with all
the extras. Note the extra curb
area in the garage.

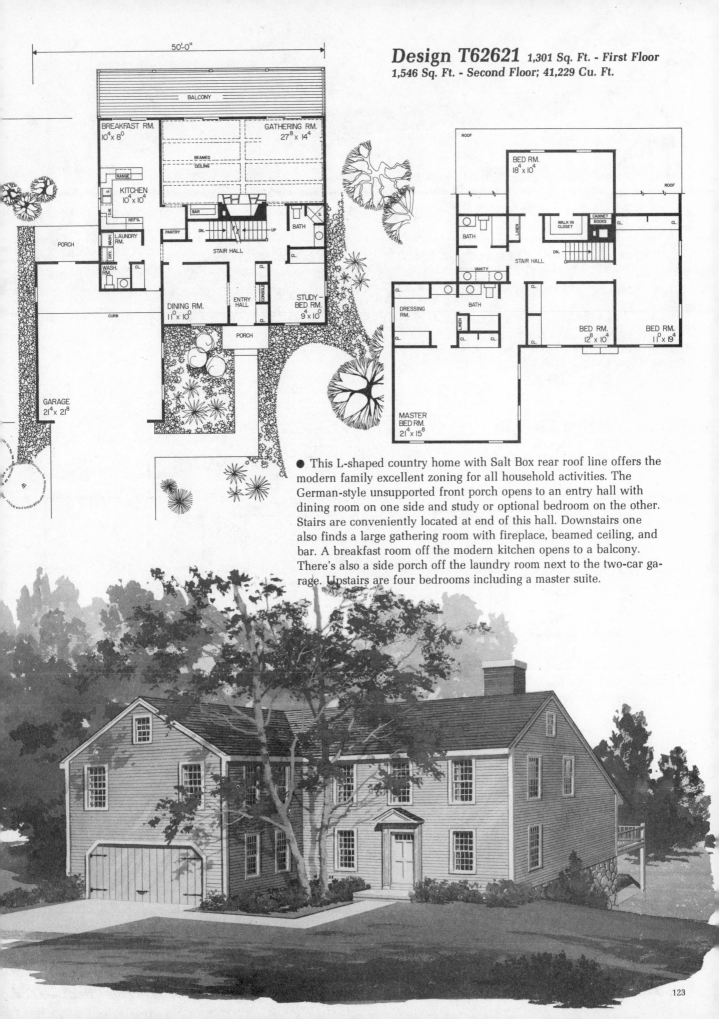

Design T62621 1,301 Sq. Ft. - First Floor
1,546 Sq. Ft. - Second Floor; 41,229 Cu. Ft.

50'-0"

BALCONY

BREAKFAST RM.
10⁴x 8⁰

GATHERING RM.
27⁸ x 14⁴

BEAMED CEILING

RANGE

KITCHEN
10⁴ x 10⁴

REF'G.

BAR

PANTRY

DN.   UP

BATH

S.

WASH LAUNDRY RM.
DRY.

STAIR HALL

CL.

PORCH

WASH. RM.   CL.

CURB

DINING RM.
11⁴x 10⁰

ENTRY HALL   CONSOLE   CL.

CL.

STUDY – BED RM.
9⁴ x 10⁰

PORCH

GARAGE
21⁴x 21⁸

ROOF

BED RM.
18⁴ x 10⁴

ROOF

BATH   LINEN

WALK-IN CLOSET   CABINET BOOKS   CL.   CL.

DN.

STAIR HALL

VANITY

CL.   CL.   CL.

DRESSING RM.   BATH   CL.

LINEN   CL.   CL.

BED RM.
12⁸ x 10⁴

BED RM.
11⁰ x 19⁴

MASTER BED RM.
21⁴ x 15⁸

● This L-shaped country home with Salt Box rear roof line offers the modern family excellent zoning for all household activities. The German-style unsupported front porch opens to an entry hall with dining room on one side and study or optional bedroom on the other. Stairs are conveniently located at end of this hall. Downstairs one also finds a large gathering room with fireplace, beamed ceiling, and bar. A breakfast room off the modern kitchen opens to a balcony. There's also a side porch off the laundry room next to the two-car garage. Upstairs are four bedrooms including a master suite.

123

Design T61996

1,056 Sq. Ft. - First Floor
1,040 Sq. Ft. - Second Floor
29,071 Cu. Ft.

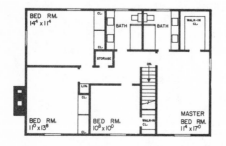

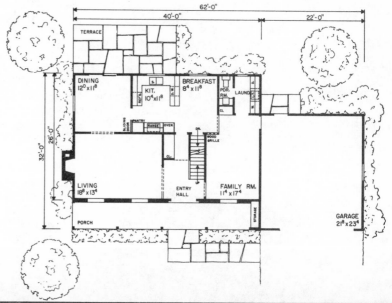

Design T61304

1,120 Sq. Ft. - First Floor
1,120 Sq. Ft. - Second Floor
31,920 Cu. Ft.

Design T61339

1,292 Sq. Ft. - First Floor
1,232 Sq. Ft. - Second Floor
34,706 Cu. Ft.

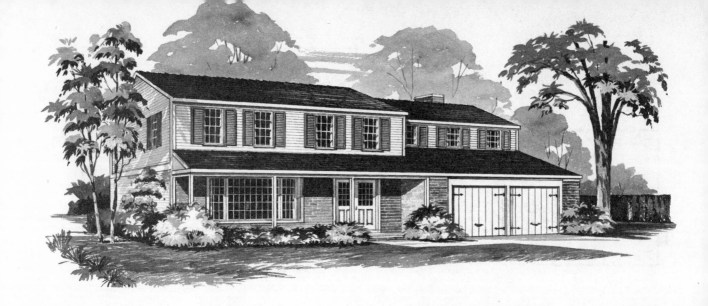

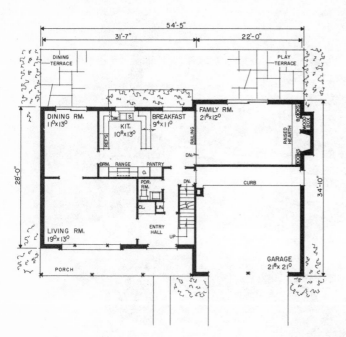

Design T61868
1,190 Sq. Ft. - First Floor
1,300 Sq. Ft. - Second Floor
32,327 Cu. Ft.

● A five bedroom Farmhouse adaptation that is truly a home for family living. The big family room will be everyone's favorite area. Note the master bedroom suite located over the garage

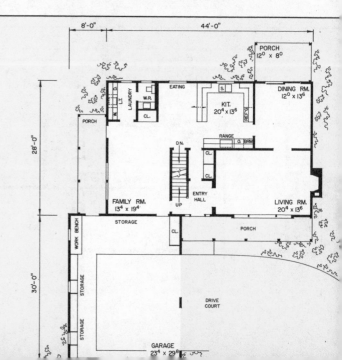

Design T61269 1,232 Sq. Ft. - First Floor
1,232 Sq. Ft. - Second Floor; 33,344 Cu. Ft.

● This practical, comfortable home offers plenty of usable space for the larger family with good bedroom space, kitchen space, dining area, double garage, and both a living room and family room. A deck and porch extend the house even more. All this modern comfort wrapped in a lovely exterior with traditional charm!

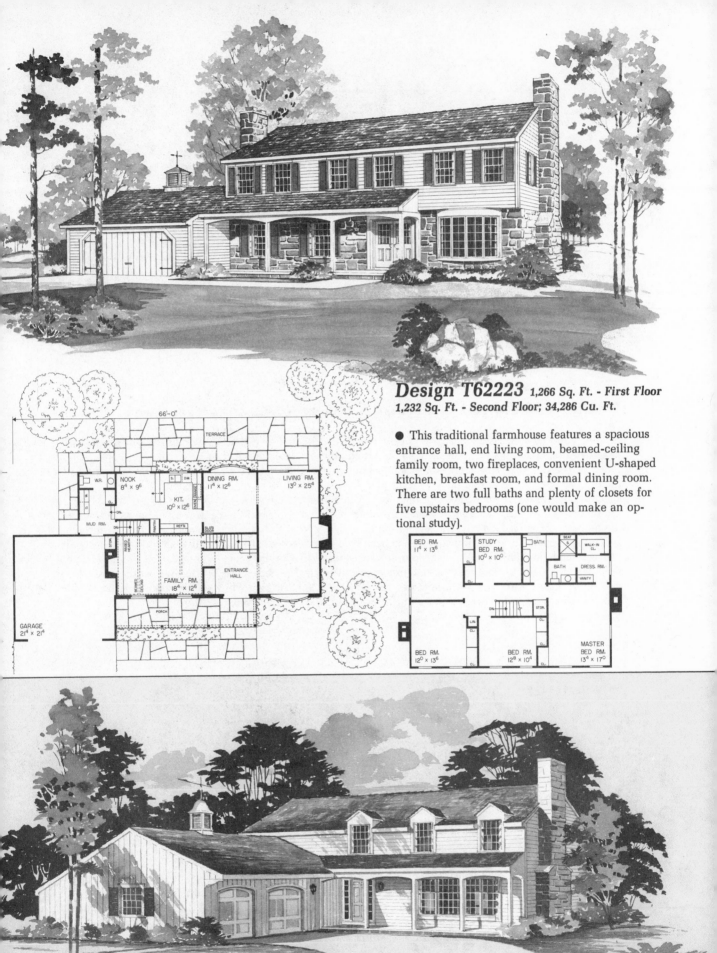

Design T62223 1,266 Sq. Ft. - *First Floor*
1,232 Sq. Ft. - *Second Floor*; 34,286 Cu. Ft.

● This traditional farmhouse features a spacious entrance hall, end living room, beamed-ceiling family room, two fireplaces, convenient U-shaped kitchen, breakfast room, and formal dining room. There are two full baths and plenty of closets for five upstairs bedrooms (one would make an optional study).

TERRACE

W.R.

NOOK
8⁴ x 9⁶

KIT.
10⁰ x 12⁶

DINING RM.
11⁴ x 12⁶

LIVING RM.
13⁰ x 25⁴

MUD RM.

FAMILY RM.
18⁴ x 12⁶

ENTRANCE HALL

UP

BEAMED CEILING

RAISED HEARTH

PORCH

GARAGE
21⁴ x 21⁴

66'-0"

BED RM.
11⁴ x 13⁶

STUDY
BED RM.
10⁰ x 10⁰

BATH

SEAT

WALK-IN CL.

BATH

DRESS. RM.

VANITY

DN.

STOR.

BED RM.
12⁰ x 13⁶

BED RM.
12⁸ x 10⁴

MASTER BED RM.
13⁴ x 17⁰

Design T62694 *2,026 Sq. Ft. - First Floor; 1,386 Sq. Ft. - Second Floor; 69,445 Cu. Ft.*

● This comfortable two-story design faithfully recalls the original 18th-Century homestead of Secretary of Foreign Affairs John Jay. Jay, born in 1745, inherited land for his homestead in Bedford, New York, from his father, a wealthy New York merchant of Huguenot descent. Our updated design captures the exterior flavor of the Jay Homestead, but adds a modern floor plan for lifestyle of today. A cozy country kitchen offers plenty of space and convenience with cook-top snack bar. A downstairs clutter room includes space for tool bench, sorting counter, pantry, freezer, and sewing. A spacious living room just off the central foyer opens to a formal dining room on one side, a music alcove on another side, and a library wing. A mud room and washroom separate the garage from the big country kitchen. That makes grocery trips from the car to the kitchen quick and easy and also allows careful backdoor entrances for kids with dirty feet. Huge covered porches stretch across the front and back of the house. Upstairs are three sizable bedrooms. The master bedroom suite is especially luxurious with large walk-in closet, dressing room, and its own whirpool. You like fireplaces? This cozy farmhouse has two of them. One's in the living room, while the other is in the spacious country kitchen, sure to be a gathering place.

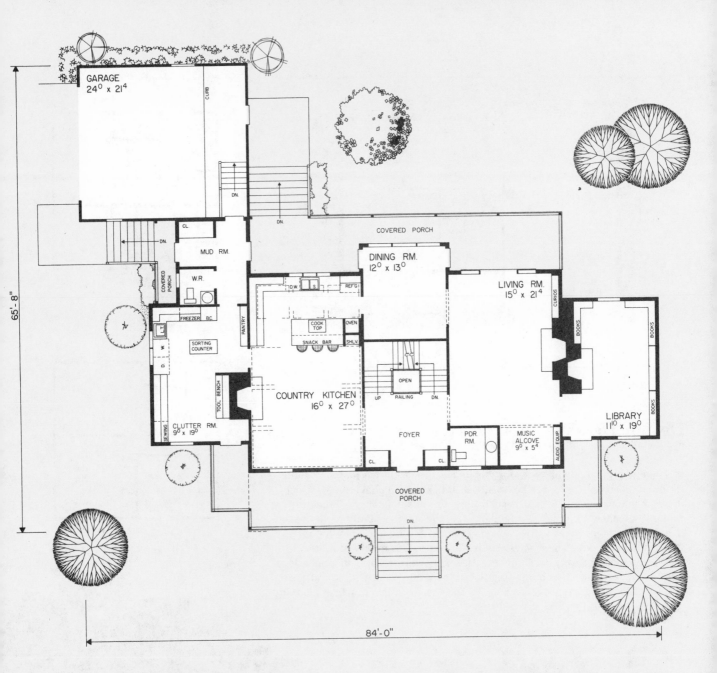

GARAGE
24⁰ x 21⁴

CURB

DN.

DN.

DN.

CL.

MUD RM.

W.R.

COVERED PORCH

FREEZER B.C.

SORTING COUNTER

SEWING

W

D

TOOL BENCH

CLUTTER RM.
9⁰ x 19⁰

PANTRY

COVERED PORCH

D.W. S

REF'G

COOK TOP

OVEN

SNACK BAR

SHLV.

DINING RM.
12⁰ x 13⁰

LIVING RM.
15⁰ x 21⁴

CURIOS

BOOKS

BOOKS

COUNTRY KITCHEN
16⁰ x 27⁰

OPEN

UP   RAILING   DN.

FOYER

PDR. RM.

MUSIC ALCOVE
9⁰ x 5⁴

AUDIO EQUIP.

BOOKS

LIBRARY
11¹⁰ x 19⁰

CL.

CL.

COVERED PORCH

DN.

65'- 8"

84'- 0"

. . . reminiscent of Historic 18th-Century Farmhouse!

CL. SEAT SEAT CL.

DRESSING RM.

BATH

WHIRLPOOL

BEDROOM
16⁰ x 13⁴

WALK-IN CLOSET

S

SEAT

CL.

OPEN

RAILING

DN.

CL.

CL.

LINEN

MASTER BEDROOM
16⁰ x 17⁴

BATH

BEDROOM
12⁰ x 15⁰

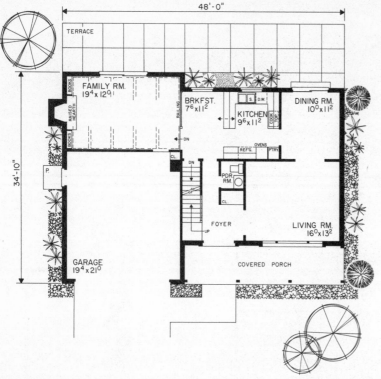

OPTIONAL 3 BEDROOM PLAN

Design T61956 *990 Sq. Ft. - First Floor*
728 Sq. Ft. - Second Floor; 23,703 Cu. Ft.

● The blueprints that you order for this four bedroom design include details for building an optional three bedroom second floor. Whichever your choice, the tremendous livability of the second floor remains unchanged. Study the fine traffic patterns throughout the plan. Note the sunken family room, tucked behind the garage, with its fireplace and beamed ceiling. Observe that the efficiently planned kitchen is conveniently flanked by the breakfast room and the dining room for ease in serving meals. The powder room is in a good location. It can serve all areas of the first floor. The living room will be traffic-free and serve those formal occasions ideally. Together with this practical plan and attractive exterior, this design is a winner.

TWO-STORY
TRADITIONAL STYLE VARIATIONS

Traditional style homes trace their roots in America to colonial days. They are designed with comfort in mind. Their simple, clean lines and efficiency are reminiscent of the traditional charm of yesteryear.

Design T62826
1,112 Sq. Ft. - First Floor
881 Sq. Ft. - Second Floor; 32,770 Cu. Ft.

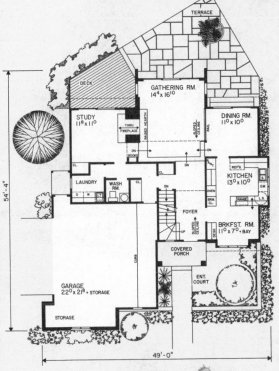

ALTERNATE KITCHEN / DINING RM./
BREAKFAST RM. FLOOR PLAN

● This is an outstanding example of the type of informal, traditional-style architecture that has captured the modern imagination. The interior plan houses all of the features that people want most - a spacious gathering room, formal and informal dining areas, efficient, U-shaped kitchen, master bedroom, two children's bedrooms, second floor lounge, entrance court and rear terrace and deck. Study all areas of this plan carefully.

Design T62561

1,655 Sq. Ft. - First Floor
943 Sq. Ft. - Second Floor; 41,738 Cu. Ft.

● A convenient living plan housed in
a distinctively appealing exterior.
Passing through the double front
doors one immediately observes a
fine functioning interior. Traffic patterns are efficient, but also flexible.
The family room area is sunken a
couple of steps below the level of the
breakfast nook and entry. The open
planning of the kitchen area, and between the living and dining rooms
add to the spaciousness. Study the
upstairs and how it is open to the
family room below. Those are folding
doors that provide the bedroom with
privacy.

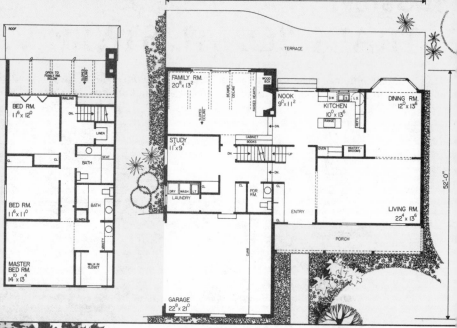

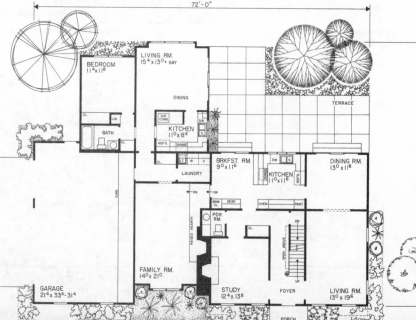

Design T62808

1,540 Sq. Ft. - First Floor; 1,117 Sq. Ft. - Second Floor
605 Sq. Ft. - Apartment; 48,075 Cu. Ft.

● A complete apartment is tucked in the back
of this Colonial home. This apartment would
be ideal for a live-in relative or supplement
your income by becoming a landlord and rent
out the apartment. The rest of this house will
serve a larger family with great ease. There is
a formal living room and an informal family
room plus a good-sized study. All of the sleeping facilities are on the efficiently planned
second floor.

Design T62609 1,543 Sq. Ft. - First Floor
1,005 Sq. Ft. - Second Floor; 36,800 Cu. Ft.

● Here is an L-shaped two-story with a variety of features that help recall the architectural charm of Colonial America. Observe the massive twin chimneys, contrasting exterior materials, window and door treatment, cupola and picket fence. The interior is designed for real family living. Four bedrooms, two full baths and plenty of closets provide excellent sleeping facilities. The large, end living room will enjoy its privacy. A study provides that often sought-after haven for the enjoyment of peace and quiet. Beamed ceilings are a highlight of the family room and kitchen. Don't miss the breakfast eating area, the separate dining room, the laundry and the stairs to the basement.

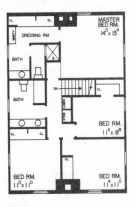

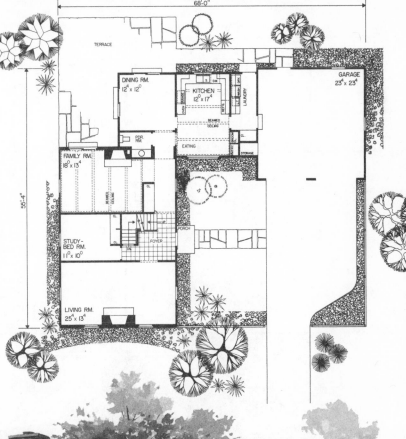

133

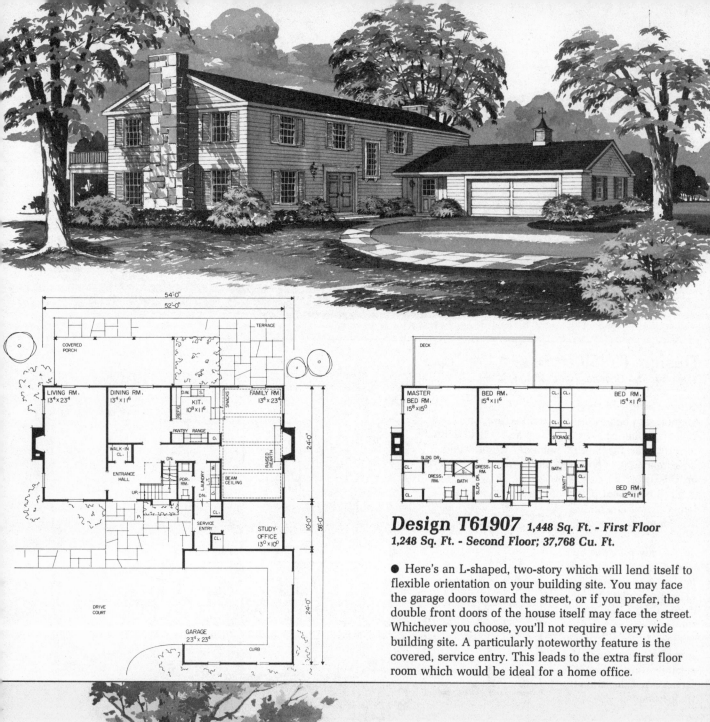

Design T61907 1,448 Sq. Ft. - First Floor
1,248 Sq. Ft. - Second Floor; 37,768 Cu. Ft.

● Here's an L-shaped, two-story which will lend itself to flexible orientation on your building site. You may face the garage doors toward the street, or if you prefer, the double front doors of the house itself may face the street. Whichever you choose, you'll not require a very wide building site. A particularly noteworthy feature is the covered, service entry. This leads to the extra first floor room which would be ideal for a home office.

Design T62598
1,016 Sq. Ft. - First Floor
890 Sq. Ft. - Second Floor; 30,000 Cu. Ft.

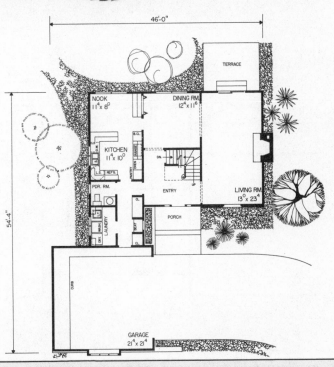

● An impressive, Early Colonial adaptation with a projecting two-car garage and front drive court. It will not demand a large, expensive piece of property. In days of high-cost building, this relatively modest-sized two-story will be a great investment. Note the huge living room. The basement lends itself to recreational facilities.

Design T62622
624 Sq. Ft. - First Floor
624 Sq. Ft. - Second Floor; 19,864 Cu. Ft.

● Appealing design can envelope little packages, too. Here is a charming, Early Colonial adaptation with an attached two-car garage to serve the young family with a modest building budget.

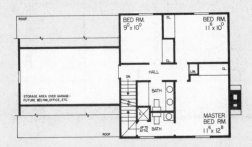

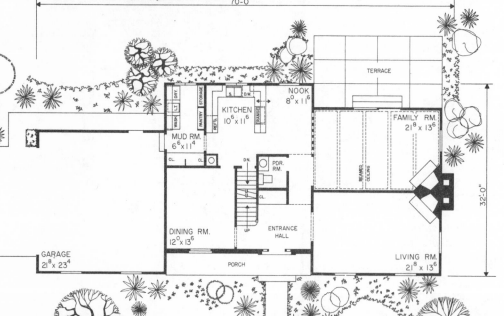

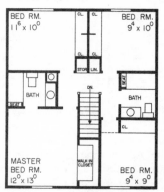

Design T62367
1,356 Sq. Ft. - First Floor
780 Sq. Ft. - Second Floor
31,230 Cu. Ft.

● This attractively proportioned two-story is a good study in effective zoning. Observe how the various areas function independently as well as together.

70'-0"

TERRACE

NOOK
8⁰ x 11⁶

KITCHEN
10⁶ x 11⁶

WASH / DRY / PANTRY / STORAGE / REF'L / RANGE

FAMILY RM.
21⁸ x 13⁶

MUD RM.
6⁶ x 11⁴

CL. CL.

BEAMED CEILING

DN. / PDR. RM.

32'-0"

DINING RM.
12⁰ x 13⁶

UP

ENTRANCE HALL

LIVING RM.
21⁸ x 13⁶

GARAGE
21⁸ x 23⁴

PORCH

BED RM.
11⁶ x 10⁰

CL. CL.

BED RM.
9⁴ x 10⁰

STOR. LIN.

BATH

SEAT

DN.

SEAT

BATH

MASTER BED RM.
12⁰ x 13⁰

WALK-IN CLOSET

CL.

BED RM.
9⁴ x 9⁰

Design T62634 1,308 Sq. Ft. - First Floor
1,047 Sq. Ft. - Second Floor; 32,600 Cu. Ft.

● The second floor of this fine home overhangs the first floor. Four bedrooms and two baths are located here. This home will be an outstanding investment.

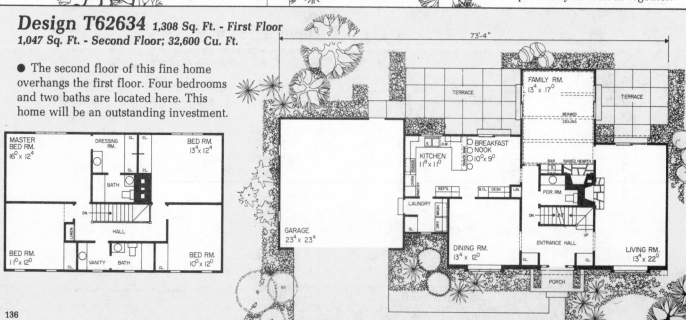

MASTER BED RM.
16⁰ x 12⁴

DRESSING RM.

CL. CL.

BED RM.
13⁴ x 12⁴

BATH

DN.

HALL

BED RM.
11⁰ x 12⁰

VANITY / BATH

LINEN

BED RM.
10⁰ x 12⁰

73'-4"

TERRACE

FAMILY RM.
13⁴ x 17⁰

TERRACE

BEAMED CEILING

GARAGE
23⁴ x 23⁴

KITCHEN
11⁸ x 11⁰

BREAKFAST NOOK
10⁰ x 9⁰

SNACK BAR

BAR / RAISED HEARTH

OVEN / RANGE / PANTRY

REF'L.

B.CL. / DESK

LIN.

S.

PDR. RM.

LAUNDRY

DRY / WASH

CL.

DN.

UP

DINING RM.
13⁴ x 12⁰

ENTRANCE HALL

LIVING RM.
13⁴ x 22⁰

PORCH

Design T62108 1,188 Sq. Ft. - First Floor
720 Sq. Ft. - Second Floor; 27,394 Cu. Ft.

● This design features a full two-story section flanked by one-story wings. The livability offered in this home is interesting and practical. It has separated the functions to assure convenient living.

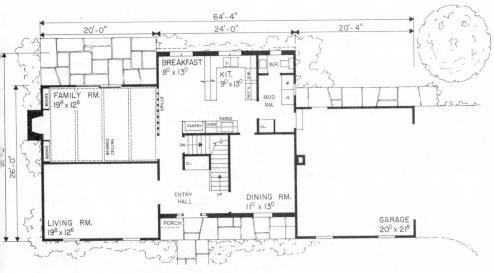

Design T62535

986 Sq. Ft. - First Floor
1,436 Sq. Ft. - Second Floor; 35,835 Cu. Ft.

● What a great package this is! An enchanting Colonial exterior and an exceptional amount of interior livability. Utilizing the space over the garage results in a fifth bedroom with bath.

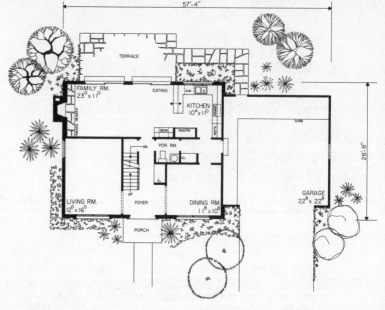

Design T62558

1,030 Sq. Ft. - First Floor
840 Sq. Ft. - Second Floor; 27,120 Cu. Ft.

● This relatively low-budget house is long on exterior appeal and interior livability. It has all the features to assure years of convenient living. Make a list of your favorite features.

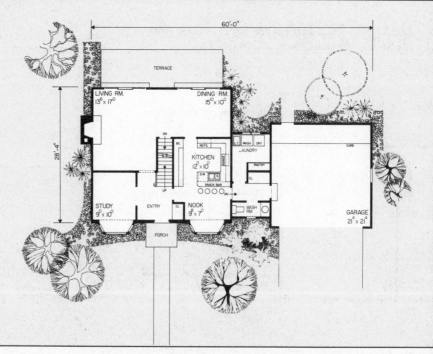

Design T62540

1,306 Sq. Ft. - First Floor
1,360 Sq. Ft. - Second Floor; 40,890 Cu. Ft.

● This efficient Colonial abounds in features. A spacious entry flanked by living areas. A kitchen flanked by eating areas. Upstairs, four bedrooms including a sitting room in the master suite.

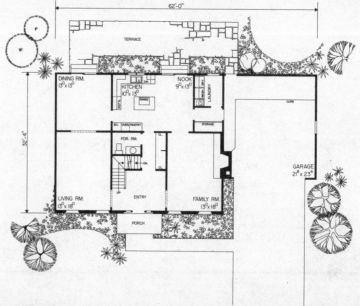

Design T62643
1,446 Sq. Ft. - First Floor
1,281 Sq. Ft. - Second Floor; 41,299 Cu. Ft.

● Four fireplaces! One to serve each of the main rooms on the first floor. Plus an impressive front and rear entrance hall to lead the way through the rest of the interior. Now note the exterior. The main house is identical from the front and back view. This house could hardly be more symmetrical.

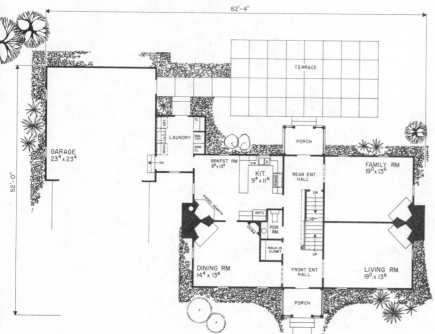

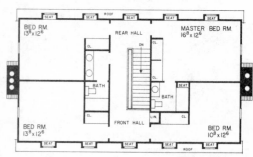

CAPE COD COTTAGES

Severe winds sweep the Cape, dictating the low profile of original 1½-story Cape Cod homes, dating back to the 17th Century. Charming, warm Cape Cod homes generally fall into three groups: (1) a half house with two windows to one side of the front door; (2) a three-quarter house with two windows to one side and one to the other; and (3) a full Cape with a center door flanked by two windows on either side. Appendages often are added to accommodate family growth.

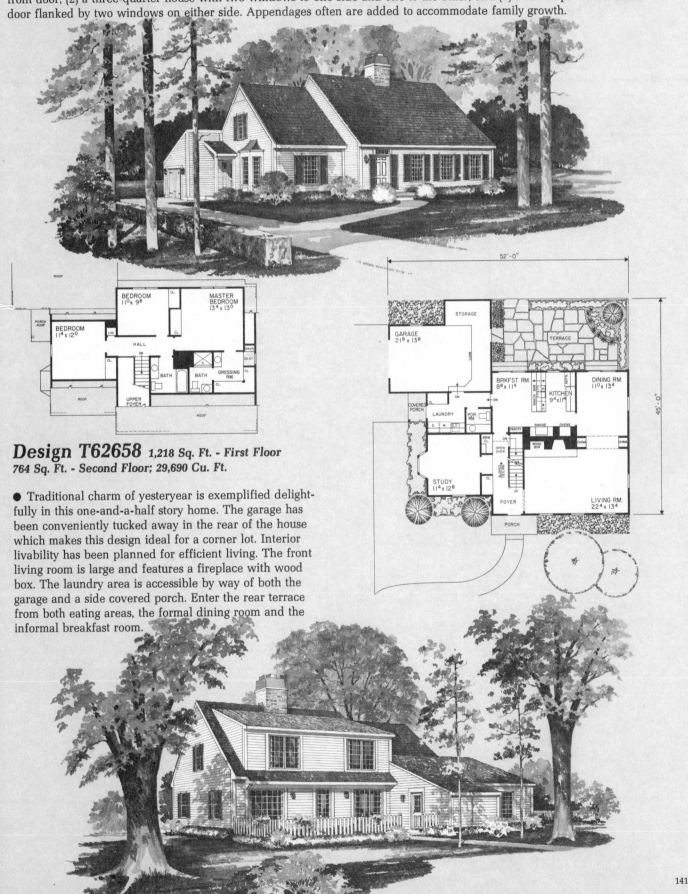

Design T62658 1,218 Sq. Ft. - First Floor
764 Sq. Ft. - Second Floor; 29,690 Cu. Ft.

● Traditional charm of yesteryear is exemplified delightfully in this one-and-a-half story home. The garage has been conveniently tucked away in the rear of the house which makes this design ideal for a corner lot. Interior livability has been planned for efficient living. The front living room is large and features a fireplace with wood box. The laundry area is accessible by way of both the garage and a side covered porch. Enter the rear terrace from both eating areas, the formal dining room and the informal breakfast room.

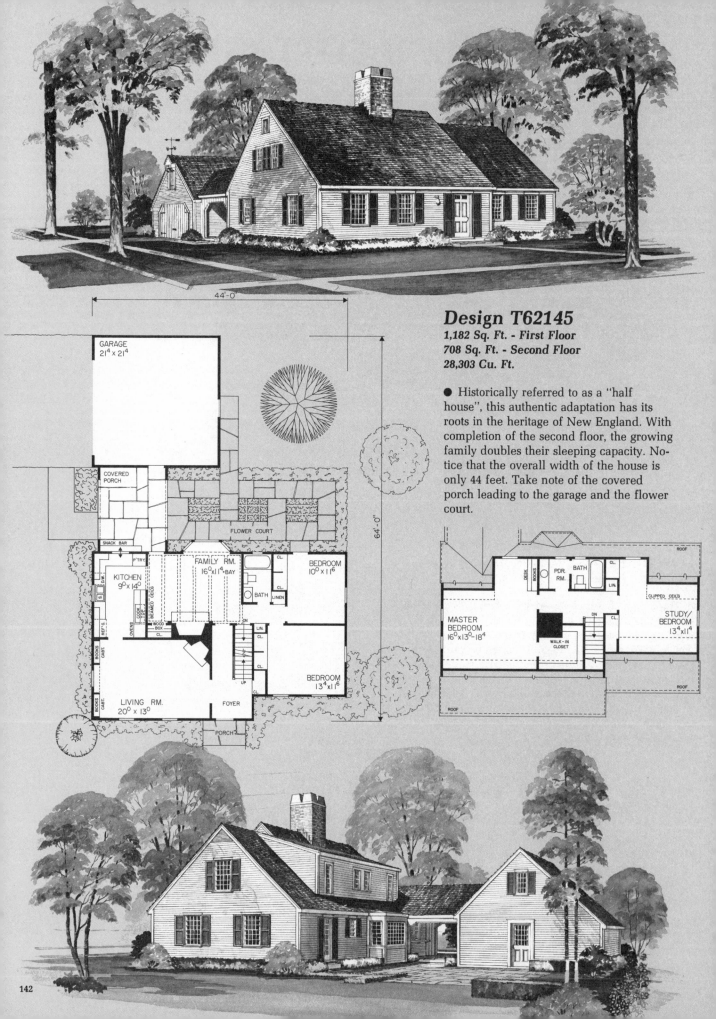

Design T62145

1,182 Sq. Ft. - First Floor
708 Sq. Ft. - Second Floor
28,303 Cu. Ft.

● Historically referred to as a "half house", this authentic adaptation has its roots in the heritage of New England. With completion of the second floor, the growing family doubles their sleeping capacity. Notice that the overall width of the house is only 44 feet. Take note of the covered porch leading to the garage and the flower court.

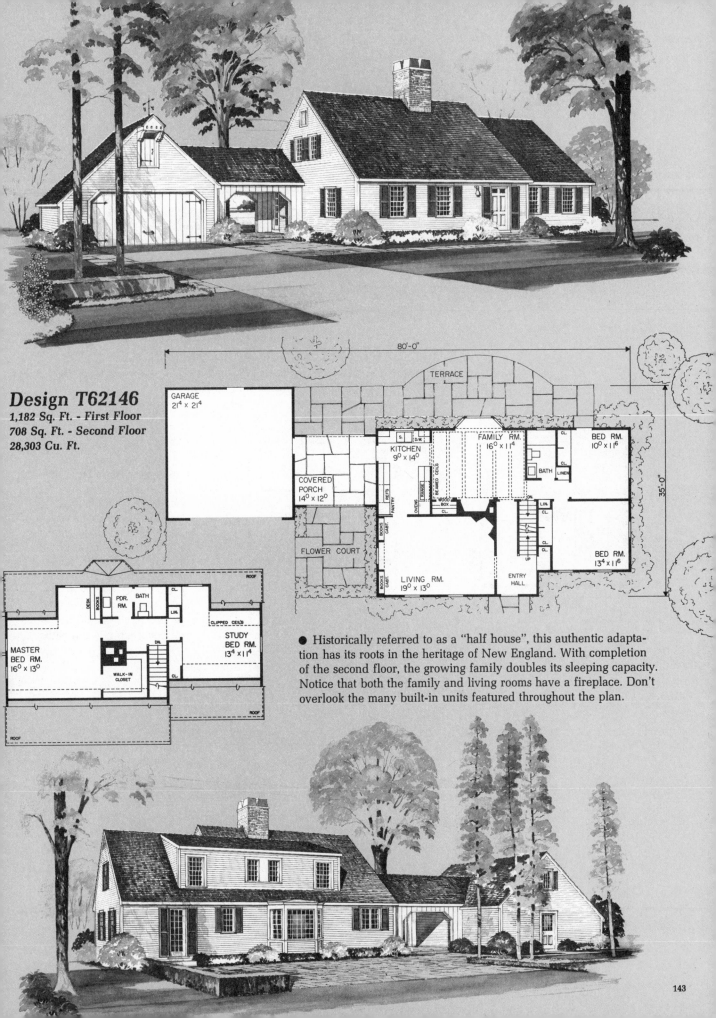

Design T62146
1,182 Sq. Ft. - First Floor
708 Sq. Ft. - Second Floor
28,303 Cu. Ft.

80'-0"

TERRACE

GARAGE
21⁴ x 21⁴

KITCHEN
9⁰ x 14⁰

FAMILY RM.
16⁰ x 11⁴

BED RM.
10⁰ x 11⁶

BATH

LINEN

COVERED
PORCH
14⁰ x 12⁰

D.W.

S.

REFR'S

PANTRY

BOOKS

CABT.

OVENS

RANGE

WOOD
BOX

BEAMED CEIL'G

CL.

CL.

CL.

CL.

LIN.

DN.

35'-0"

BOOKS

CABT.

FLOWER COURT

LIVING RM.
19⁰ x 13⁰

ENTRY
HALL

UP

BED RM.
13⁴ x 11⁶

ROOF

DESK

BOOKS

PDR.
RM.

BATH

CL.

LIN.

CLIPPED CEIL'G

ROOF

MASTER
BED RM.
16⁰ x 13⁰

DN.

WALK-IN
CLOSET

STUDY
BED RM.
13⁴ x 11⁴

CL.

ROOF

ROOF

● Historically referred to as a "half house", this authentic adaptation has its roots in the heritage of New England. With completion of the second floor, the growing family doubles its sleeping capacity. Notice that both the family and living rooms have a fireplace. Don't overlook the many built-in units featured throughout the plan.

Expanding the Half-House

Design T62682
976 Sq. Ft. - First Floor (Basic Plan)
1,230 Sq. Ft. - First Floor (Expanded Plan); 744 Sq. Ft. - Second Floor (Both Plans)
29,355 Cu. Ft. Basic Plan; 35,084 Cu. Ft. Expanded Plan

32'-0"

TERRACE

DINING RM.
10⁸ x 12⁰

COUNTRY KITCHEN
20⁰ x 13⁰-15⁸

30'-0"

DN

PDR. RM.

PTRY

BRM CL.

UP

FOYER

BOOKS

LIVING RM.
20⁰ x 13⁰

PORCH

ROOF

BEDROOM
12¹⁰ x 9⁸

BEDROOM
12¹⁰ x 9⁸

DN

BATH

LINEN

BATH

MASTER BEDROOM
11¹⁰ x 14⁰

ROOF

● Here is an expandable Colonial with a full measure of Cape Cod Charm. For those who wish to build the basic house, there is an abundance of low-budget livability. Twin fireplaces serve the formal living room and the informal country kitchen. Note the spaciousness of both areas. A dining room and powder room are also on the first floor of this basic plan. Upstairs three bedrooms and two full baths.

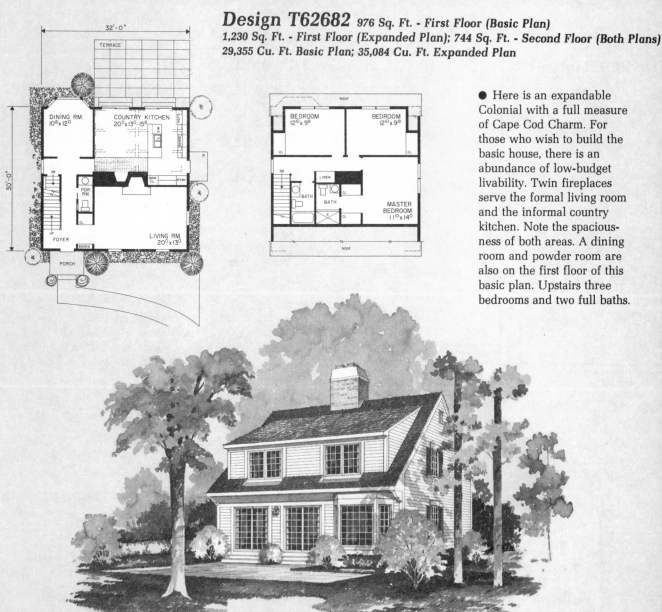

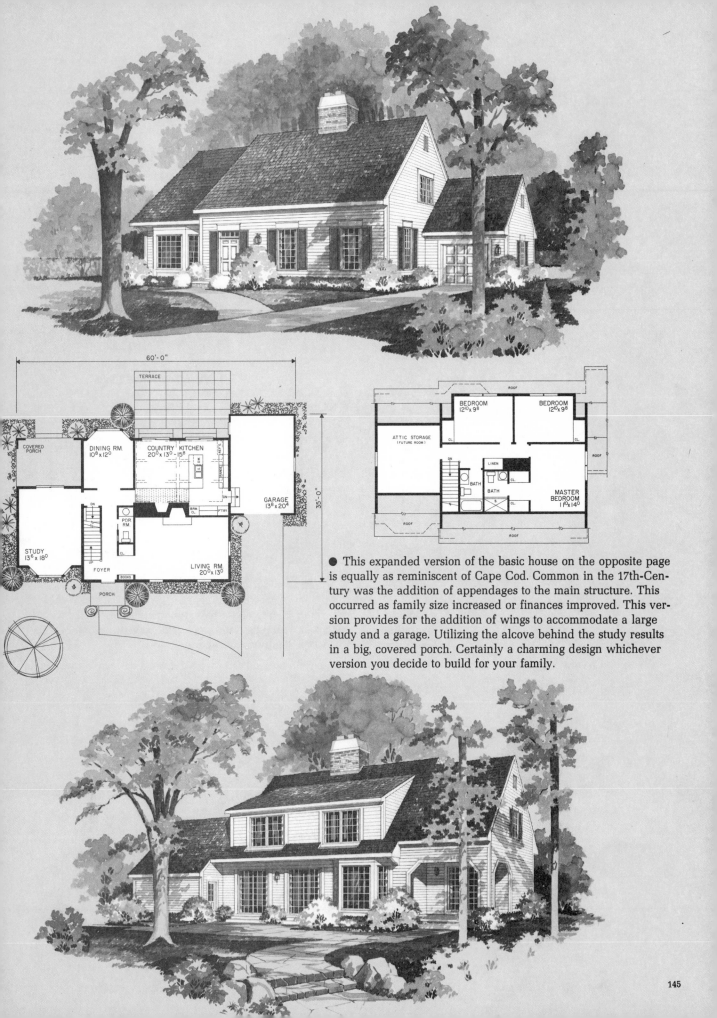

COVERED PORCH

DINING RM.
10⁸ x 12⁰

COUNTRY KITCHEN
20⁰ x 13⁰ -15⁸

REF'G.

RANGE

DW

GARAGE
13⁸ x 20⁴

60'-0"

TERRACE

35'-0"

DN

UP

PDR. RM.

BRM. CL.

CL.

PTRY.

DN

STUDY
13⁶ x 18⁰

FOYER

BOOKS

LIVING RM.
20⁰ x 13⁰

PORCH

ATTIC STORAGE
(FUTURE ROOM)

BEDROOM
12¹⁰ x 9⁸

BEDROOM
12¹⁰ x 9⁸

CL.

CL.

ROOF

DN

LINEN

BATH

CL.

BATH

MASTER BEDROOM
11⁰ x 14⁰

CL.

ROOF

ROOF

ROOF

● This expanded version of the basic house on the opposite page is equally as reminiscent of Cape Cod. Common in the 17th-Century was the addition of appendages to the main structure. This occurred as family size increased or finances improved. This version provides for the addition of wings to accommodate a large study and a garage. Utilizing the alcove behind the study results in a big, covered porch. Certainly a charming design whichever version you decide to build for your family.

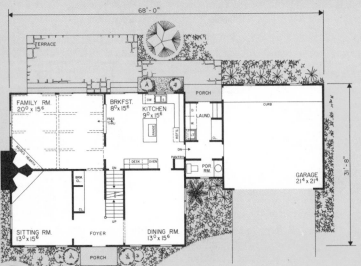

Design T62644
1,349 Sq. Ft. - First Floor
836 Sq. Ft. - Second Floor
36,510 Cu. Ft.

● What a delightful, compact, one-and-a-half story home. This design has many fine features tucked within its framework. The bowed roofline of this house stems from late 17th-Century architecture.

Design T62661

1,020 Sq. Ft. - First Floor
777 Sq. Ft. - Second Floor; 30,745 Cu. Ft.

● Any other starter house or retirement home couldn't have more charm than this design. Its compact frame houses a very livable plan. An outstanding feature of the first floor is the large country kitchen. Its fine attractions include a beamed ceiling, raised hearth fireplace, built-in window seat and a door leading to the outdoors. A living room is in the front of the plan and has another fireplace which shares the single chimney. The rear dormered second floor houses the sleeping and bath facilities.

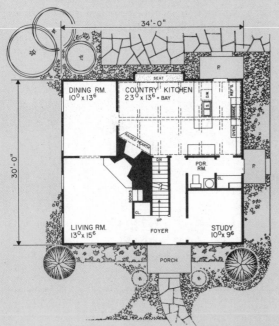

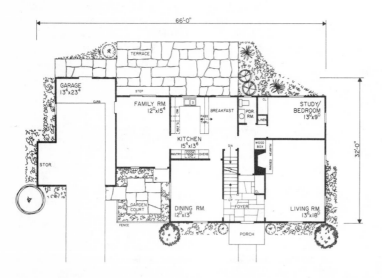

● Colonial charm could hardly be more appealingly captured than it is by this winsome design. List the features and study the living patterns.

Design T61901
1,200 Sq. Ft. - First Floor
744 Sq. Ft. - Second Floor; 27,822 Cu. Ft.

Design T61104
1,396 Sq. Ft. - First Floor
574 Sq. Ft. - Second Floor; 31,554 Cu. Ft.

● Here is a home whose front elevation makes one think of early New England. The frame exterior is highlighted by authentic double-hung windows with charming shutters. The attractive front entrance detail, flanked by the traditional side lites, and the projecting two-car garage with its appealing double doors are more exterior features.

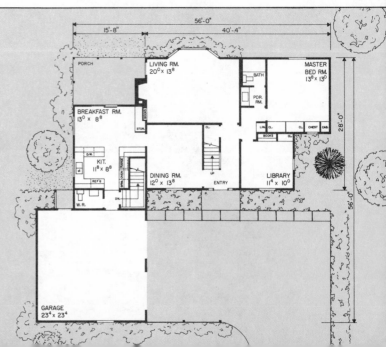

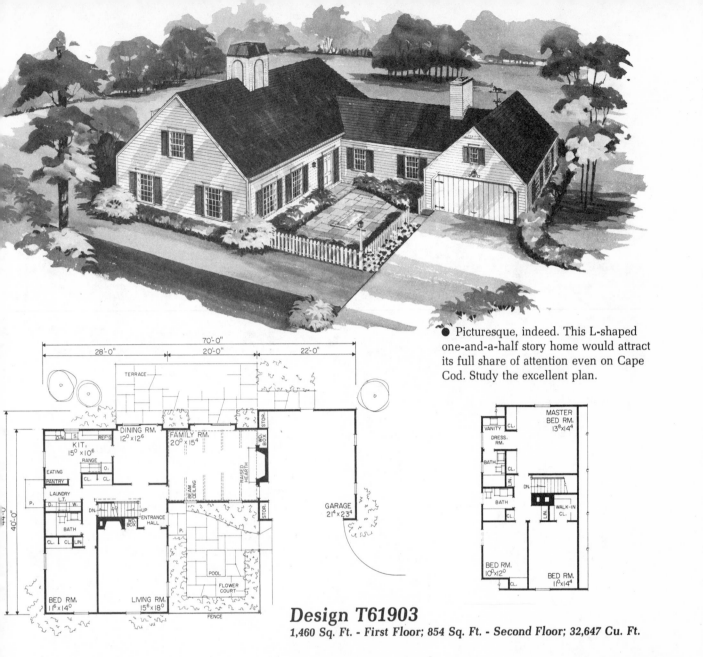

TERRACE

28'-0" | 20'-0" | 22'-0"
70'-0"

DINING RM.
12'⁰ x 12'⁶

KIT.
15'⁰ x 10'⁶

RANGE
O.

EATING
PANTRY
CL. CL.

LAUNDRY
D. W.
L.T.

DN.
WD.
BOX
ENTRANCE
HALL
UP

BATH
CL. CL. LIN.

BED RM.
11'⁶ x 14'⁰

FAMILY RM.
20'⁰ x 15'⁴

BEAM CEILING

RAISED HEARTH

P.

POOL

FLOWER COURT

LIVING RM.
15'⁶ x 18'⁰

FENCE

STOR.

WD. BOX

STOR.

GARAGE
21'⁴ x 23'⁴

40'-0" 44'-0"

● Picturesque, indeed. This L-shaped one-and-a-half story home would attract its full share of attention even on Cape Cod. Study the excellent plan.

MASTER BED RM.
13'⁸ x 14'⁴

VANITY
CL.

DRESS. RM.

BATH
CL.

BATH
CL.

LIN.

DN.
LIN.
WALK-IN CL.

BED RM.
10'⁰ x 12'⁰

BED RM.
11'⁰ x 14'⁴

CL.

Design T61903
1,460 Sq. Ft. - First Floor; 854 Sq. Ft. - Second Floor; 32,647 Cu. Ft.

Design T62631

1,634 Sq. Ft. - First Floor
1,011 Sq. Ft. - Second Floor; 33,720 Cu. Ft.

● Two fireplaces and much more! Notice how all the rooms are accessible from the main hall. That keeps traffic in each room to a minimum, saving you work by preserving your furnishings. There's more. A large family room featuring a beamed ceiling, a fireplace with built-in wood box and double doors onto the terrace. An exceptional U-shaped kitchen is ready to serve you. It has an adjacent breakfast nook. Built-ins, too . . a desk, storage pantry, oven and range. Plus a first floor laundry close at hand.

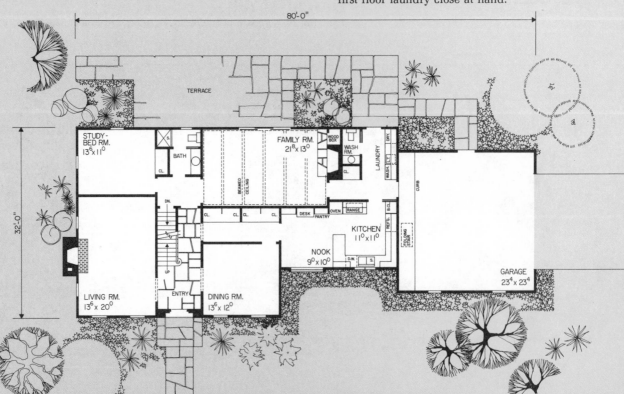

Design T61970

1,664 Sq. Ft. - First Floor
1,116 Sq. Ft. - Second Floor
41,912 Cu. Ft.

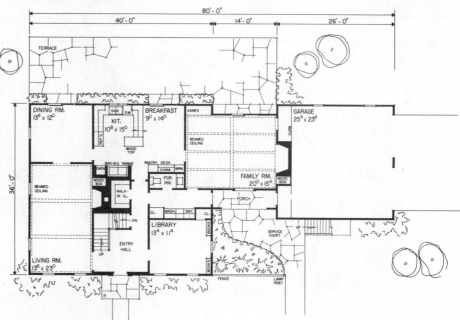

● The prototype of this Colonial house was an integral part of the 18th-Century New England landscape; the updated version is a welcome addition to any suburban scene. The main entry wing, patterned after a classic Cape Cod cottage design, is two stories high but has a pleasing groundhugging look. The steeply pitched roof, triple dormers, and a massive central chimney anchor the house firmly to its site. Entry elevation is symmetrically balanced; doorway, middle dormer, and chimney are in perfect alignment. The one story wing between the main house and the garage is a spacious, beam-ceilinged family room with splay-walled entry porch at the front elevation and sliding glass windows at the rear opening to terrace, which is the full length of the house.

Design T62563

1,500 Sq. Ft. - First Floor
690 Sq. Ft. - Second Floor; 38,243 Cu. Ft.

● You'll have all kinds of fun deciding just how your family will function in this dramatically expanded half-house. There is a lot of attic storage, too. Observe the three-car garage.

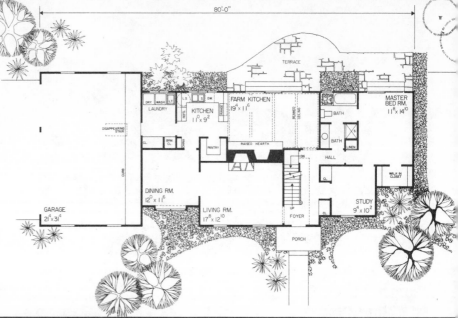

Design T62395

1,481 Sq. Ft. - First Floor
861 Sq. Ft. - Second Floor; 34,487 Cu. Ft.

● New England revisited. The appeal of this type of home is ageless. As for its livability, it will serve its occupants admirably for generations to come. With two bedrooms downstairs, you may want to finish off the second floor at a later date.

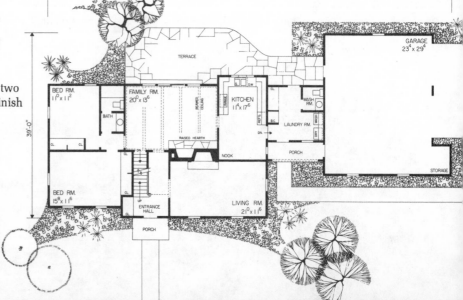

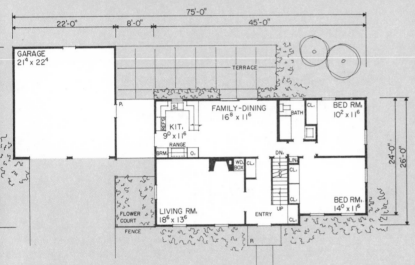

Design T63126 1,141 Sq. Ft. - First Floor
630 Sq. Ft. - Second Floor; 25,533 Cu. Ft.

● This New England adaptation has a lot to offer. There is the U-shaped kitchen, family-dining room, four bedrooms, two full baths, fireplace, covered porch and two-car garage. A delightful addition to any neighborhood.

Design T61791

1,157 Sq. Ft. - First Floor
875 Sq. Ft. - Second Floor; 27,790 Cu. Ft.

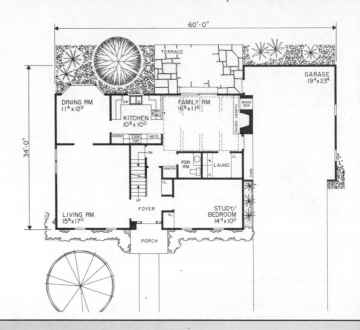

● Wherever you build this moderately sized house an aura of Cape Cod is sure to unfold. The symmetry is pleasing, indeed. The authentic center entrance seems to project a beckoning call.

Design T61870

1,136 Sq. Ft. - First Floor
936 Sq. Ft. - Second Floor; 26,312 Cu. Ft.

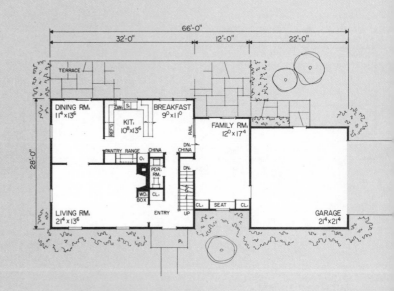

● Besides an enchanting exterior, this home has formal dining and living rooms, plus informal family and breakfast rooms. Built-ins are located in both of these informal rooms. U-shaped, the kitchen will efficiently service both of the dining areas. Study the sleeping facilities of the second floor.

Design T62396

1,616 Sq. Ft. - First Floor
993 Sq. Ft. - Second Floor; 30,583 Cu. Ft.

● Another picturesque facade right from the pages of our Colonial heritage. The authentic features are many. Don't miss the stairs to area over the garage.

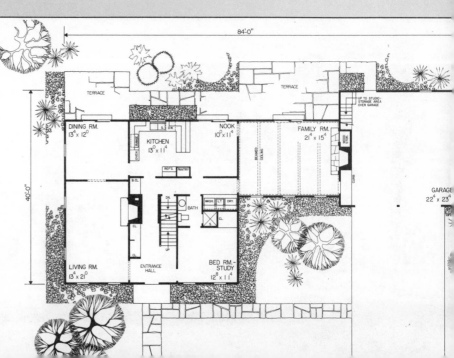

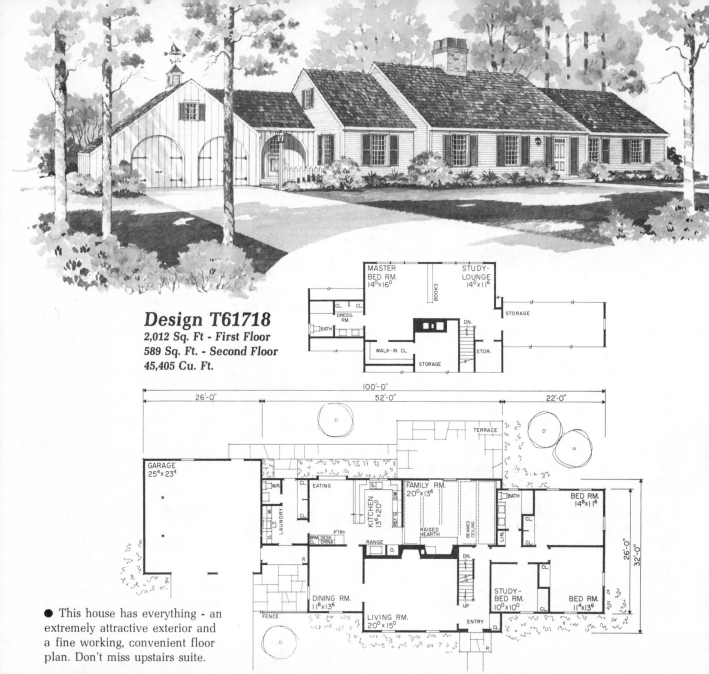

Design T61718

2,012 Sq. Ft - First Floor
589 Sq. Ft - Second Floor
45,405 Cu. Ft.

Second Floor Plan:
MASTER BED RM. 14⁰x16⁰
STUDY-LOUNGE 14⁰x11⁶
BOOKS
CL. CL.
DRESS. RM.
BATH
STORAGE
DN.
WALK-IN CL.
STORAGE
STOR.

First Floor Plan:
100'-0"
26'-0" | 52'-0" | 22'-0"
GARAGE 25⁴x23⁴
TERRACE
W.R.
CL.
EATING
CL.
S.
FAMILY RM. 20⁰x13⁶
BATH
BED RM. 14⁸x11⁶
CL.
D. W.
LT. LAUNDRY
KITCHEN 13⁶x20⁰
REF. FRZ.
DW
CL.
LIN.
BRM. DESK CL. CHINA
P'TRY
RANGE
RAISED HEARTH
BEAMED CEILING
LIN.
P.
O.
DN.
DINING RM. 11⁸x13⁶
FENCE
UP
STUDY-BED RM. 10⁰x10⁰
CL.
BED RM. 11⁴x13⁶
CL.
LIVING RM. 20⁰x15⁰
ENTRY
CL.
P.
26'-0"
32'-0"

● This house has everything - an extremely attractive exterior and a fine working, convenient floor plan. Don't miss upstairs suite.

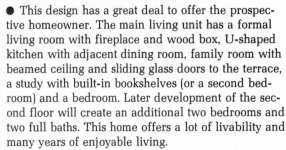

Design T61902 1,312 Sq. Ft. - First Floor
850 Sq. Ft. - Second Floor; 31,375 Cu. Ft.

● This design has a great deal to offer the prospective homeowner. The main living unit has a formal living room with fireplace and wood box, U-shaped kitchen with adjacent dining room, family room with beamed ceiling and sliding glass doors to the terrace, a study with built-in bookshelves (or a second bedroom) and a bedroom. Later development of the second floor will create an additional two bedrooms and two full baths. This home offers a lot of livability and many years of enjoyable living.

Design T61987
1,632 Sq. Ft. - First Floor
980 Sq. Ft. - Second Floor
35,712 Cu. Ft.

● The comforts of home will be endless and enduring when experienced and enjoyed in this Colonial adaptation. What's your favorite feature?

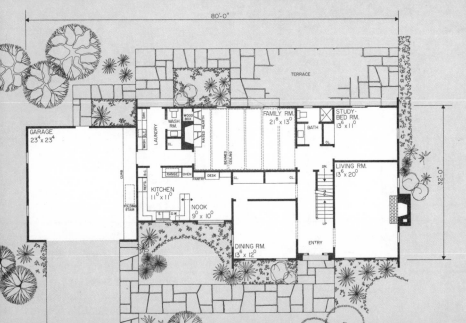

157

● Captivating as a New England village! From the weather vane atop the garage to the roofed side entry and paned windows, this home is perfectly detailed. Inside, there is a lot of living space. An exceptionally large family room which is more than 29' by 13' including a dining area. The adjoining kitchen has a laundry just steps away. Two formal rooms are in the front.

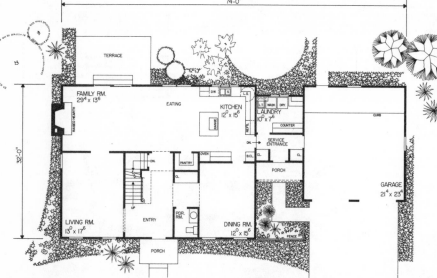

Design T62596
1,489 Sq. Ft. - First Floor
982 Sq. Ft. - Second Floor; 38,800 Cu.

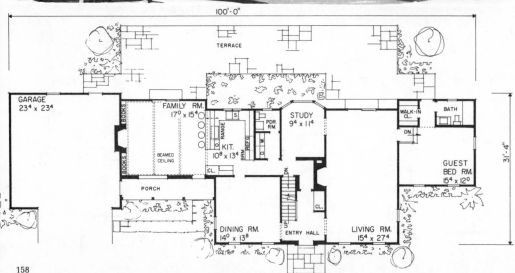

Design T61163
1,758 Sq. Ft. - First Floor
716 Sq. Ft. - Second Floor
34,747 Cu. Ft.

● The warmth of this exterior is characterized by the effective use of materials. The front entry hall routes traffic efficiently. Note the two fireplaces and study. Like so many one-and-a-half story designs, this home lends itself to building in stages. The guest bedroom may be made to function as the master bedroom, while leaving the completion of the second floor until a later date.

Design T62657 1,217 Sq. Ft. - First Floor
868 Sq. Ft. - Second Floor; 33,260 Cu. Ft.

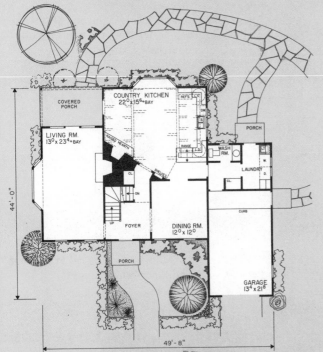

● Deriving its design from the traditional Cape Cod style, this facade features clapboard siding, small-paned windows and a transom-lit entrance flanked by carriage lamps. A central chimney services two fireplaces, one in the country-kitchen and the other in the formal living room which is removed from the disturbing flow of traffic. The master suite is located to the left of the upstairs landing. A full bathroom services two additional bedrooms on the second floor.

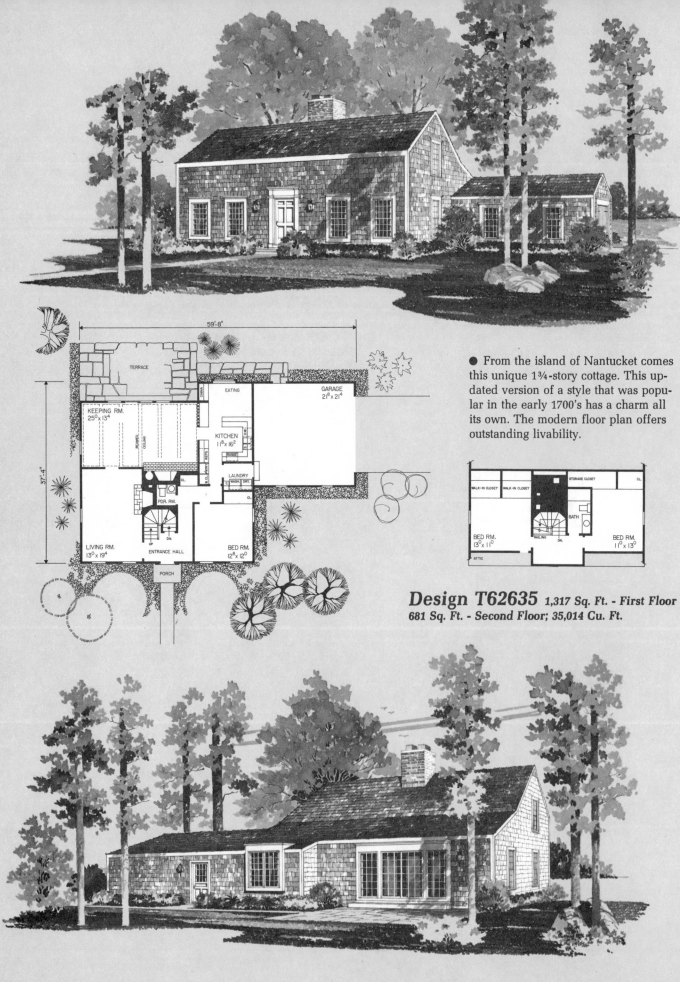

TERRACE

CHINA

EATING

GARAGE
21⁸ x 21⁴

KEEPING RM.
25⁰ x 13⁴

BEAMED CEILING

KITCHEN
11⁸ x 16²

RANGE

REFR.

LAUNDRY

WASH. DRY.

PDR. RM.

CL.

B. CL.

UP DN.

LIVING RM.
13⁰ x 19⁴

ENTRANCE HALL

BED RM.
12⁸ x 12⁰

PORCH

59'-8"

37'-4"

WALK-IN CLOSET   WALK-IN CLOSET   STORAGE CLOSET   CL.

BED RM.
13⁰ x 11⁰

RAILING   DN.

BATH

BED RM.
11⁰ x 13⁰

ATTIC

● From the island of Nantucket comes this unique 1¾-story cottage. This updated version of a style that was popular in the early 1700's has a charm all its own. The modern floor plan offers outstanding livability.

Design T62635 1,317 Sq. Ft. - First Floor
681 Sq. Ft. - Second Floor; 35,014 Cu. Ft.

● Another 1¾-story home - a
type of house favored by many
of Cape Cod's early whalers.
The compact floor plan will be
economical to build and surely
an energy saver. An excellent
house to finish-off in stages.

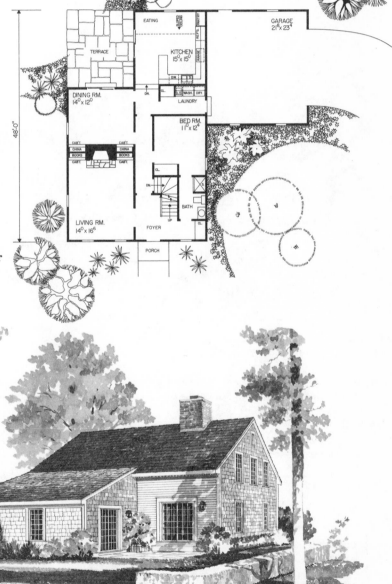

Design T62636 1,211 Sq. Ft. - First Floor
747 Sq. Ft. - Second Floor; 28,681 Cu. Ft.

Design T62569 1,102 Sq. Ft. - First Floor
764 Sq. Ft. - Second Floor; 29,600 Cu. Ft.

● What an enchanting updated version of the popular Cape Cod cottage. There are facilities for both formal and informal living pursuits. Note the spacious family area, the formal dining/living room, the first floor laundry and the efficient kitchen. The second floor houses the three bedrooms and two economically located baths.

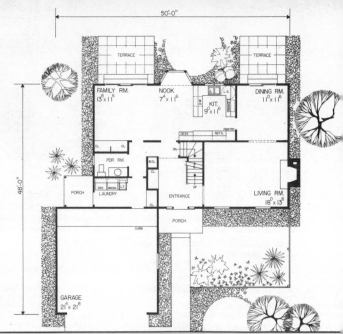

Design T62559 1,388 Sq. Ft. - First Floor
809 Sq. Ft. - Second Floor; 36,400 Cu. Ft.

● Imagine, a 26 foot living room with fireplace, a quiet study with built-in bookshelves and excellent dining facilities. All of this, plus much more, is within an appealing, traditional exterior. Study the rest of this plan and list its numerous features.

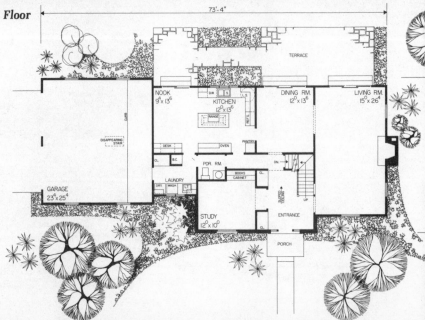

Design T61365 975 Sq. Ft. - First Floor
583 Sq. Ft. - Second Floor; 20,922 Cu. Ft.

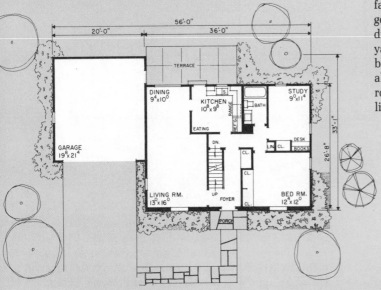

● This cozy, story-and-a-half home will suit a small family nicely. Upon entering this home, you will find a good sized living room. A few steps away is the formal dining area which has an excellent view of the backyard. Adjacent is the nice sized kitchen. A bedroom, bath and a study with a built-in desk and bookshelves also will be found on this floor. There are two bedrooms upstairs and a full bath. This home is big on livability; light on your building budget.

Design T62655
893 Sq. Ft. - First Floor
652 Sq. Ft. - Second Floor; 22,555 Cu. Ft.

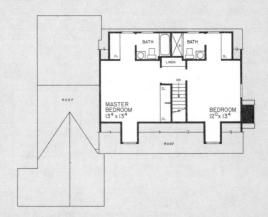

● Wonderful things can be enclosed in small packages. This is the case for this one-and-a-half story design. The total square footage is a mere 1,545 square feet yet its features are many, indeed. Its exterior appeal is very eye-pleasing with horizontal lines and two second story dormers. Livability will be enjoyed in this plan. The front study is ideal for a quiet escape. Nearby is a powder room also convenient to the kitchen and breakfast room. Two bedrooms and two full baths are located on the second floor.

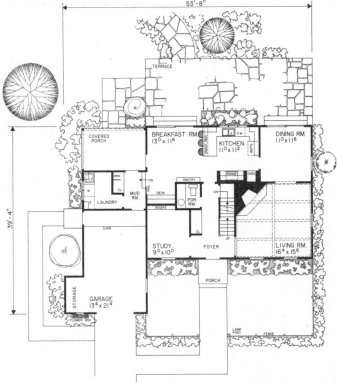

Design T62656 1,122 Sq. Ft. - First Floor
884 Sq. Ft. - Second Floor; 31,845 Cu. Ft.

● This charming Cape cottage possesses a great sense of shelter through its gambrel roof. Dormers at front and rear pierce the gambrel roof to provide generous, well-lit living space on the second floor which houses three bedrooms. This design's first floor layout is not far different from that of the Cape cottages of the 18th century. The large kitchen and adjoining dining room recall cottage keeping rooms both in function and in location at the rear of the house.

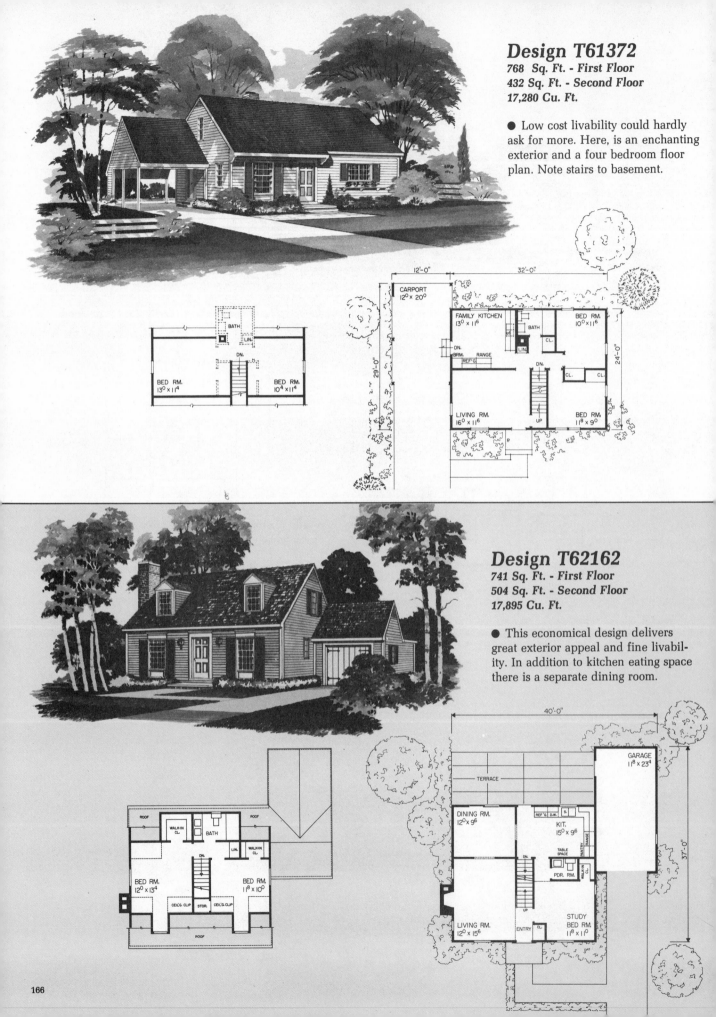

Design T61372
768 Sq. Ft. - First Floor
432 Sq. Ft. - Second Floor
17,280 Cu. Ft.

● Low cost livability could hardly ask for more. Here, is an enchanting exterior and a four bedroom floor plan. Note stairs to basement.

BATH
LIN.
DN.
BED RM.
13⁰ x 11⁴
BED RM.
10⁴ x 11⁴

12'-0"   32'-0"
CARPORT
12⁰ x 20⁰
29'-0"
FAMILY KITCHEN
13⁰ x 11⁶
BATH
CL.
BED RM.
10⁰ x 11⁶
24'-0"
DN.
BRM. RANGE
REF'G
LIN.
DN.
CL.   CL.
LIVING RM.
16⁰ x 11⁶
UP
BED RM.
11⁸ x 9⁰
R

Design T62162
741 Sq. Ft. - First Floor
504 Sq. Ft. - Second Floor
17,895 Cu. Ft.

● This economical design delivers great exterior appeal and fine livability. In addition to kitchen eating space there is a separate dining room.

ROOF
ROOF
WALK-IN CL
BATH
LIN.
WALK-IN CL
DN.
BED RM.
12⁰ x 13⁴
BED RM.
11⁸ x 10⁰
CEIL'G. CLIP.   STOR.   CEIL'G. CLIP.
ROOF

40'-0"
GARAGE
11⁸ x 23⁴
TERRACE
DINING RM.
12⁰ x 9⁶
REF'G. D.W. S.
KIT.
15⁰ x 9⁶
RANGE
PANTRY
TABLE SPACE
37'-0"
DN.
PDR. RM.
WALK-IN
LIVING RM.
12⁰ x 15⁶
UP
ENTRY
CL.
STUDY
BED RM.
11⁸ x 11⁰

Design T61394

832 Sq. Ft. - First Floor
512 Sq. Ft. - Second Floor
19,385 Cu. Ft.

● The growing family with a restricted building budget will find this a great investment - a convenient living floor plan inside an attractive facade.

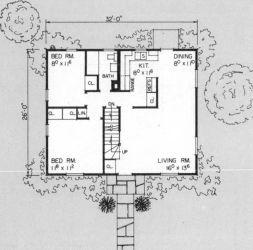

Design T62510

1,191 Sq. Ft. - First Floor
533 Sq. Ft. - Second Floor
27,500 Cu. Ft.

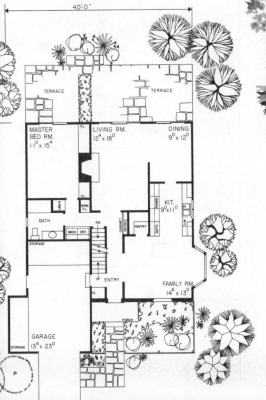

● The pleasant in-line kitchen is flanked by a separate dining room and a family room. The master bedroom is on the first floor with two more bedrooms upstairs.

Design T62852 919 Sq. Ft. - First Floor
535 Sq. Ft. - Second Floor; 24,450 Cu. Ft.

● Compact enough for even the smallest lot, this cozy design provides comfortable living space for a small family. At the heart of the plan is a spacious country kitchen. It features a cooking is-land - snack bar and a dining area that opens to a house-wide rear terrace. The nearby dining room also opens to the terrace. At the front of the plan is the living room, warmed by a fire-place. Across the cen-tered foyer is a cozy study. Two second floor bedrooms are ser-viced by two baths. Note the first floor powder room and stor-age closet located next to the side entrance. This home will be a delight.

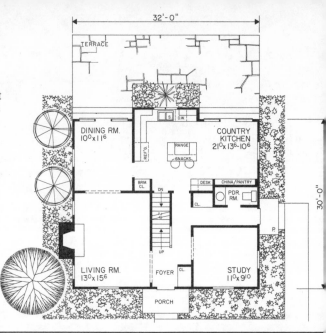

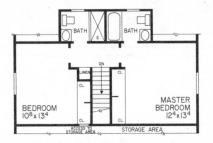

Design T62571 1,137 Sq. Ft. - First Floor
795 Sq. Ft. - Second Floor; 28,097 Cu. Ft.

● Cost-efficient space! That's the bonus with this attractive Cape Cod. Start in the living room. It is spacious and inviting with full-length paned win-dows. In the formal dining room, a bay window adds the appropriate touch. For more living space, a delightfully appointed family room. The efficient kitchen has a snack bar for casual meals. Three bedrooms are on the second floor.

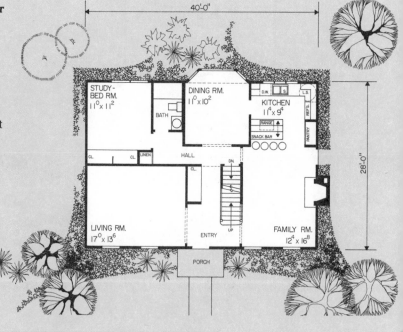

Design T63189 884 Sq. Ft. - First Floor
598 Sq. Ft. - Second Floor; 18,746 Cu. Ft.

● A large kitchen/dining area and living room are the living areas of this design. Four bedrooms, two up and two down, compose the sleeping zone. Each floor also has a full bath. A full basement and an attached garage will provide plenty of storage areas.

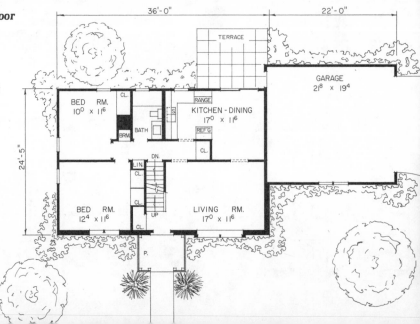

Design T62488
543 Sq. Ft. - Second Floor; 36,055 Cu. Ft.

● A cozy cottage for the young at heart! Whether called upon to serve the young, active family as a leisure-time retreat at the lake, or the retired couple as a quiet haven in later years, this charming design will perform well. As a year round second home, the upstairs with its two sizable bedrooms, full bath and lounge area, looking down into the gathering room below, will ideally accommodate the younger generation.

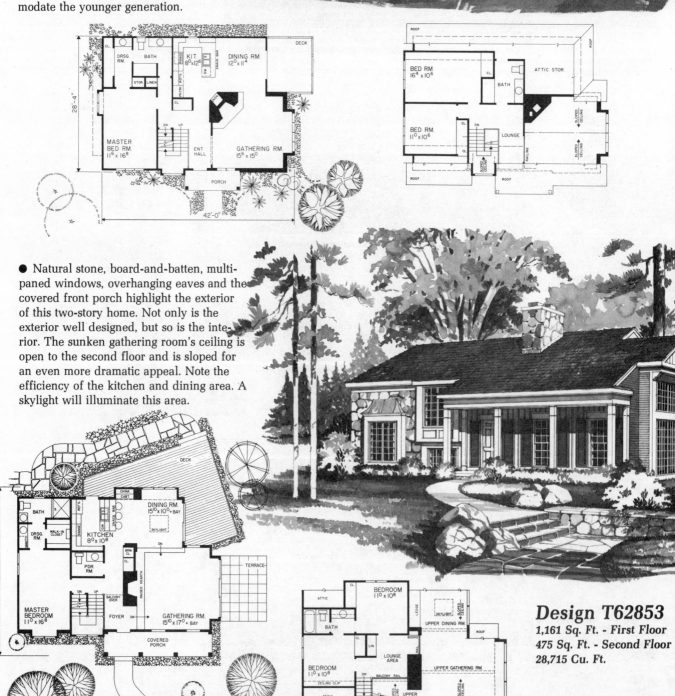

● Natural stone, board-and-batten, multi-paned windows, overhanging eaves and the covered front porch highlight the exterior of this two-story home. Not only is the exterior well designed, but so is the interior. The sunken gathering room's ceiling is open to the second floor and is sloped for an even more dramatic appeal. Note the efficiency of the kitchen and dining area. A skylight will illuminate this area.

Design T62853
1,161 Sq. Ft. - First Floor
475 Sq. Ft. - Second Floor
28,715 Cu. Ft.

1½-STORY
GEORGIAN & FARMHOUSE THEMES

These designs combine formal grace of Georgian facade with informal warmth of Farmhouse living. These Georgian adaptations often are marked by symmetry of window treatment, massive twin chimneys, dentil work at cornices, ornamented front entrance detailing, and sometimes Greek columns. Structure may be brick or frame exterior. More casual facade of the 1½-story Farmhouse may feature Gable or Gambrel roof. Unadorned pillars often support sweeping front porches, sometimes with railing.

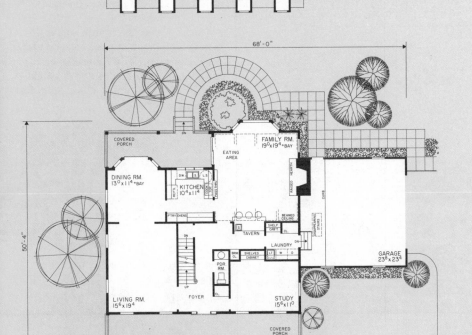

Design T62890
1,612 Sq. Ft. - First Floor
1,356 Sq. Ft. - Second Floor
47,010 Cu. Ft.

● An appealing Farmhouse that is complimented by an inviting front porch. Many memorable summer evenings will be spent here. Entering this house, you will notice a nice-sized study to your right and spacious living room to the left. The adjacent dining room is enriched by an attractive bay window. Just a step away, an efficient kitchen will be found. Many family activities will be enjoyed in the large family room. The tavern/ snack bar will make entertaining guests a joy. A powder room and laundry are also on the first floor. Upstairs you'll find a master bedroom suite featuring a bath with an oversized tub and shower and a dressing room. Also on this floor; two bedrooms, full bath and a large attic.

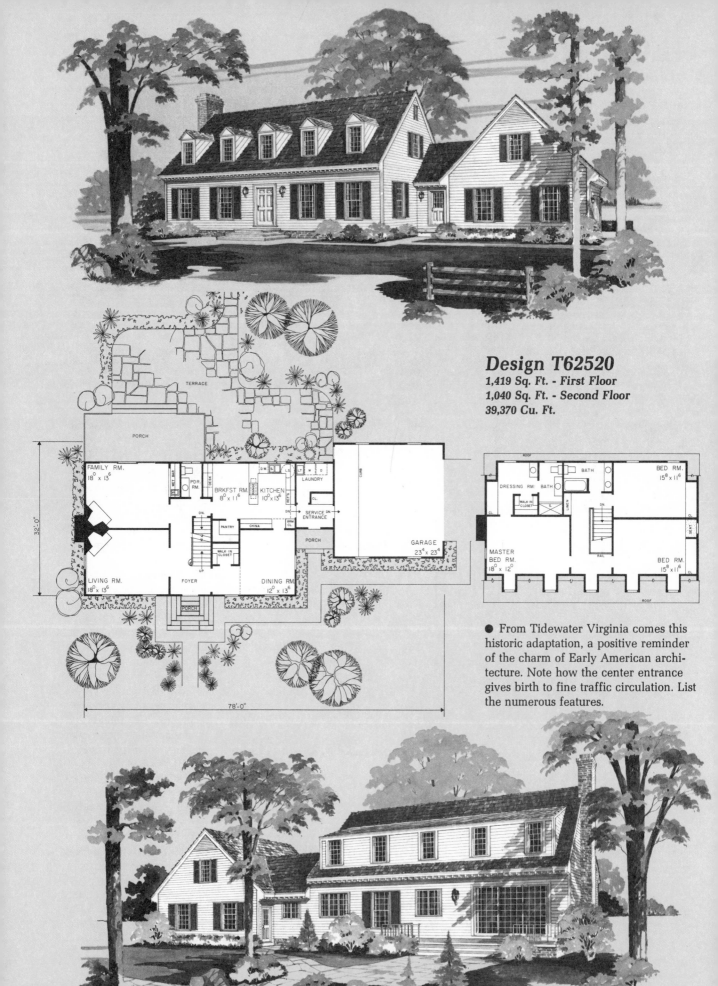

Design T62520

1,419 Sq. Ft. - First Floor
1,040 Sq. Ft. - Second Floor
39,370 Cu. Ft.

● From Tidewater Virginia comes this historic adaptation, a positive reminder of the charm of Early American architecture. Note how the center entrance gives birth to fine traffic circulation. List the numerous features.

Design T62684 1,600 Sq. Ft. - First Floor
498 Sq. Ft. - Second Floor; 47,395 Cu. Ft.

Highlighting this plan is the spacious, country kitchen. Its features are many, indeed. Also worth a special note is the second floor studio/office. It is accessible by way of a staircase in the back of the plan. Just imagine the many uses for this area. There is a great deal of livability in this plan. Don't miss the three fireplaces or the first floor laundry.

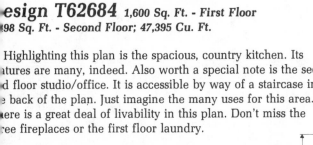

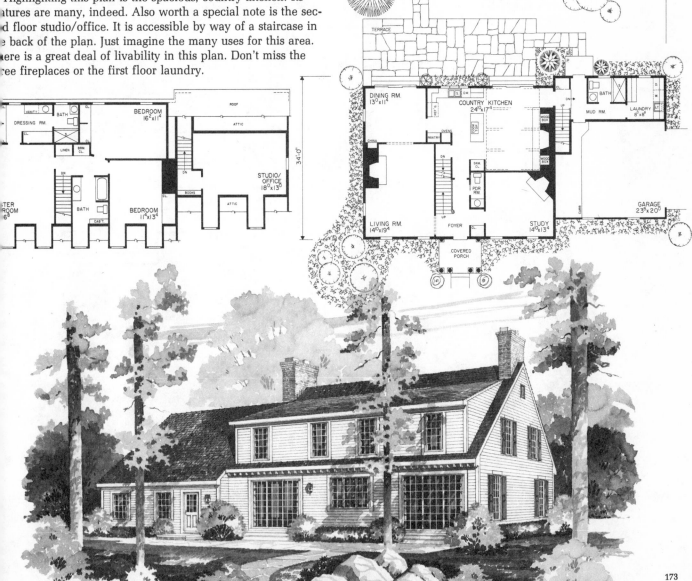

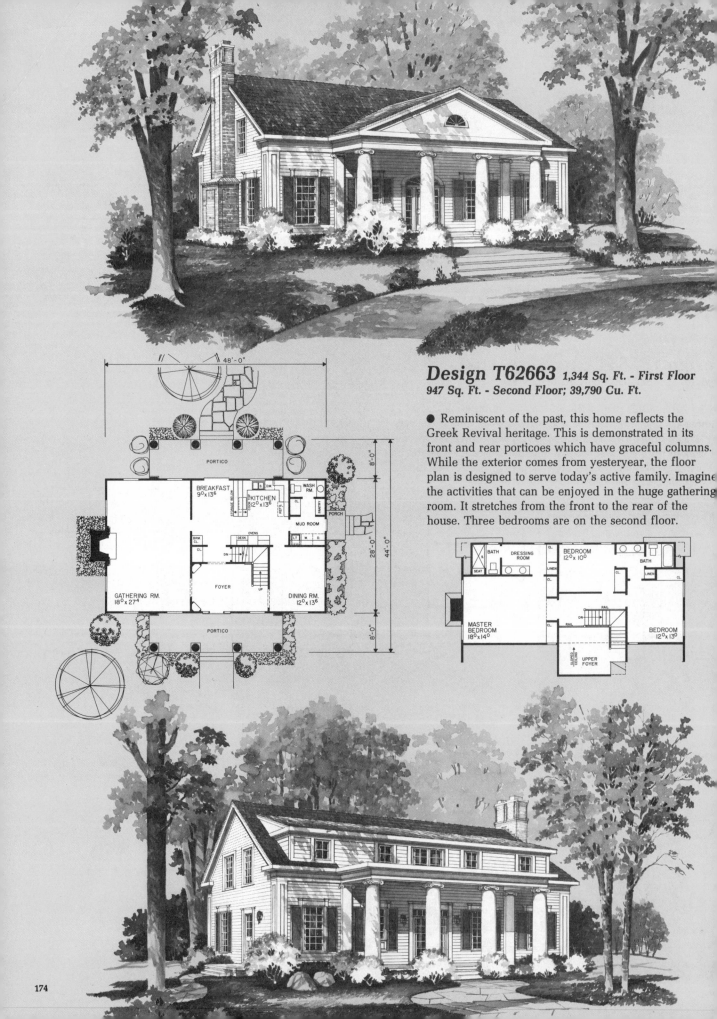

Design T62663 1,344 Sq. Ft. - First Floor
947 Sq. Ft. - Second Floor; 39,790 Cu. Ft.

● Reminiscent of the past, this home reflects the Greek Revival heritage. This is demonstrated in its front and rear porticoes which have graceful columns. While the exterior comes from yesteryear, the floor plan is designed to serve today's active family. Imagine the activities that can be enjoyed in the huge gathering room. It stretches from the front to the rear of the house. Three bedrooms are on the second floor.

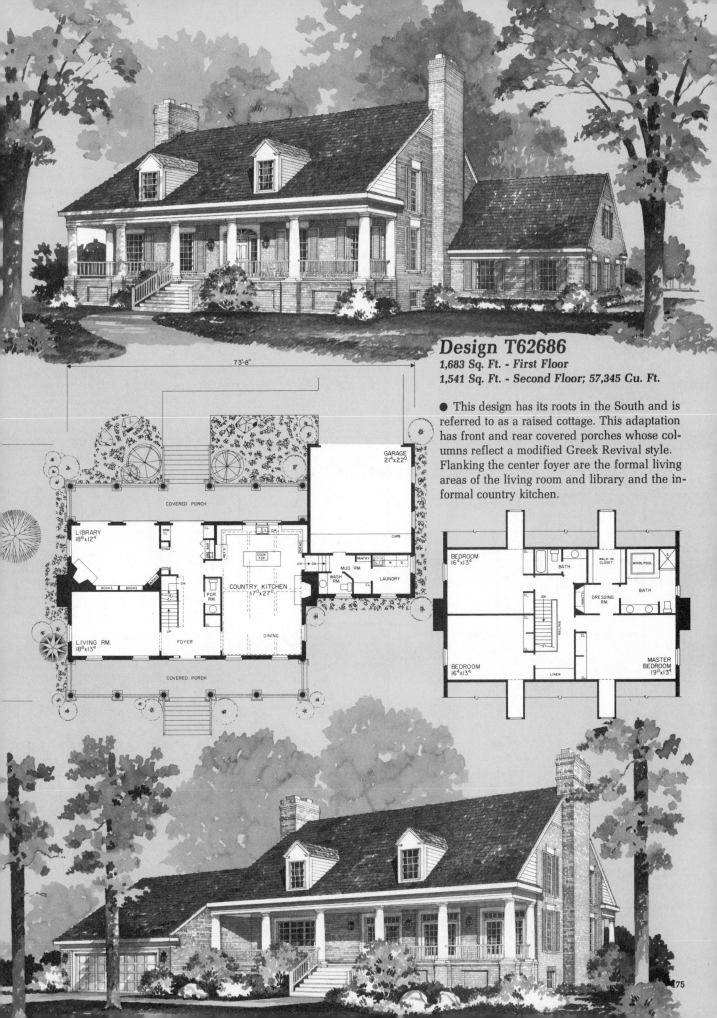

Design T62686

1,683 Sq. Ft. - First Floor
1,541 Sq. Ft. - Second Floor; 57,345 Cu. Ft.

● This design has its roots in the South and is referred to as a raised cottage. This adaptation has front and rear covered porches whose columns reflect a modified Greek Revival style. Flanking the center foyer are the formal living areas of the living room and library and the informal country kitchen.

73'-8"

COVERED PORCH

LIBRARY
18⁸x12⁴

GARAGE
21⁴x22⁰

CURB

PANTRY

CHINA

LAUNDRY

COUNTRY KITCHEN
17⁰x27⁰

COOK TOP

MUD RM.

WASH RM.

BOOKS   BOOKS

PDR. RM.

DINING

LIVING RM.
18⁸x13⁴

FOYER

UP

COVERED PORCH

BEDROOM
16⁴x13⁴

BATH

WALK-IN CLOSET

WHIRLPOOL

BATH

DRESSING RM.

DN

BEDROOM
16⁴x13⁴

LINEN

MASTER BEDROOM
19⁰x13⁴

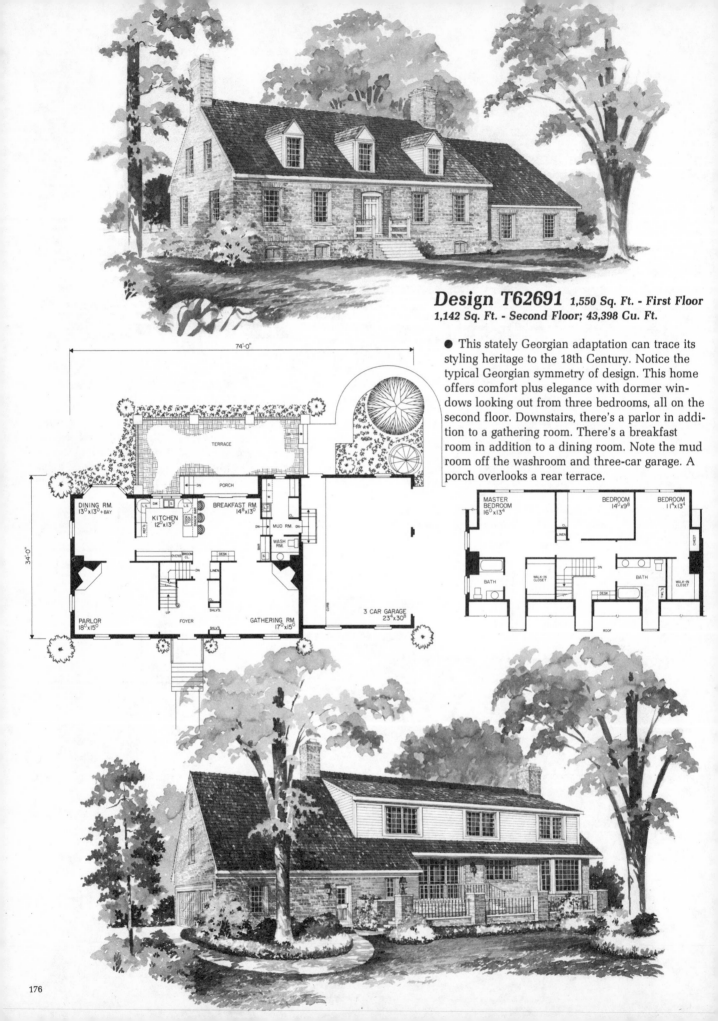

Design T62691 *1,550 Sq. Ft. - First Floor*
1,142 Sq. Ft. - Second Floor; 43,398 Cu. Ft.

● This stately Georgian adaptation can trace its styling heritage to the 18th Century. Notice the typical Georgian symmetry of design. This home offers comfort plus elegance with dormer windows looking out from three bedrooms, all on the second floor. Downstairs, there's a parlor in addition to a gathering room. There's a breakfast room in addition to a dining room. Note the mud room off the washroom and three-car garage. A porch overlooks a rear terrace.

74'-0"

34'-0"

TERRACE

PORCH

DINING RM.
13⁰x13⁰ + BAY

KITCHEN
12⁰x13⁰

BREAKFAST RM.
14⁸x13⁰

MUD RM.

WASH RM.

OVENS

DESK

LINEN

BROOM CL.

CL.

SHLVS.

PARLOR
18⁰x15⁰

FOYER

GATHERING RM.
17⁰x15⁰

3 CAR GARAGE
23⁴x30⁸

MASTER BEDROOM
16⁰x13⁴

BEDROOM
14⁴x9⁸

BEDROOM
11⁴x13⁴

LINEN

CL.

WALK-IN CLOSET

BATH

BATH

WALK-IN CLOSET

CHEST

DESK

ROOF

Design T62132
1,958 Sq. Ft. - First Floor
1,305 Sq. Ft. - Second Floor; 51,428 Cu. Ft.

● Another Georgian adaptation with a great heritage dating back to 18th-Century America. Exquisite and symmetrical detailing set the character of this impressive home. Don't overlook such features as the two fireplaces, the laundry, the beamed ceiling, the built-in china cabinets and the oversized garage.

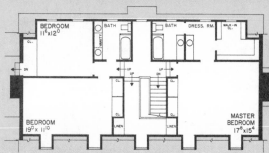

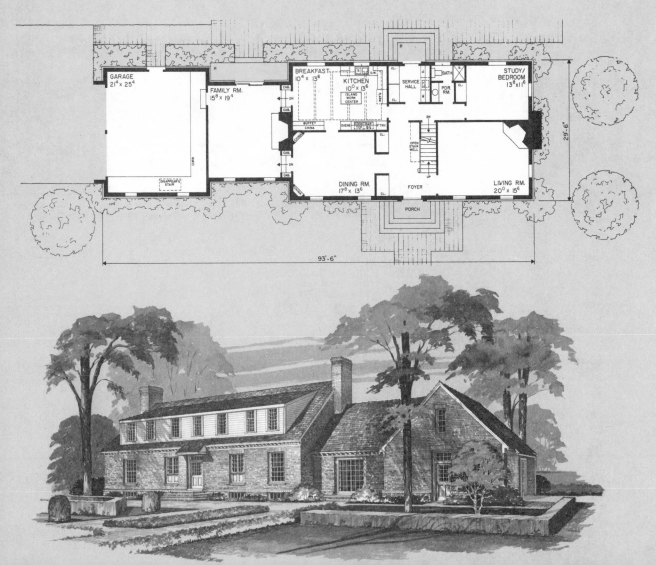

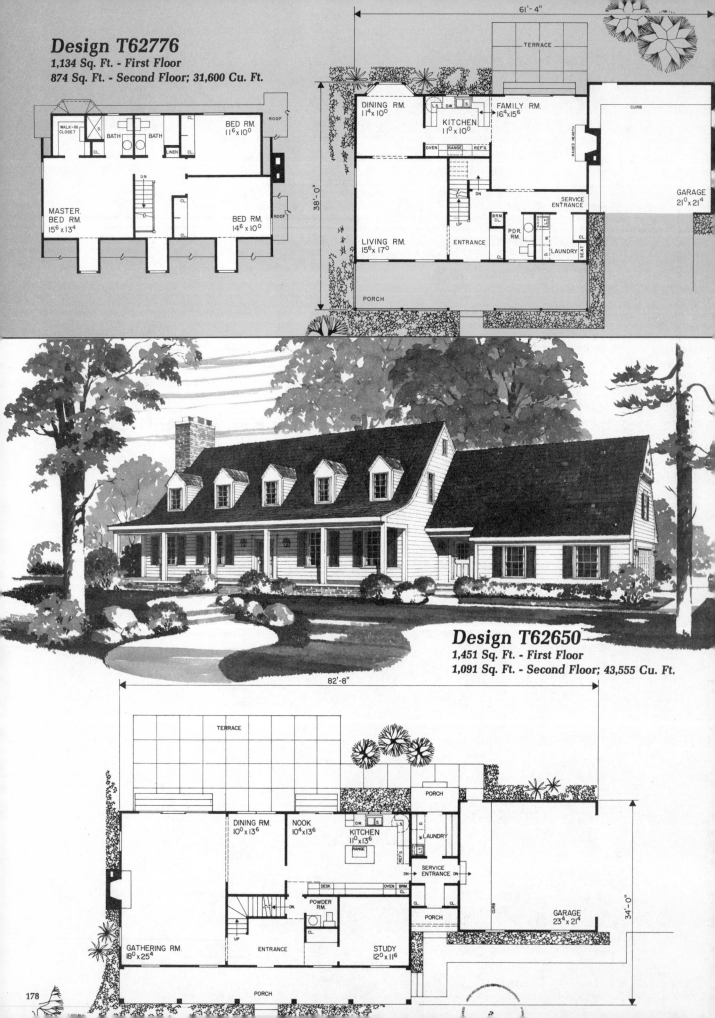

Design T62776
1,134 Sq. Ft. - First Floor
874 Sq. Ft. - Second Floor; 31,600 Cu. Ft.

WALK-IN CLOSET
BATH
BATH
LINEN
CL.
CL.
CL.
ROOF
BED RM.
11⁶ x 10⁰
DN
CL.
MASTER. BED RM.
15⁶ x 13⁴
BED RM.
14⁶ x 10⁰
ROOF

61'-4"

TERRACE
CURB

DINING RM.
11⁴ x 10⁰
L.S. D.W. S
KITCHEN
11⁰ x 10⁰
FAMILY RM.
16⁴ x 15⁶
OVEN RANGE REF'G
RAISED HEARTH
GARAGE
21⁰ x 21⁴
38'-0"
DN
SERVICE ENTRANCE
LIVING RM.
15⁶ x 17⁰
BRM. CL.
UP
PDR. RM.
W.
CL.
LAUNDRY
SEAT
CL.
ENTRANCE
CL.
PORCH

Design T62650
1,451 Sq. Ft. - First Floor
1,091 Sq. Ft. - Second Floor; 43,555 Cu. Ft.

82'-8"

TERRACE
PORCH
DINING RM.
10⁰ x 13⁶
NOOK
10⁴ x 13⁶
D.W. S
KITCHEN
11⁰ x 13⁶
LAUNDRY
RANGE
REF'G
SERVICE ENTRANCE
DN
DN
34'-0"
GARAGE
23⁴ x 21⁴
DESK
OVEN BRM. CL.
UP
POWDER RM.
CL.
PORCH
GATHERING RM.
18⁰ x 25⁴
ENTRANCE
STUDY
12⁰ x 11⁶
CURB
PORCH

● The rear view of this design is just as appealing as the front. The dormers and the covered porch with pillars is a charming way to introduce this house to the on-lookers. Inside, the appeal is also outstanding. Note the size (18 x 25 foot) of the gathering room which is open to the dining room. Kitchen-nook area is very spacious and features an island range, built-in desk and more. Great convenience having the laundry in service area close to the kitchen. Imagine, a fireplace in both the gathering room and the master bedroom! Make special note of the service entrance doors leading to both the front and back of the house.

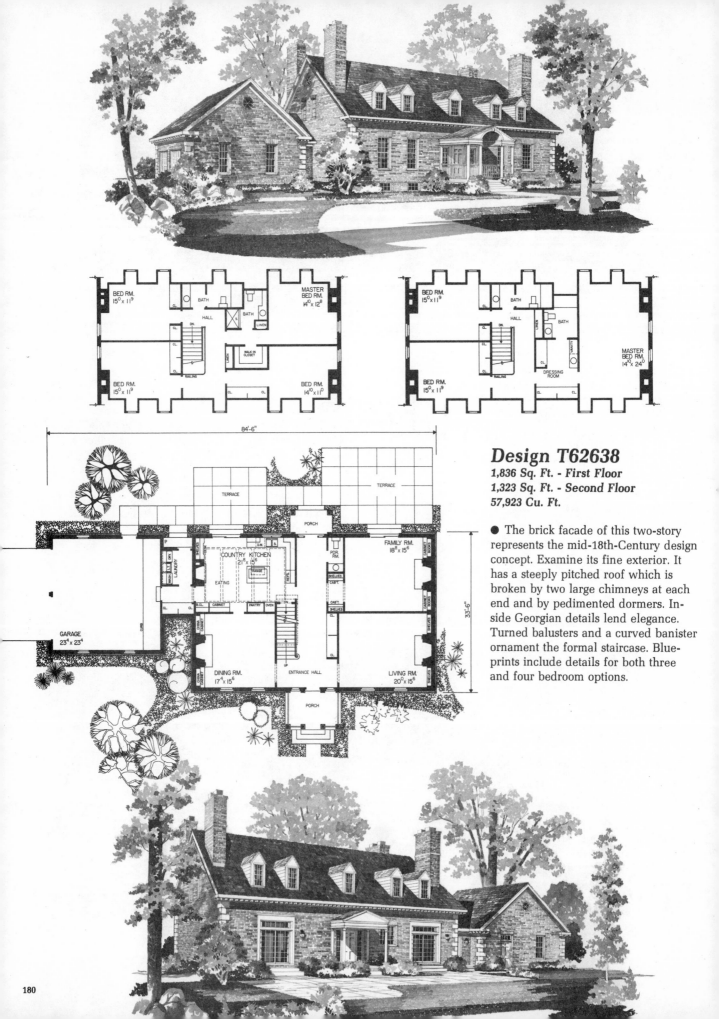

Design T62638

1,836 Sq. Ft. - First Floor
1,323 Sq. Ft. - Second Floor
57,923 Cu. Ft.

● The brick facade of this two-story represents the mid-18th-Century design concept. Examine its fine exterior. It has a steeply pitched roof which is broken by two large chimneys at each end and by pedimented dormers. Inside Georgian details lend elegance. Turned balusters and a curved banister ornament the formal staircase. Blueprints include details for both three and four bedroom options.

66'-0"

48'-0"

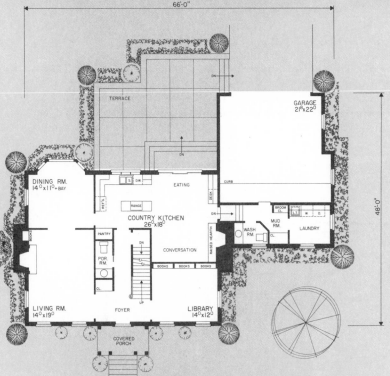

TERRACE

GARAGE
21⁰x22⁰

DINING RM.
14⁰x11⁰+BAY

EATING

CURB

BROOM CL.

LT. W. D.

DW.

RANGE

COUNTRY KITCHEN
26⁰x18

PANTRY

WASH RM.

MUD RM.

LAUNDRY

CONVERSATION

RAISED HEARTH

PDR. RM.

BOOKS BOOKS BOOKS

CL.

LIVING RM.
14⁰x19⁰

FOYER

UP

LIBRARY
14⁰x12⁰

COVERED PORCH

Design T62688 1,588 Sq. Ft. - First Floor
1,101 Sq. Ft. - Second Floor; 44,021 Cu. Ft.

● Here are two floors of excellent livability. Start at the country kitchen. It will be the center for family activities. It has an island, desk, raised hearth fireplace, conversation area and sliding glass doors to the terrace. Adjacent to this area is the washroom and laundry. Quieter areas are available in the living room and library. Three bedrooms are housed on the second floor.

ROOF

BEDROOM
13⁰x12⁴

BATH

BATH

LINEN

DRESSING RM

ROOF

BEDROOM
15⁰x11⁴

DN

RAILING

MASTER BEDROOM
14⁰x13⁴

ROOF

Design T62221 1,726 Sq. Ft. - First Floor; 1,440 Sq. Ft. - Second Floor; 50,204 Cu. Ft.

● A Georgian Colonial adaptation on the grand scale! The authentic front entrance is delightfully detailed. Two massive end chimneys that house four fireplaces are in keeping with the architecture of its day. Notice the Georgian symmetry in design. Downstairs there's a library in addition to a living room plus a family room with beam ceiling. There's also a formal dining room in addition to a breakfast nook. Notice the country porch that overlooks the rear terrace and also the spacious master bedroom suite — one of three bedrooms upstairs. There's plenty of storage in a sizable upstairs attic, too.

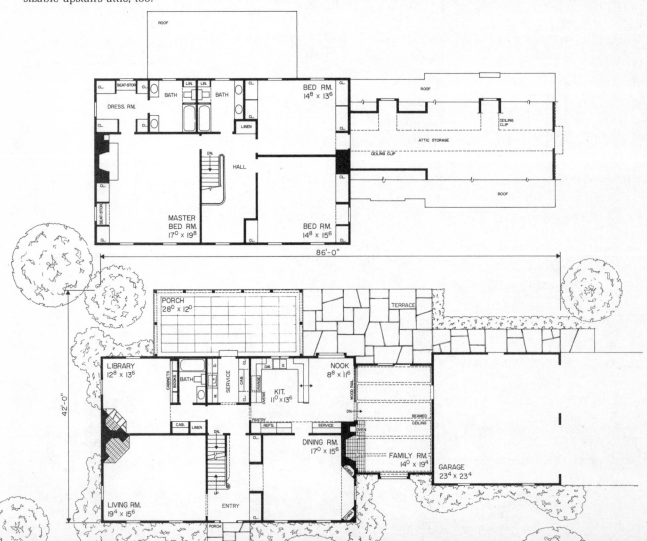

1½-STORY
TRADITIONAL STYLE VARIATIONS

The 1½-story home was born in Colonial America. Early 17th-Century houses featured one room with fireplace and a staircase that led upstairs to a large sleeping room under a sloping roof rafters. The 1½-story home enjoys a lot of the economic benefits of two levels of livability sandwiched between minimal roof and foundation areas.

Design T62174
1,506 Sq. Ft. - First Floor
1,156 Sq. Ft. - Second Floor
37,360 Cu. Ft.

● Your building budget could hardly buy more charm, or greater livability. The appeal of the exterior is wrapped up in a myriad of design features. They include: the interesting roof lines; the effective use of brick and horizontal siding; the delightful window treatment; the covered front porch; the chimney and dovecote detailing. The livability of the interior is represented by a long list of convenient living features. There is a formal area consisting of a living room with fireplace and dining room. The family room has a raised hearth fireplace, wood box and beamed ceiling. Also on the first floor is a kitchen, laundry and bedroom with adjacent bath. Three bedrooms, lounge and two baths upstairs plus plenty of closets and bulk storage over garage. Don't overlook the sliding glass doors, the breakfast area and the basement. An excellent plan.

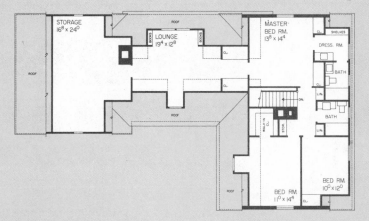

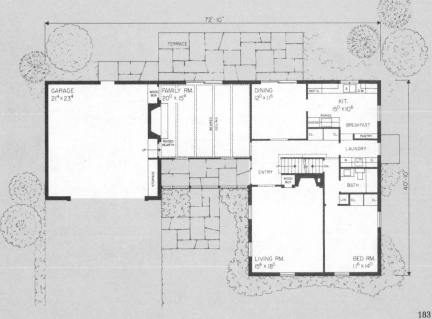

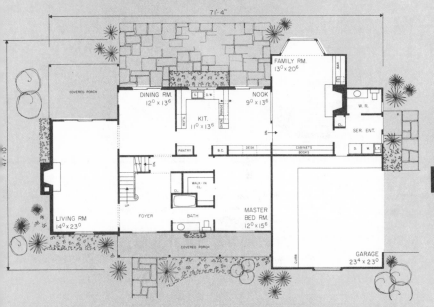

Design T62500
1,851 Sq. Ft. - First Floor
762 Sq. Ft. - Second Floor
43,052 Cu. Ft.

● The large family will enjoy the wonderful living patterns offered by this charming home. Don't miss the covered rear porch and the many features of the family room.

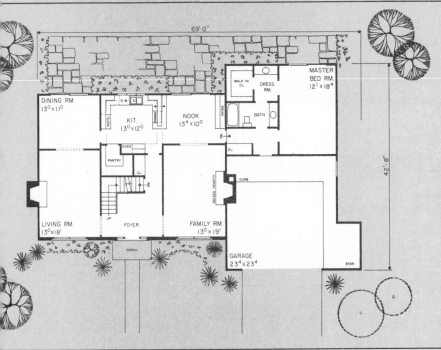

Design T62501
1,699 Sq. Ft. - First Floor
758 Sq. Ft. - Second Floor
37,693 Cu. Ft.

● Whether you build this inviting home with a fieldstone front, or substitute with a different material of your choice, you can be assured that you've selected a great home for your family.

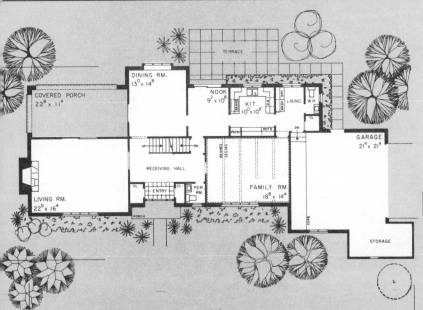

Design T62338
1,505 Sq. Ft. - First Floor
1,219 Sq. Ft. - Second Floor
38,878 Cu. Ft.

● A spacious receiving hall is a fine setting for the welcoming of guests. Here traffic flows effectively to all areas of the plan. Outstanding livability throughout the entire plan.

185

● If symmetry means any-
thing, this pleasant house
has it. The projecting wings
of the sleeping zone and the
garage are virtually identical.
However, the appeal of this
charmer does not end with
its symmetrical beauty.
There is a world of livability
to be fostered by this home.

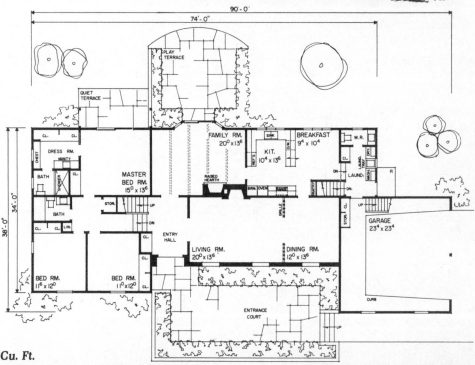

Design T61964
2,150 Sq. Ft. - First Floor
680 Sq. Ft. - Second Floor; 39,927 Cu. Ft.

Design T61780 2,018 Sq. Ft. - First Floor
568 Sq. Ft - Second Floor; 37,586 Cu. Ft.

● Here is a U-shaped story-and-a-half
which has an abundance of livable floor
area. Imagine, here are five bedrooms and
three full baths, plus plenty of storage to
serve the large family. There will be a
choice of eating places: kitchen, dining room
or snack bar.

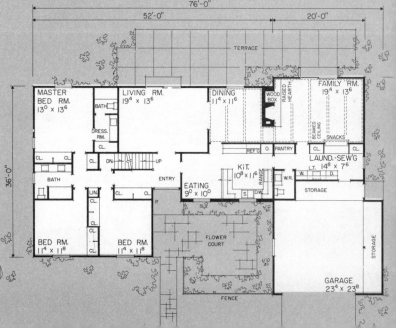

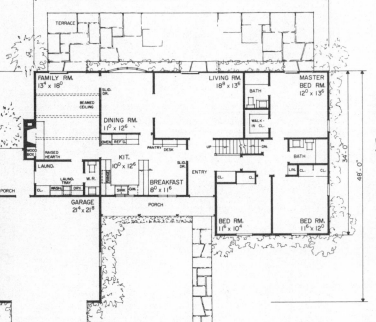

Design T61967 1,804 Sq. Ft. - First Floor
496 Sq. Ft. - Second Floor; 40,173 Cu. Ft.

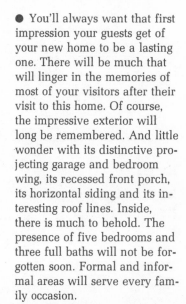

● You'll always want that first impression your guests get of your new home to be a lasting one. There will be much that will linger in the memories of most of your visitors after their visit to this home. Of course, the impressive exterior will long be remembered. And little wonder with its distinctive projecting garage and bedroom wing, its recessed front porch, its horizontal siding and its interesting roof lines. Inside, there is much to behold. The presence of five bedrooms and three full baths will not be forgotten soon. Formal and informal areas will serve every family occasion.

● A versatile plan, wrapped in a pleasing traditional facade, to cater to the demands of even the most active of families. There is plenty of living space for both formal and informal activities. With two bedrooms upstairs and two down, sleeping accommodations are excellently planned to serve all.

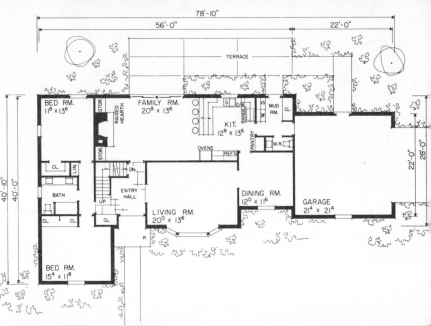

● A study of the first and second floors of this charming design will reveal that nothing has been omitted to assure convenient living. List your family's living requirements and then observe how this house will proceed to satisfy them. Features galore.

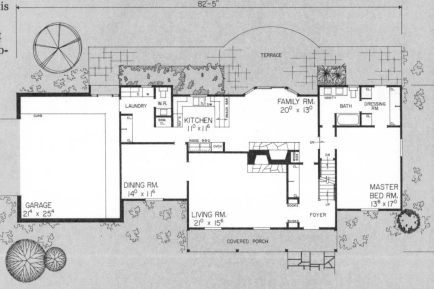

● A great plan! The large family will find its living requirements satisfied admirably all throughout those active years of growing up. This would make a fine expansible house. The upstairs may be finished off as the size of the family increases and budget permits. Complete living requirements can be obtained on the first floor.

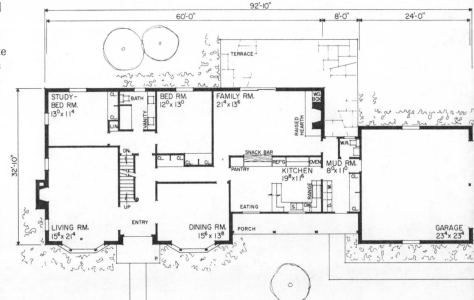

Design T61790 1,782 Sq. Ft. - First Floor; 920 Sq. Ft. - Second Floor; 37,359 Cu. Ft.

Design T61736 1,618 Sq. Ft. - First Floor; 952 Sq. Ft. - Second Floor; 34,106 Cu. Ft.

Design T61793 1,986 Sq. Ft. - First Floor; 944 Sq. Ft. - Second Floor; 35,800 Cu. Ft.

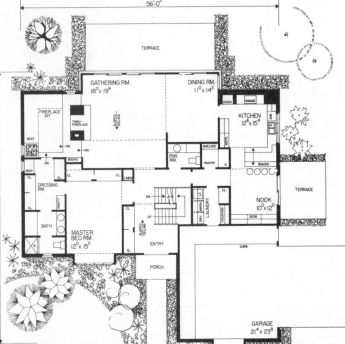

● You and your family will love the new living patterns you'll experience in this story-and-a-half home. The front entry hall features an impressive open staircase to the upstairs and basement. Adjacent is the master bedroom which has a compartmented bath with both tub and stall shower. The spacious dressing room steps down into a unique, sunken conversation pit. This cozy area has a planter, built-in seat and a view of the thru-fireplace, opening to the gathering room as well. Here, the ceiling slopes to the top of the second floor lounge which looks down into the gathering room.

Design T62718 1,941 Sq. Ft. - First Floor
791 Sq. Ft. - Second Floor; 49,895 Cu. Ft.

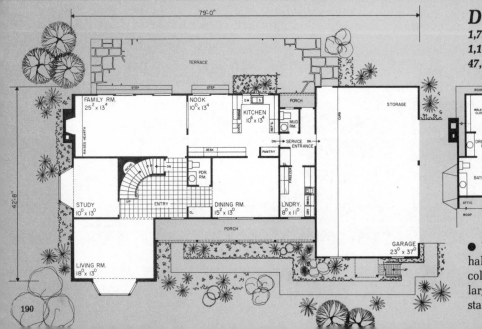

Design T62513
1,799 Sq. Ft. - First Floor
1,160 Sq. Ft. - Second Floor
47,461 Cu. Ft.

● What an appealing story-and-a-half design. Delightful, indeed, is the colonial detailing of the garage. The large entry hall with its open curving staircase is dramatic.

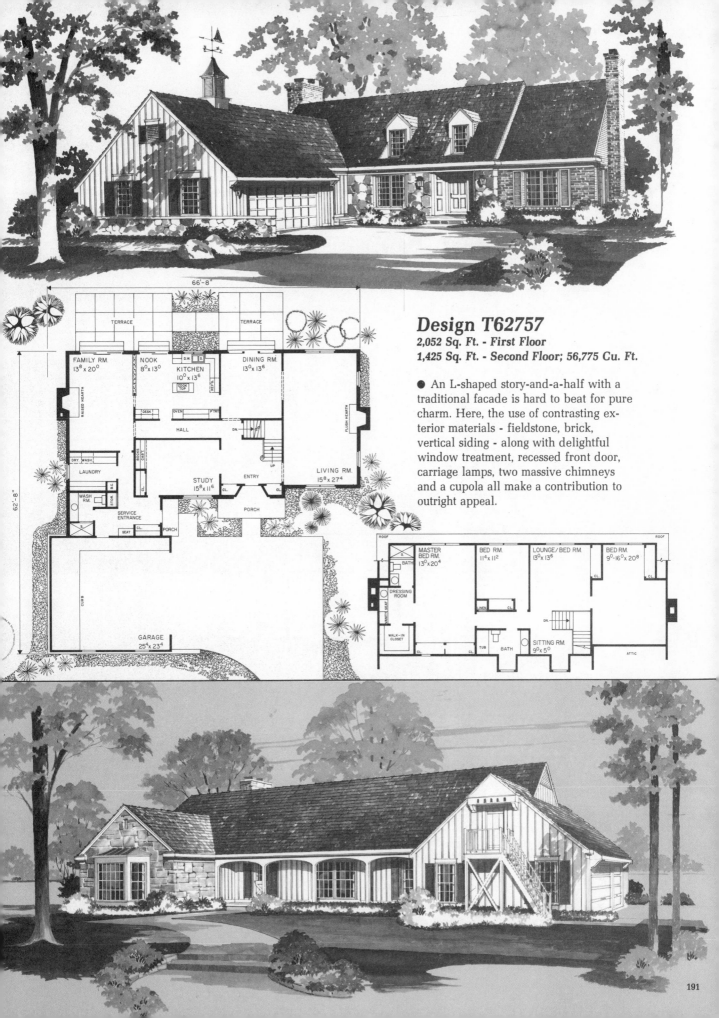

Design T62757
2,052 Sq. Ft. - First Floor
1,425 Sq. Ft. - Second Floor; 56,775 Cu. Ft.

● An L-shaped story-and-a-half with a traditional facade is hard to beat for pure charm. Here, the use of contrasting exterior materials - fieldstone, brick, vertical siding - along with delightful window treatment, recessed front door, carriage lamps, two massive chimneys and a cupola all make a contribution to outright appeal.

Design T61242 1,872 Sq. Ft. - First Floor
982 Sq. Ft. - Second Floor; 29,221 Cu. Ft.

● Here are three long, low one-and-a-half story designs with all the traditional charm one would wish for a new home. The floor plans offer all the livability an active family would want. Which is your favorite design?

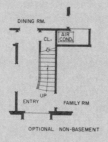

OPTIONAL NON-BASEMENT

982 SQ. FT. SECOND FLOOR

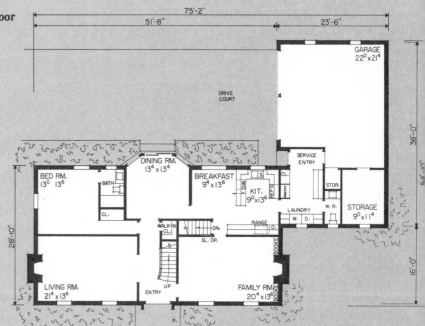

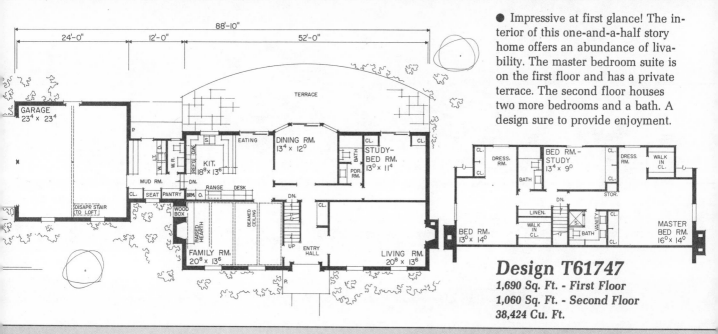

Dimensions: 88'-10" (24'-0", 12'-0", 52'-0")

GARAGE 23⁴ x 23⁴

TERRACE

MUD RM.

KIT. 18⁸ x 13⁶

DISAPP STAIR TO LOFT

EATING

DINING RM. 13⁴ x 12⁰

STUDY-BED RM. 13⁰ x 11⁴

BATH

CL.

PDR. RM.

DN.

RANGE DESK

WOOD BOX

RAISED HEARTH

BEAMED CEILING

FAMILY RM. 20⁸ x 13⁶

UP

ENTRY HALL

DN.

CL.

LIVING RM. 20⁰ x 13⁶

CL.

DRESS. RM.

BATH

BED RM.-STUDY 13⁴ x 9⁰

DRESS. RM.

WALK IN CL.

STOR.

LINEN.

WALK IN CL.

DN.

S.

BATH

VANITY

CL.

CL.

BED RM. 13⁰ x 14⁰

MASTER BED RM. 16⁰ x 14⁰

● Impressive at first glance! The interior of this one-and-a-half story home offers an abundance of livability. The master bedroom suite is on the first floor and has a private terrace. The second floor houses two more bedrooms and a bath. A design sure to provide enjoyment.

Design T61747
1,690 Sq. Ft. - First Floor
1,060 Sq. Ft. - Second Floor
38,424 Cu. Ft.

Design T61906 1,514 Sq. Ft. - First Floor
992 Sq. Ft. - Second Floor; 37,311 Cu. Ft.

● This charming, one-and-a-half story home definitely extends an invitation of warmth in appearance. Once inside this home, you will be surprised at its many fine features. Study the floor plan and list your favorite features.

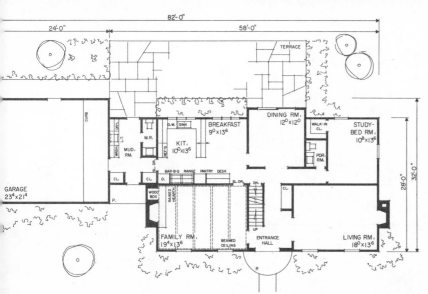

Dimensions: 82'-0" (24'-0", 58'-0"); 32'-0"; 28'-0"

GARAGE 23⁴ x 21⁴

TERRACE

CURB

MUD RM.

KIT. 10⁰ x 13⁶

DW SINK

BREAKFAST 9⁰ x 13⁶

DINING RM. 12⁰ x 12⁰

WALK-IN CL.

STUDY-BED RM. 10⁸ x 13⁶

PDR. RM.

WOOD BOX

RAISED HEARTH

BAR-B-Q RANGE PANTRY DESK

CL.

SL. DR.

DN.

UP

CL.

FAMILY RM. 19⁴ x 13⁶

BEAMED CEILING

ENTRANCE HALL

LIVING RM. 18⁰ x 13⁶

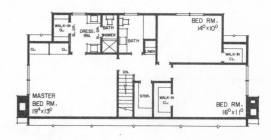

WALK-IN CL.

DRESS. CL.

BATH

SHOWER

BATH

LINEN

BED RM. 14⁰ x 10⁰

WALK-IN CL.

MASTER BED RM. 19⁴ x 13⁰

DN.

STOR.

WALK-IN CL.

BED RM. 16⁰ x 11⁰

Design T61766 1,638 Sq. Ft. - First Floor; 1,006 Sq. Ft. - Second Floor; 35,352 Cu. Ft.

● Here is a home that truly fits the description of traditional charm. The symmetry is, indeed, delightful. A certain magnetic aura seems to reach out with a whisper of welcome. Observe the spacious family-kitchen area, the study, the separate dining room and the extra bath.

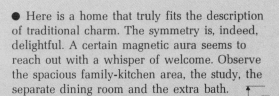

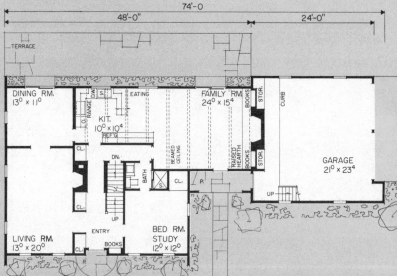

Design T62124

1,176 Sq. Ft. - First Floor
922 Sq. Ft. - Second Floor; 29,854 Cu. Ft.

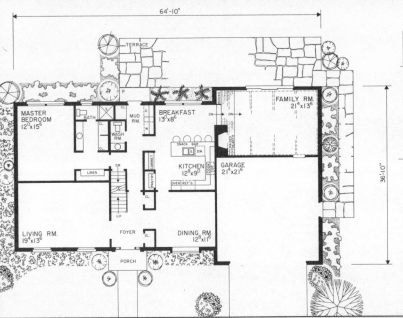

● This cozy home has over 2,600 square feet of livable floor area! And the manner in which this space is put to work to function conveniently for the large family is worth studying. Imagine five bedrooms, three full baths, living, dining and family rooms. Note large kitchen.

Design T61701 1,344 Sq. Ft. - First Floor; 948 Sq. Ft. - Second Floor; 33,952 Cu. Ft.

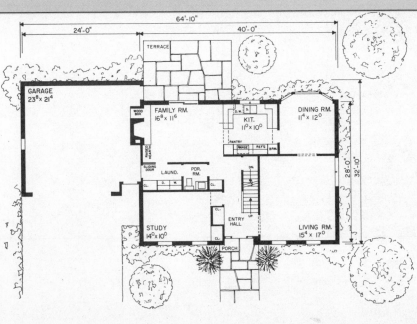

● Surely your list of favorite features will be fun to compile. It certainly will be a long one. The center entry hall helps establish excellent traffic patterns and good zoning. The formal living and dining rooms function well together, as do the kitchen and family room. Note laundry and study.

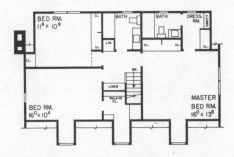

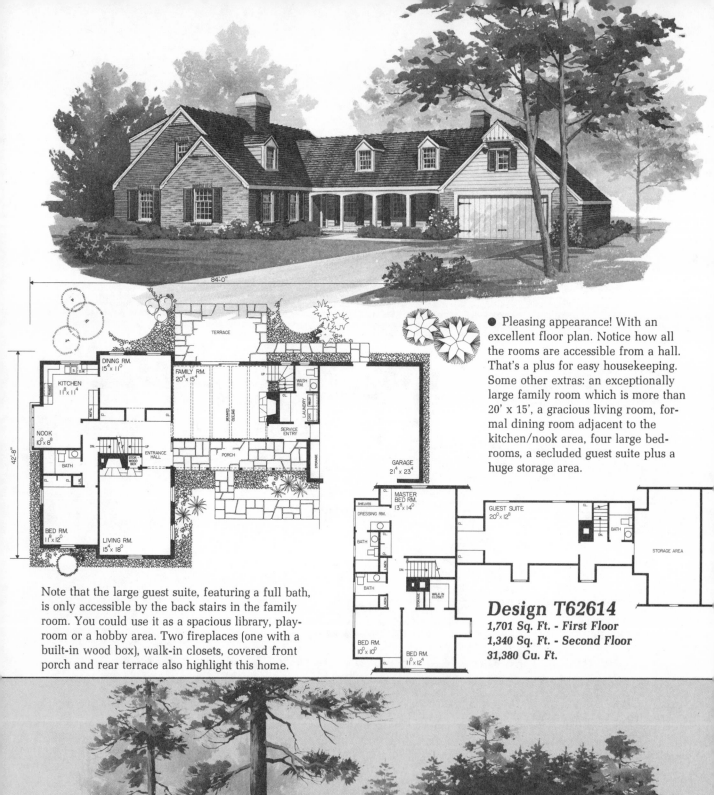

● Pleasing appearance! With an excellent floor plan. Notice how all the rooms are accessible from a hall. That's a plus for easy housekeeping. Some other extras: an exceptionally large family room which is more than 20' x 15', a gracious living room, formal dining room adjacent to the kitchen/nook area, four large bedrooms, a secluded guest suite plus a huge storage area.

Note that the large guest suite, featuring a full bath, is only accessible by the back stairs in the family room. You could use it as a spacious library, playroom or a hobby area. Two fireplaces (one with a built-in wood box), walk-in closets, covered front porch and rear terrace also highlight this home.

Design T62614
1,701 Sq. Ft. - *First Floor*
1,340 Sq. Ft. - *Second Floor*
31,380 Cu. Ft.

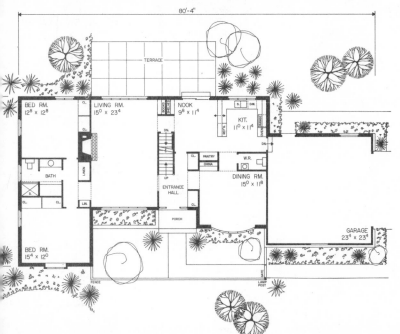

Design T62284
1,677 Sq. Ft. - First Floor
897 Sq. Ft. - Second Floor; 40,413 Cu. Ft.

● This low-slung traditional design features four bedrooms, two up and two down, plus three baths and a washroom. The spacious living room will efficiently serve all of the family activities. There is a basement for family recreational and hobby space.

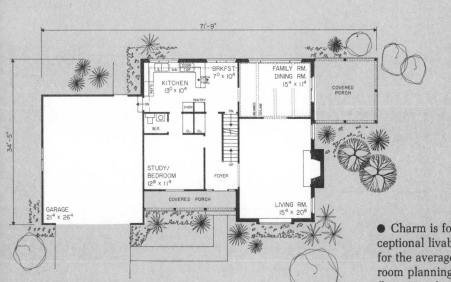

Design T62285
1,118 Sq. Ft. - First Floor
821 Sq. Ft. - Second Floor
28,585 Cu. Ft.

● Charm is found in this appealing home. There is exceptional livability in this one-and-a-half story design for the average sized family. Note the flexibility in the room planning. Rooms have optional usage on the first floor. You decide how your family will live.

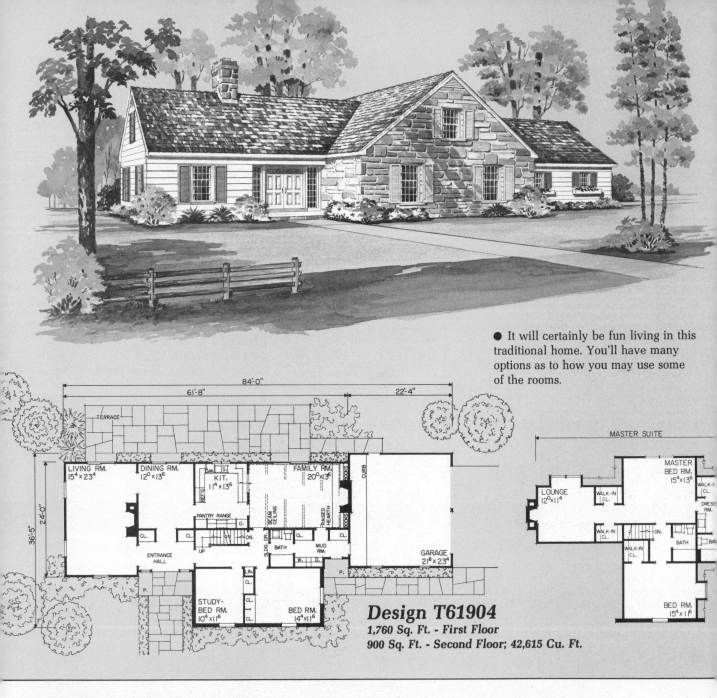

● It will certainly be fun living in this traditional home. You'll have many options as to how you may use some of the rooms.

TERRACE

LIVING RM.
15⁴ x 23⁴

DINING RM.
12⁰ x 13⁶

KIT.
11⁴ x 13⁶

FAMILY RM.
20⁰ x 13⁶

CURB

GARAGE
21⁸ x 23⁴

PANTRY RANGE

BEAM CEILING

RAISED HEARTH

CL.

BATH

MUD RM.

CL.

ENTRANCE HALL

UP

DN.

LIN.

CL.

CL.

CL.

W.

D.

STUDY-BED RM.
10⁴ x 11⁶

BED RM.
14⁴ x 11⁶

84'-0"
61'-8"
22'-4"
36'-5"
24'-0"

MASTER SUITE

LOUNGE
12⁰ x 11⁴

WALK-IN CL.

MASTER BED RM.
15⁴ x 13⁶

WALK-IN CL.

DRESS RM.

WALK-IN CL.

WALK-IN CL.

BATH

DN.

BED RM.
15⁴ x 11⁶

Design T61904
1,760 Sq. Ft. - First Floor
900 Sq. Ft. - Second Floor; 42,615 Cu. Ft.

Design T61794 2,122 Sq. Ft. - First Floor
802 Sq. Ft. - Second Floor; 37,931 Cu. Ft.

● The inviting warmth of this delightful home catches the eye of even the most casual observer. Imagine, four big bedrooms! Formal and informal living can be enjoyed throughout this charming plan. A private, formal dining room is available for those very special occasions.

BED RM.
17⁰ x 15⁰

BATH

BATH

LIN.

CL.

DN.

WALK-IN CL.

BED RM.
12⁰ x 18⁰

CL.

CL.

QUIET TERRACE

MASTER BED RM.
15⁰ x 15⁶

CL.

CL.

VANITY

DRESS RM.

BATH

PDR. RM.

BED RM.
12⁰ x 13⁰

BATH

CL.

LIN.

PLAY TERRACE

FAMILY RM.
20⁰ x 15⁰

RAISED HEARTH

WD. BOX

CURB

GARAGE
23⁴ x 23⁴

W.R.

CL.

DN.

CL.

LINEN

SNACKS

KITCHEN
20⁰ x 10⁰

MUD RM.

LIVING RM.
23⁰ x 15⁶

ENTRY HALL

UP

DINING RM.
12⁰ x 12⁰

EATING

RANGE

FENCE

44'-0"
88'-10"
20'-0"
24'-0"
40'-10"
32'-0"

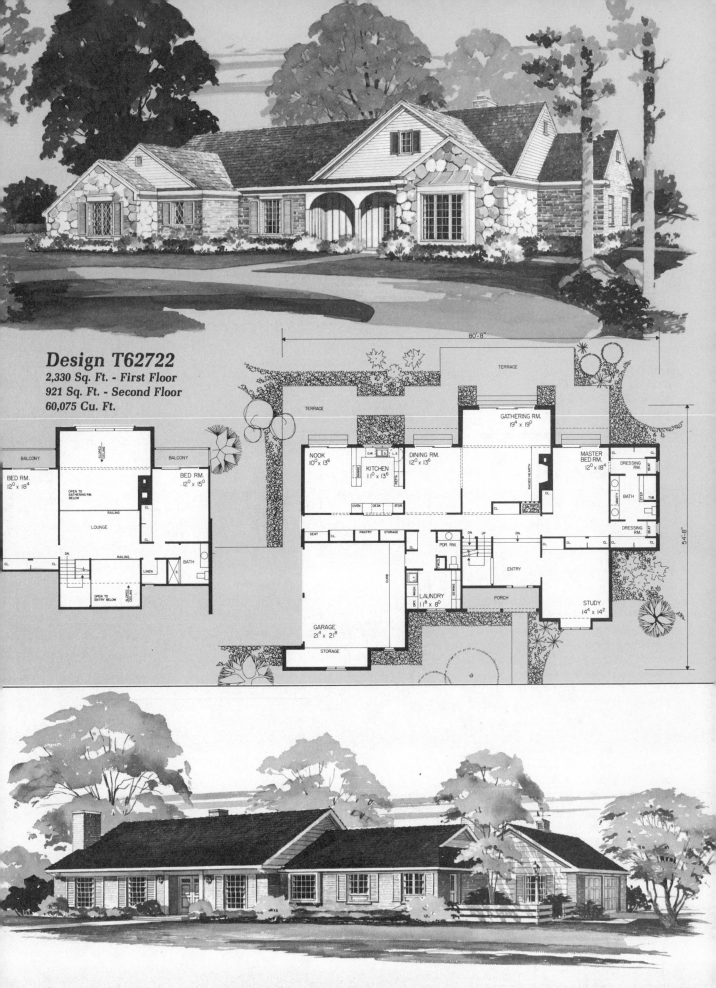

Design T62722

2,330 Sq. Ft. - First Floor
921 Sq. Ft. - Second Floor
60,075 Cu. Ft.

BALCONY

BALCONY

BED RM.
12⁰ x 18⁴

OPEN TO
GATHERING RM.
BELOW

BED RM.
12⁰ x 15⁰

RAILING

CL.

LOUNGE

CL.

DN.

RAILING

OPEN TO ENTRY BELOW

LINEN

BATH

80'-8"

TERRACE

TERRACE

54'-8"

GATHERING RM.
19⁴ x 19⁰

NOOK
10⁰ x 13⁶

DINING RM.
12⁰ x 13⁶

MASTER
BED RM.
12⁰ x 18⁴

DRESSING
RM.

KITCHEN
11⁰ x 13⁶

RAISED HEARTH

BATH

VANITY

STEP

TUB

OVEN

DESK

STOR.

CL.

DRESSING
RM.

SEAT

CL.

PANTRY

STORAGE

CL.

PDR. RM.

DN.

UP

DN.

CL.

CL.

CURB

ENTRY

DRY.

WASH.

LAUNDRY
11⁸ x 8⁰

PORCH

STUDY
14⁴ x 14²

GARAGE
21⁴ x 21⁸

STORAGE

199

Design T62724
2,543 Sq. Ft. - First Floor
884 Sq. Ft. - Second Floor
53,640 Cu. Ft.

● Impressive at first glance! The interior of this one-and-a-half story home offers an abundance of livability. The master bedroom suite is on the first floor and has a private terrace. The second floor houses two more bedrooms and a bath. A design sure to provide enjoyment.

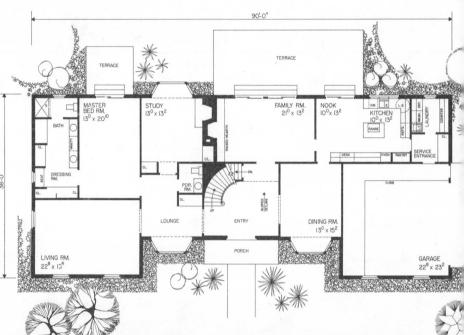

Design T62676 **1,889 Sq. Ft. - First Floor**
872 Sq. Ft. - Second Floor; 39,003 Cu. Ft.

● Here is the perfect home for those who want lots of livability. Note the easy access to each room. A luxurious master bedroom suite will provide all of the comforts you deserve. Take note of the sitting room, his/her dressing and closet areas and the raised tub. Upstairs, two nice sized bedrooms and a full bath.

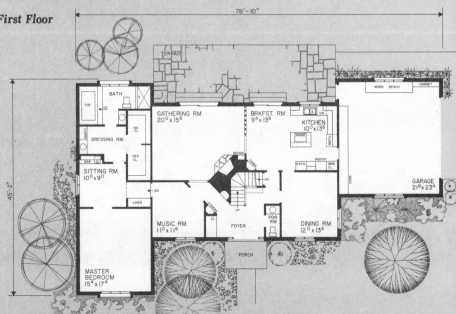

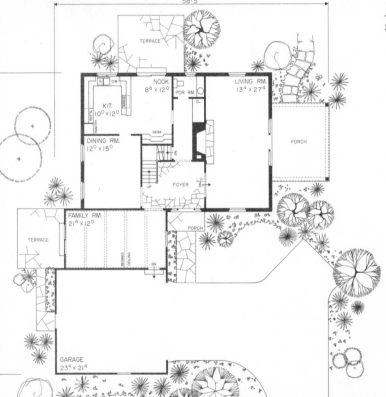

58'-5"

TERRACE

NOOK
8⁸ x 12⁰

LIVING RM.
13⁴ x 27⁴

KIT.
10⁰ x 12⁰

PDR. RM.

PORCH

DINING RM.
12⁰ x 15⁰

DESK

FOYER

FAMILY RM.
21⁴ x 12⁰

PORCH

TERRACE

BEAMED CEILING

DN

GARAGE
23⁴ x 21⁴

BED RM.
14⁰ x 11⁰

BATH BATH

LINEN

CL'S CLIP

MASTER BED RM.
12⁴ x 20⁴

BED RM.
14⁰ x 11⁸

Design T62313 1,446 Sq. Ft. - First Floor
985 Sq. Ft. - Second Floor; 33,544 Cu. Ft.

● This charming, one-and-a-half story house will embrace you with its cozy appeal. A spacious living room is to the right after entering this home. It has a fireplace that is sure to bring many hours of pleasure in the cold winter months. Note its easy access to the covered porch. Left of the foyer, you will find a good sized family room with beamed ceiling and a formal dining room. Nearby is an efficient kitchen and adjacent nook. Note the built-in desk. Upstairs, a master bedroom, two smaller bedrooms and a bath will serve the family. Because of its configuration, this design is ideal for a corner lot.

Design T61115 1,440 Sq. Ft. - First Floor
740 Sq. Ft. - Second Floor; 33,516 Cu. Ft.

● A most distinctive exterior with an equally distinctive interior. A study of the plan reveals all of the elements to assure convenient living. The main living unit, the first floor, functions very efficiently. Two bedrooms and a full bath comprise the sleeping zone. The U-shaped kitchen is very efficient. The family/dining room will serve the family admirably. Adjacent to the kitchen is the laundry area, washroom and entrance from the garage. This living unit is definitely complete. Now add the second floor. Absolutely fantastic! The whole second floor is a master bedroom.

Design T61196 1,008 Sq. Ft. - First Floor
648 Sq. Ft. - Second Floor; 23,884 Cu. Ft.

● This cozy home is ideal for a small family. Upon entering this house, you will find a nice sized living room with a fireplace. Adjacent, the formal dining area has sliding glass doors leading to the terrace. The kitchen and informal eating area are just a few steps away. A full bath and an optional bedroom/study also are on this floor. A full bath and two good sized bedrooms, each with its own dressing area, are on the second floor.

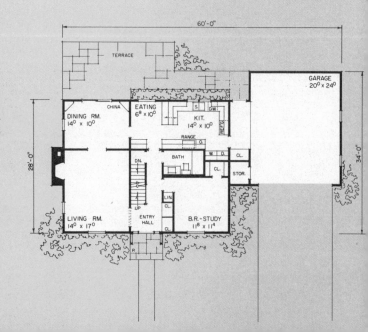

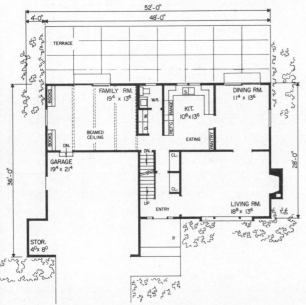

Design T61241 *1,064 Sq. Ft. - First Floor*
898 Sq. Ft. - Second Floor; 24,723 Cu. Ft.

● You don't need a mansion to live graciously. What you do need is a practical floor plan which takes into consideration the varied activities of the busy family. This plan does that! This story-and-a-half design will not require a large piece of property while it returns the maximum per construction dollar. Its living potential is tremendous.

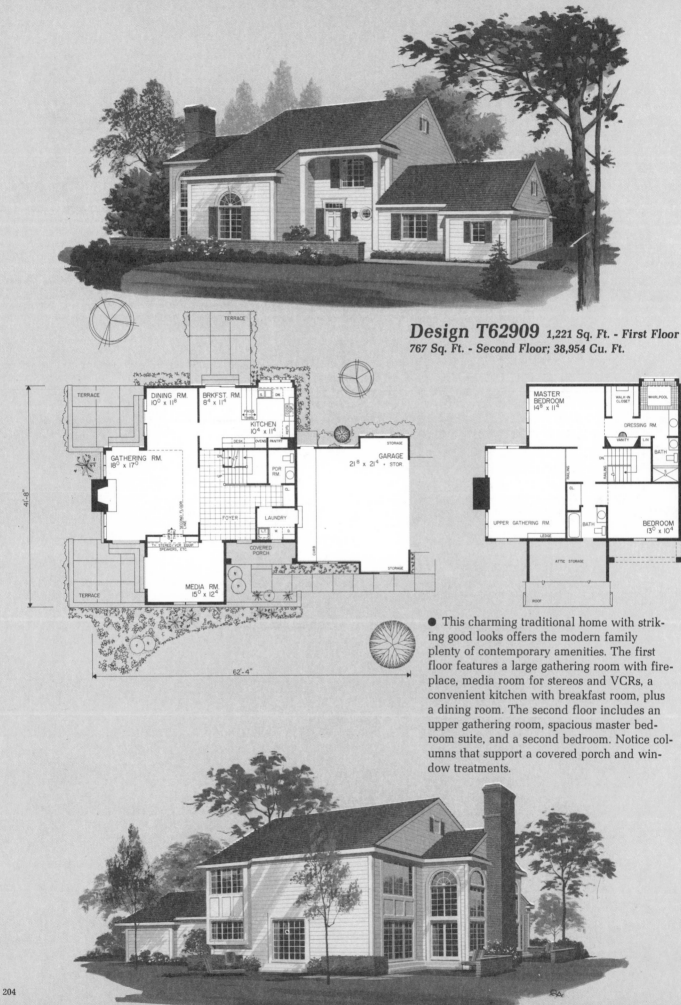

Design T62909 1,221 Sq. Ft. - First Floor
767 Sq. Ft. - Second Floor; 38,954 Cu. Ft.

● This charming traditional home with striking good looks offers the modern family plenty of contemporary amenities. The first floor features a large gathering room with fireplace, media room for stereos and VCRs, a convenient kitchen with breakfast room, plus a dining room. The second floor includes an upper gathering room, spacious master bedroom suite, and a second bedroom. Notice columns that support a covered porch and window treatments.

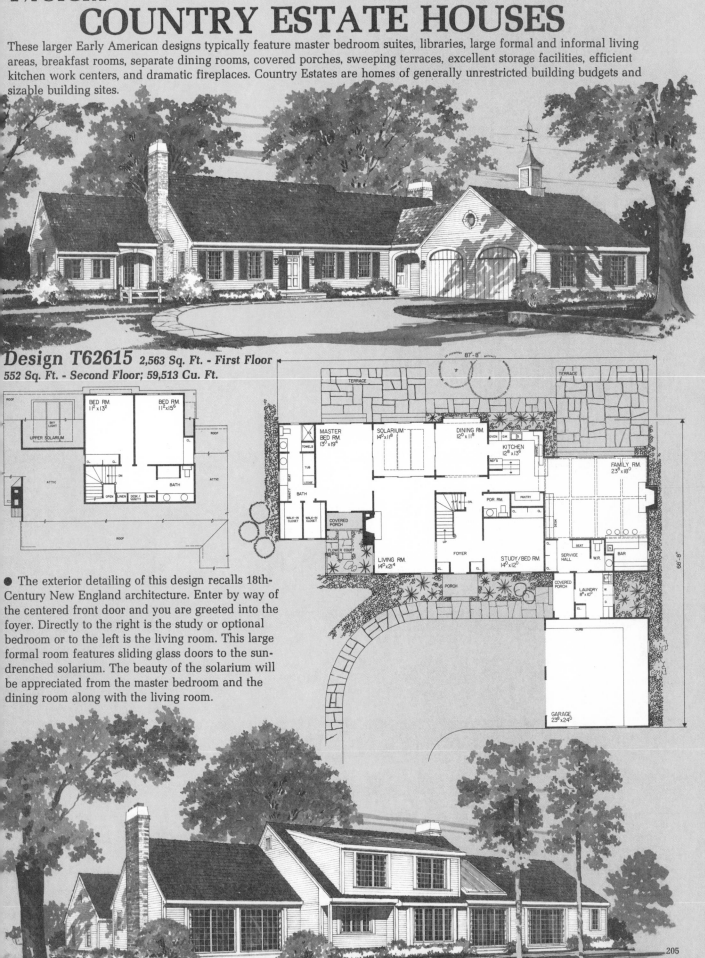

1½-STORY
COUNTRY ESTATE HOUSES

These larger Early American designs typically feature master bedroom suites, libraries, large formal and informal living areas, breakfast rooms, separate dining rooms, covered porches, sweeping terraces, excellent storage facilities, efficient kitchen work centers, and dramatic fireplaces. Country Estates are homes of generally unrestricted building budgets and sizable building sites.

Design T62615 2,563 Sq. Ft. - First Floor
552 Sq. Ft. - Second Floor; 59,513 Cu. Ft.

● The exterior detailing of this design recalls 18th-Century New England architecture. Enter by way of the centered front door and you are greeted into the foyer. Directly to the right is the study or optional bedroom or to the left is the living room. This large formal room features sliding glass doors to the sun-drenched solarium. The beauty of the solarium will be appreciated from the master bedroom and the dining room along with the living room.

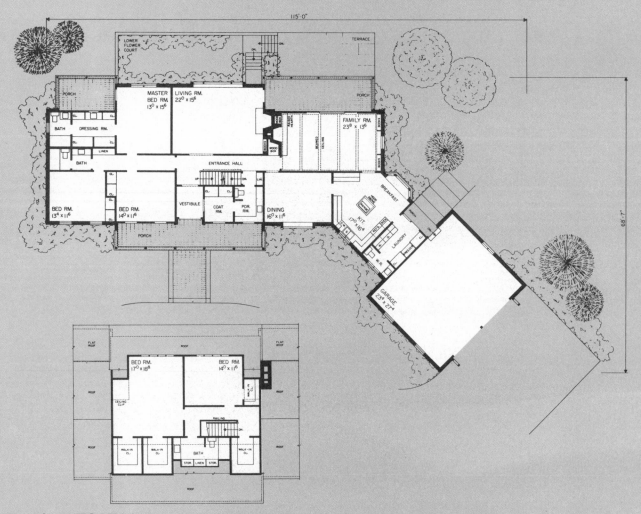

Design T61711 *2,580 Sq. Ft. - First Floor; 938 Sq. Ft. - Second Floor; 46,788 Cu. Ft.*

● If the gracious charm of the Colonial South appeals to you, this may be just the house you've been waiting for. There is something solid and dependable in its well-balanced facade and wide, pillared front porch. Much of the interest generated by this design comes from its interesting expanses of roof and angular projection of its kitchen and garage. The feeling of elegance is further experienced upon stepping inside, through double doors, to the spacious entrance hall where there is the separate coat room. Adjacent to this is the powder room, also convenient to the living areas. The work area of the kitchen and laundry room is truly outstanding. Designed as a five bedroom house, each is large. Storage and bath facilities are excellent.

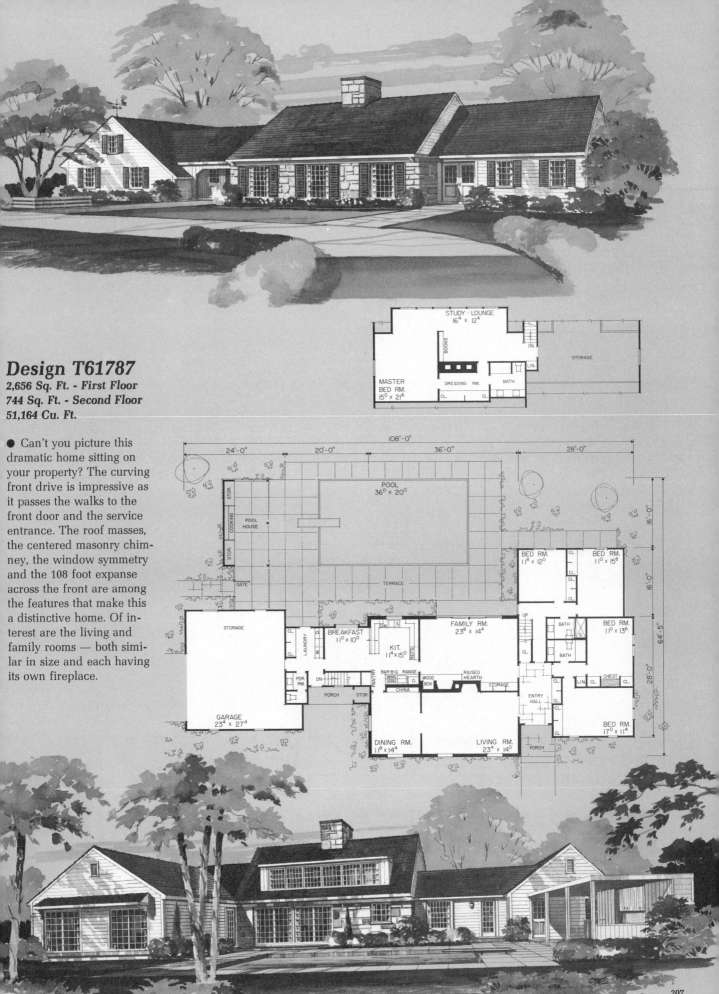

Design T61787

2,656 Sq. Ft. - First Floor
744 Sq. Ft. - Second Floor
51,164 Cu. Ft.

● Can't you picture this dramatic home sitting on your property? The curving front drive is impressive as it passes the walks to the front door and the service entrance. The roof masses, the centered masonry chimney, the window symmetry and the 108 foot expanse across the front are among the features that make this a distinctive home. Of interest are the living and family rooms — both similar in size and each having its own fireplace.

Second Floor Plan:
STUDY - LOUNGE 16⁴ x 12⁴
BOOKS
DN.
STORAGE
MASTER BED RM. 15⁰ x 21⁶
DRESSING RM.
BATH
LIN.
CL.
CL.

First Floor Plan:
108'-0"
24'-0" 20'-0" 36'-0" 28'-0"
16'-0"
64'-5"
28'-0"

POOL 36⁰ x 20⁰
POOL HOUSE
STOR.
COOKING
STOR.
GATE
TERRACE
STORAGE
BED RM. 11⁸ x 12⁰
BED RM. 11⁰ x 15⁸
BED RM. 11⁰ x 13⁶
BED RM. 17⁰ x 11⁴
CL.
LAUNDRY
BREAKFAST 11⁰ x 10⁰
KIT. 11⁴ x 15⁰
FAMILY RM. 23⁸ x 14⁴
UP
BATH
BATH
ENTRY HALL
LIN.
CHEST
PDR. RM.
DN.
PORCH
STOR.
PANTRY
BAR-B-Q RANGE
CHINA
WOOD BOX
RAISED HEARTH
STORAGE
GARAGE 23⁴ x 27⁴
DINING RM. 11⁸ x 14⁴
LIVING RM. 23⁴ x 14⁰
PORCH

Design T62133 *3,024 Sq. Ft. - First Floor; 826 Sq. Ft. - Second Floor; 54,883 Cu. Ft.*

● A country-estate home which will command all the attention it truly deserves. The projecting pediment gable supported by the finely proportioned columns lends an aura of elegance. The window treatment, the front door detailing, the massive, capped chimney, the cupola, the brick veneer exterior and the varying roof planes complete the characterization of an impressive home. Inside, there are 3,024 square feet on the first floor. In addition, there is a two bedroom second floor should its development be necessary. However, whether called upon to function as one, or 1-1/2 story home it will provide a lifetime of gracious living. Don't overlook the compartment baths, the big library, the coat room, the beamed ceiling family room, the two fireplaces, the breakfast room and the efficient kitchen. Note pass-thru to breakfast room.

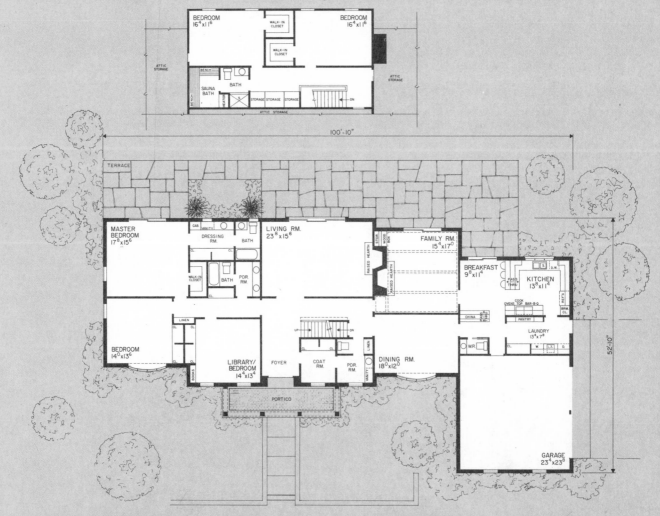

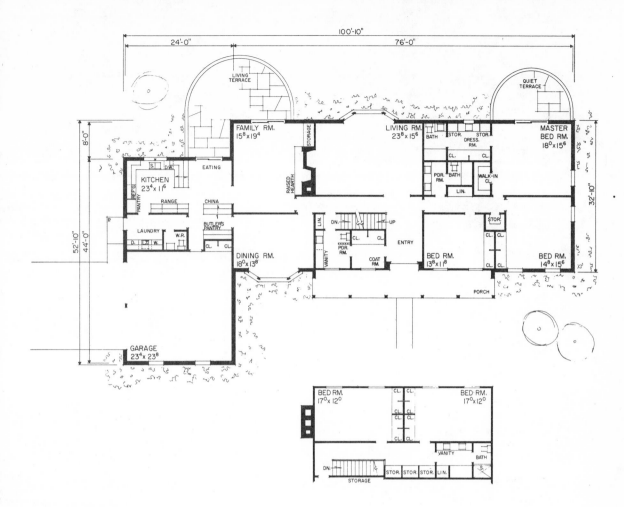

Design T61796
3,006 Sq. Ft. - First Floor
794 Sq. Ft. - Second Floor; 44,240 Cu. Ft.

● Five big bedrooms! Or make it three if you prefer not to develop the second floor. When viewing this home the initial lingering look turns into something of a studied analysis; for here is a positively outstanding design. The columned porch creates an at-

mosphere of charming country-estate living. Note that there is a living terrace plus a quiet terrace off the master bedroom. The floor plan will surely permit the fulfillment of such a way of life. Each and every member of the family will love the spaciousness of

the interior. In addition to such big and obvious features as the delightful living, dining and family rooms, the fireplaces, kitchen and three baths, there is a multitude of little features. Be sure to list them, you'll find them most interesting.

Design T61060
3,190 Sq. Ft. - First Floor
1,024 Sq. Ft. - Second Floor
52,189 Cu. Ft.

● Truly a home of disti-
tion for the large family.
Study this plan carefull
List its many features f
is certainly a unique ho
with unrestricted livabi
will serve your family's
mal and informal living
terns for many years. D
overlook the bath facili
or the extra maid's roo
use it as a family hobby
room if you wish.

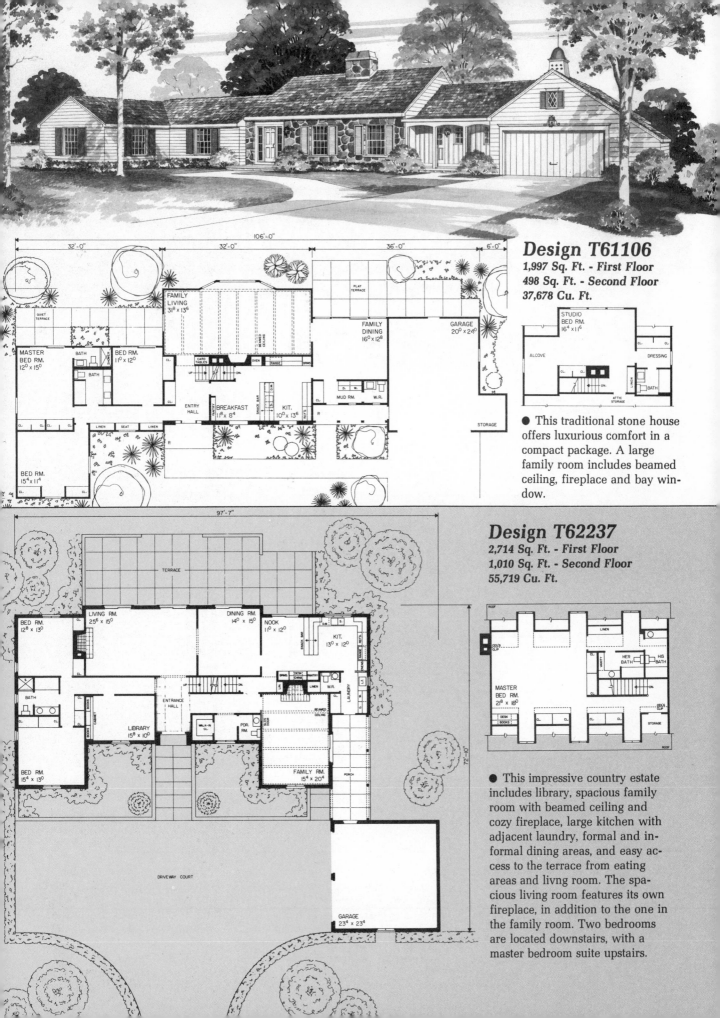

Design T61106
1,997 Sq. Ft. - First Floor
498 Sq. Ft. - Second Floor
37,678 Cu. Ft.

● This traditional stone house offers luxurious comfort in a compact package. A large family room includes beamed ceiling, fireplace and bay window.

Design T62237
2,714 Sq. Ft. - First Floor
1,010 Sq. Ft. - Second Floor
55,719 Cu. Ft.

● This impressive country estate includes library, spacious family room with beamed ceiling and cozy fireplace, large kitchen with adjacent laundry, formal and informal dining areas, and easy access to the terrace from eating areas and livng room. The spacious living room features its own fireplace, in addition to the one in the family room. Two bedrooms are located downstairs, with a master bedroom suite upstairs.

STUDY ALCOVE
10'⁰ x 10'²

BED RM.
13'² x 16'⁸

BED RM.
12'⁸ x 16'⁸

LINEN

BATH

Design T62342
2,824 Sq. Ft. - First Floor
1,013 Sq. Ft. - Second Floor
59,882 Cu. Ft.

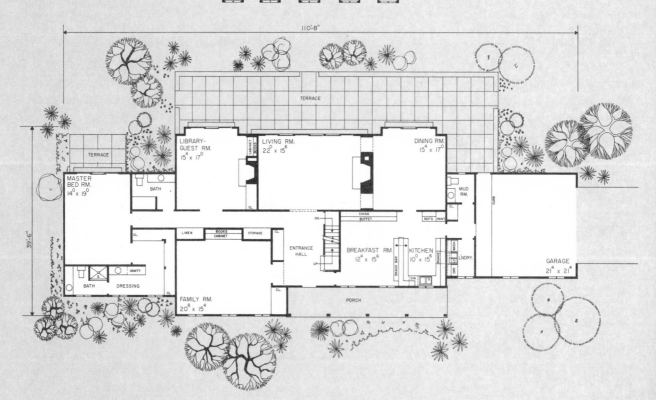

110'-8"

TERRACE

TERRACE

LIBRARY-
GUEST RM.
15'⁴ x 17'⁰

LIVING RM.
22'⁰ x 15'⁶

DINING RM.
15'⁴ x 17'⁰

MASTER
BED RM.
14' x 19'⁰

BATH

MUD.
RM.

CHINA
BUFFET

REF'G

LINEN

BOOKS
CABINET

STORAGE

ENTRANCE
HALL

BREAKFAST RM.
12'⁴ x 15'⁶

KITCHEN
10'⁰ x 15'⁶

LNDRY.

GARAGE
21'⁴ x 21'⁴

BATH

DRESSING

VANITY

FAMILY RM.
20'⁰ x 15'⁴

PORCH

39'-6"

● A distinctive exterior characterized by varying roof planes, appealing window treatment, attractive chimneys and a covered front porch with prominent vertical columns. The main portion of the house is effectively balanced by the master bedroom wing on the one side and the garage wing on the other. As a buffer between house and garage is the mud room and the laundry. The kitchen is U-shaped, efficient, and strategically located to serve the breakfast and dining rooms. Notice how the rooms at the rear function through sliding glass doors with the outdoor terrace areas. Fireplaces highlight both the spacious living room and the large library. The big family room features built-in bookshelves and cabinet. Upstairs, two bedrooms and a study alcove will be found.

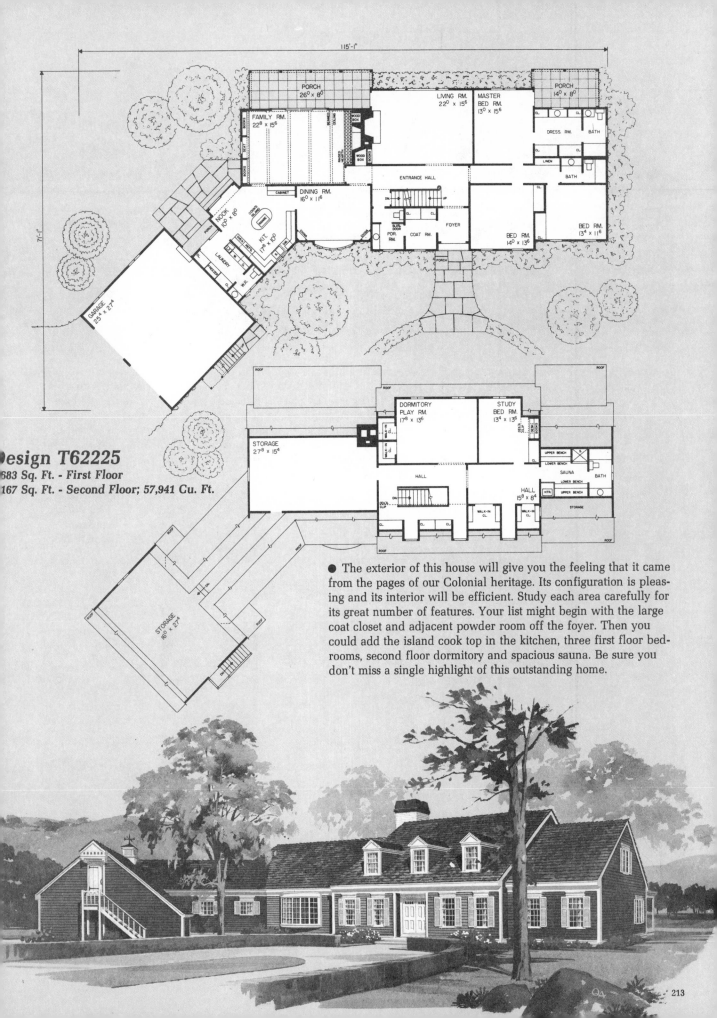

Design T62225

683 Sq. Ft. - First Floor
167 Sq. Ft. - Second Floor; 57,941 Cu. Ft.

● The exterior of this house will give you the feeling that it came from the pages of our Colonial heritage. Its configuration is pleasing and its interior will be efficient. Study each area carefully for its great number of features. Your list might begin with the large coat closet and adjacent powder room off the foyer. Then you could add the island cook top in the kitchen, three first floor bedrooms, second floor dormitory and spacious sauna. Be sure you don't miss a single highlight of this outstanding home.

● Organized zoning by room functions makes this Traditional design a comfortable home for living, as well as classic in its styling. A central foyer facilitates flexible traffic patterns. Quiet areas of the house include a media room and luxurious master bedroom suite with fitness area, spacious closet space and bath, as well as a lounge or writing area. Informal living areas of the house include a sun room, large country kitchen, and efficient kitchen with an island. Service areas include a room just off the garage for laundry, sewing, or hobbies. The second floor garage can double as a practical shop. Formal living areas include a living area and formal dining room. The second floor holds two bedrooms that would make a wonderful children's suite, with a study or TV area also upstairs.

Design T62921

3,215 Sq. Ft. - First Floor
296 Sq. Ft. - Sun Room
711 Sq. Ft. - Second Floor
69,991 Cu. Ft.

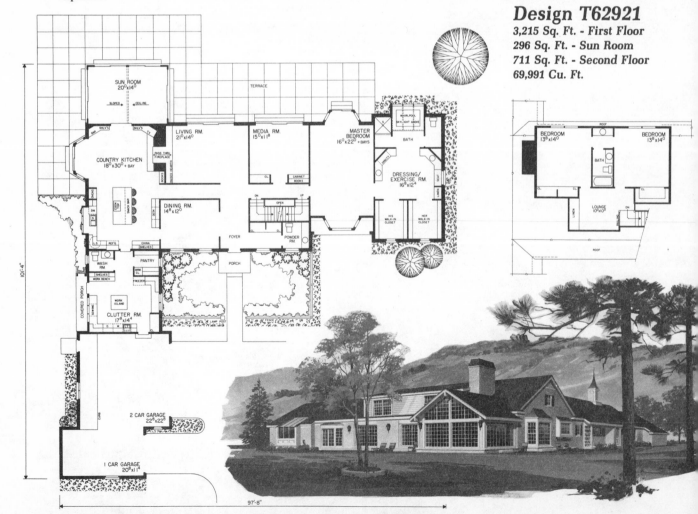

ONE-STORY
TRADITIONAL ADAPTATIONS UNDER 2,000 SQ. FT.

These delightful smaller Early American homes offer plenty of efficiency of design along with styling of the Colonial era. Everything is compacted on one floor for accessibility ease.

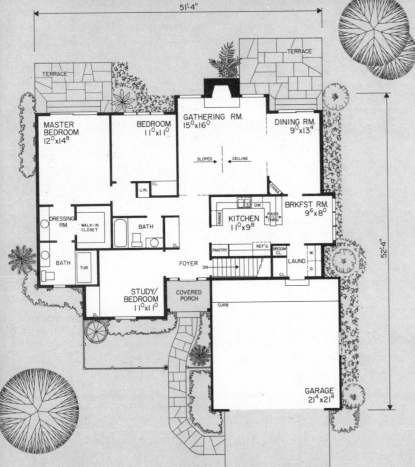

Design T62878
1,521 Sq. Ft.; 34,760 Cu. Ft.

● This charming one-story Traditional design offers plenty of livability in a compact size. Thoughtful zoning puts all bedroom sleeping areas to one side of the house apart from household activity in the living and service areas. The home includes a spacious gathering room with sloped ceiling, in addition to formal dining room and separate breakfast room. There's also a handy pass-thru between the breakfast room and an efficient, large kitchen. The laundry is strategically located adjacent to garage and breakfast/kitchen areas for handy access. A master bedroom enjoys its own suite with private bath and walk-in closet. A third bedroom can double as a sizable study just off the central foyer. This design offers the elegance of Traditional styling with the comforts of modern lifestyle.

Design T62505
1,366 Sq. Ft.; 29,329 Cu. Ft.

● This one-story traditionally styled design captures all the coziness and appeal of its more authentic 1½ and two-story counterparts. A study of the floor plans reveals a fine measure of livability. In less than 1,400 square feet, there are features galore. In addition to the two eating areas and the open planning of the gathering room, the indoor-outdoor relationships are of great interest. The basement may be developed for recreational activities. Blueprints for this design include two optional Contemporary exteriors. An excellent return on your construction dollars.

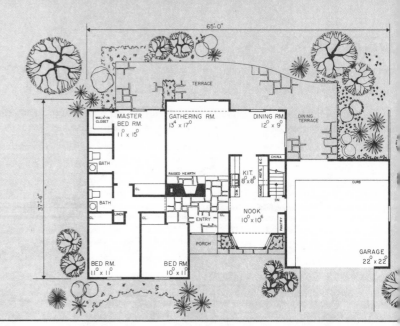

Design T62565
1,540 Sq. Ft.; 33,300 Cu. Ft.

● This modest sized floor plan has much to offer in the way of livability. It may function as either a two or three bedroom home. The family room is huge and features a fine, raised hearth fireplace. The open stairway to the basement is handy and will lead to what may be developed as the recreation area. In addition to the two full baths, there is an extra laundry room and the service entrance from the garage. The blueprints you receive for this design include details for building optional Tudor and Contemporary elevations. You'll have fun deciding upon your favorite.

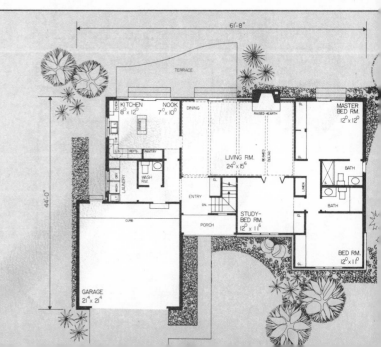

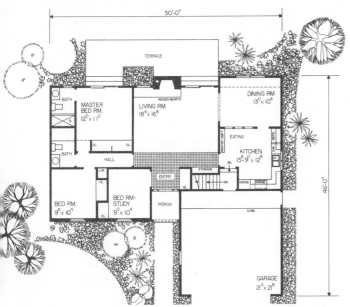

Design T62707
1,267 Sq. Ft.; 27,125 Cu. Ft.

● Here is a charming Early American adaptation that will serve as a picturesque and practical retirement home. Also, it will serve admirably those with a small family in search of an efficient, economically built home. The living area, highlighted by the raised hearth fireplace, is spacious. The kitchen features eating space; the bedroom area, two full baths. The dining room views the rear yard. Then, there is the basement for recreation and hobby pursuits. The bedroom wing offers three bedrooms and two full baths. Don't miss the sliding doors to terrace and the storage and pantry units.

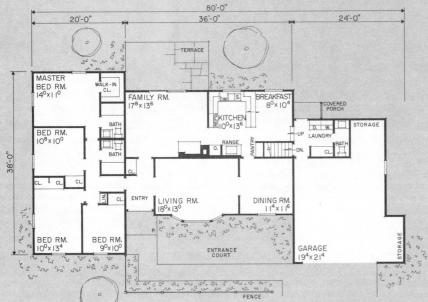

Design T61829
1,800 Sq. Ft.; 32,236 Cu. Ft.

● All the charm of a traditional heritage is wrapped up in this U-shaped home with its narrow, horizontal siding, delightful window treatment and high-pitched roof. The massive center chimney, the bay window and the double front doors are plus features. Inside, the living potential is outstanding. The sleeping wing is self-contained and has four bedrooms and two baths. The large family and living rooms cater to the divergent age groups.

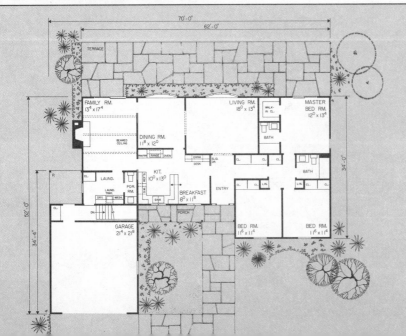

Design T61980
1,901 Sq. Ft.; 36,240 Cu. Ft.

● Planned for easy living, the daily living patterns of the active family will be pleasant ones, indeed. All the elements are present to assure a wonderful family life. The impressive exterior is enhanced by the recessed front entrance area with its covered porch. The center entry results in a convenient and efficient flow of traffic. A secondary entrance leads from the covered side porch, or the garage, into the first floor laundry. Note the powder room nearby.

Design T62360
1,936 Sq. Ft.; 37,026 Cu. Ft.

● There is no such thing as taking a fleeting glance at this charming home. Fine proportion and pleasing lines assure a long and rewarding study. Inside, the family's everyday routine will enjoy all the facilities which will surely guarantee pleasurable living. Note the sunken living room with its fireplace flanked by storage cabinets and bookshelves. Observe the excellent kitchen just a step from the dining room and the nook.

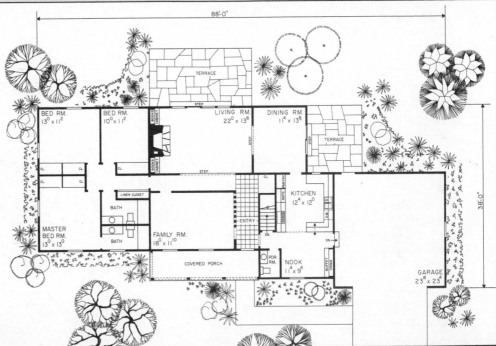

Design T61346
1,644 Sq. Ft.; 19,070 Cu. Ft.

● Whether you enter through the service door of the attached garage, or throught the centered front entry your appreciation of what this plan has to offer will grow. The mud room area is certainly an outstanding feature. Traffic flows from this area to the informal family room with its fireplace and access to the rear terrace.

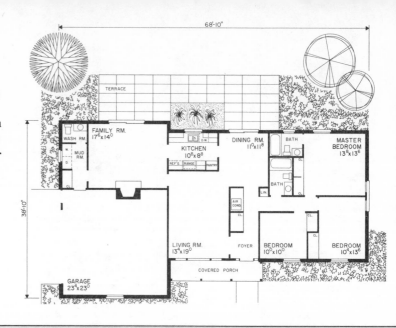

Design T62597
1,515 Sq. Ft.; 32,000 Cu. Ft.

● Whether it be a starter house you are after, or one in which to spend your retirement years, this pleasing frame home will provide a full measure of pride in ownership. The contrast of vertical and horizontal lines, the double front doors and the coach lamp post at the garage create an inviting exterior. The floor plan functions in an orderly and efficient manner. The 26 foot gathering room has a delightful view of the rear yard and will take care of those formal dining occasions. There are two full baths serving the three bedrooms. There are plenty of storage facilities, two sets of glass doors to the terraces, a fireplace in the gathering room, a basement and an attached two-car garage.

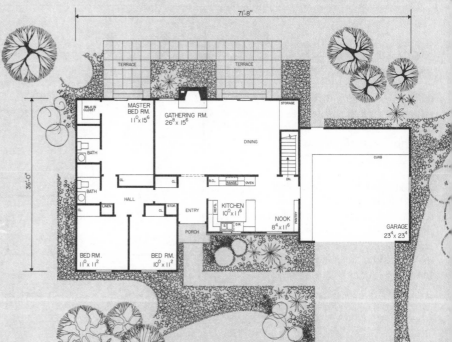

Design T61939
1,387 Sq. Ft.; 28,000 Cu. Ft.

❂ A finely proportioned house with more than its full share of charm. The brick veneer exterior contrasts pleasingly with the narrow horizontal siding of the over-sized attached two-car garage. Perhaps the focal point of the exterior is the recessed front entrance with its double Colonial styled doors. The secondary service entrance through the garage to the kitchen area is a handy feature. Study the plan. It features three bedrooms, two full baths, living room with fireplace, front kitchen with an eating area, formal dining room, plenty of storage potential plus a basement for additional storage or perhaps to be developed as a recreational area.

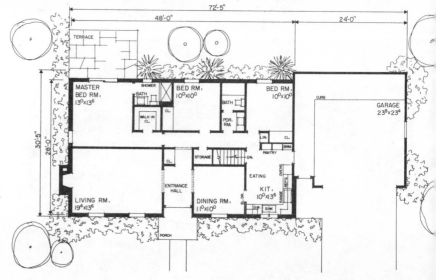

Design T61337
1,606 Sq. Ft.; 31,478 Cu. Ft.

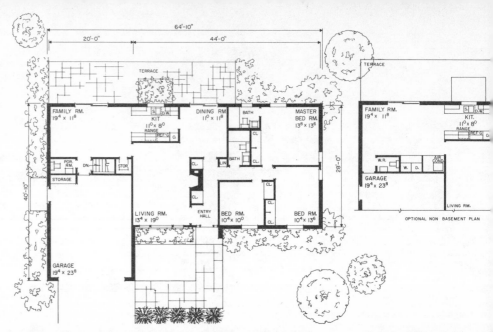

● A pleasantly traditional facade which captures a full measure of warmth. Its exterior appeal results from a symphony of such features as: the attractive window detailing; the raised planter; the paneled door, carriage light and cupola of the garage; the use of both horizontal siding and brick. The floor plan has much to recommend this design to the family whose requirements include formal and informal living areas. There is an exceptional amount of livability in this modest-sized design.

Design T61890
1,628 Sq. Ft.; 20,350 Cu. Ft.

● The pediment gable and columns help set the charm of this modestly sized home. Here is graciousness normally associated with homes twice its size. The pleasant symmetry of the windows and the double front doors complete the picture. Inside, each square foot is wisely planned to assure years of convenient living. There are three bedrooms, each with twin wardrobe closets. There are two full baths economically grouped with the laundry and heating equipment. A fine feature.

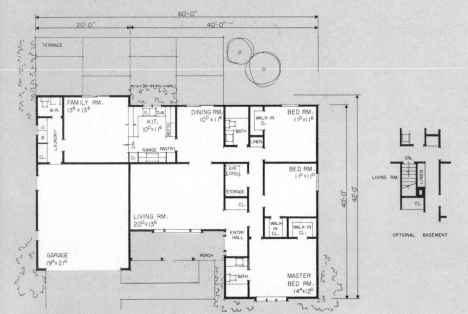

TERRACE

60'-0"

20'-0"   40'-0"

FAMILY RM.
13⁸ x 13⁶

KIT.
10⁰ x 11⁶

DINING RM.
10⁰ x 11⁶

BATH

WALK-IN CL.

LINEN

BED RM.
11⁰ x 11⁶

RANGE PANTRY

AIR COND.

BED RM.
11⁰ x 11⁰

STORAGE

LIVING RM.
20⁰ x 13⁶

CL.

ENTRY HALL

WALK IN CL.   WALK-IN CL.

GARAGE
19⁴ x 21⁶

PORCH

BATH

MASTER BED RM.
14⁴ x 12⁰

40'-0"   42'-0"

OPTIONAL BASEMENT

DN.

LINEN

LIVING RM.

CL.

Design T61920
1,600 Sq. Ft.; 18,966 Cu. Ft.

● A charming exterior with a truly great floor plan. The front entrance with its covered porch seems to herald all the outstanding features to be found inside. Study the sleeping zone with its three bedrooms and two full baths. Each of the bedrooms has its own walk-in closet. Note the efficient U-shaped kitchen with the family and dining rooms to each side. Observe the laundry and the extra washroom. Blueprints for this design include details for both basement and non-basement construction.

Design T61075
1,232 Sq. Ft.; 24,123 Cu. Ft.

● This picturesque traditional one-story home has much to offer the young family. Because of its rectangular shape and its predominantly frame exterior, construction costs will be economical. Passing through the front entrance, visitors will be surprised to find so much livability in only 1,232 square feet. Consider these features: spacious formal living and dining area; two full baths; efficient kitchen; and large, rear family room. In addition there is the full basement for further recreational facilities and bulk storage. The attached garage is extra long to accommodate the storage of garden equipment, lawn furniture, bicycles, etc.

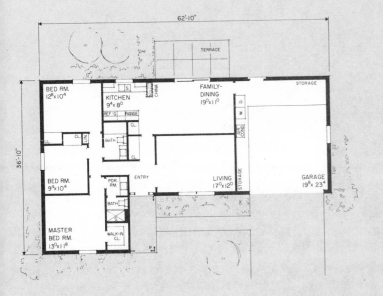

Design T61366
1,280 Sq. Ft.; 14,848 Cu. Ft.

● The extension of the main roof, along with the use of ornamental iron, vertical siding and glass side lites flanking the paneled door, all contribute to a delightful and inviting front entrance to this L-shaped design. There is much to recommend this design—from the attached two-car garage to the walk-in closet of the master bedroom. Don't overlook the compartmented master bath with its stall shower and powder room; the built-in china cabinet with an attractive planter above or the two closets right in the center of the house.

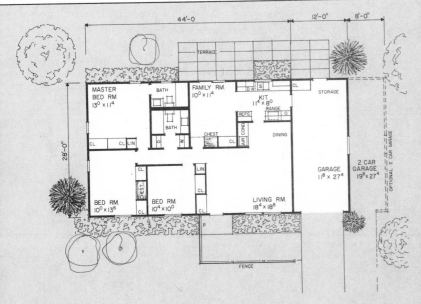

Design T61191
1,232 Sq. Ft.; 15,400 Cu. Ft.

● A careful study of the floor plan for this cozy appearing traditional home reveals a fine combination of features which add tremendously to convenient living. For instance, observe the wardrobe and storage facilities of the bedroom area. A built-in chest in the one bedroom and also one in the family room. Then, notice the economical plumbing of the two full back-to-back baths. Postively a great money saving feature for today and in the future. Further, don't overlook the location of the washer and dryer which have cupboards above the units themselves. Observe storage facilities. Optional two-car garage is available if necessary.

Design T62742
1,907 Sq. Ft.; 38,950 Cu. Ft.

● Colonial charm is expressed in this one-story design by the vertical siding, the post pillars, the cross fence, paned glass windows and the use of stone. A 19' wide living room, a sloped ceilinged family room with a raised hearth fireplace and its own terrace, a kitchen with many built-ins and a dining room with built-in china cabinets are just some of the highlights. The living terrace is accessible from the dining room and master bedroom. There are two more bedrooms and a full bath in addition to the master bedroom.

Design T61222
1,657 Sq. Ft.; 32,444 Cu. Ft.

● How will you call upon this home to function? As a three or four bedroom home? The study permits all kinds of flexibility in your living patterns. If you wish, the extra room could serve the family as a TV area or an area for sewing, hobbies or guests. The 27 foot living room features a formal dining area which is but a step from the secluded, covered dining porch and efficient kitchen. There is a strategically located mud room which houses the washer and dryer and adjacent washroom. The stairs leading to the basement are also in this area.

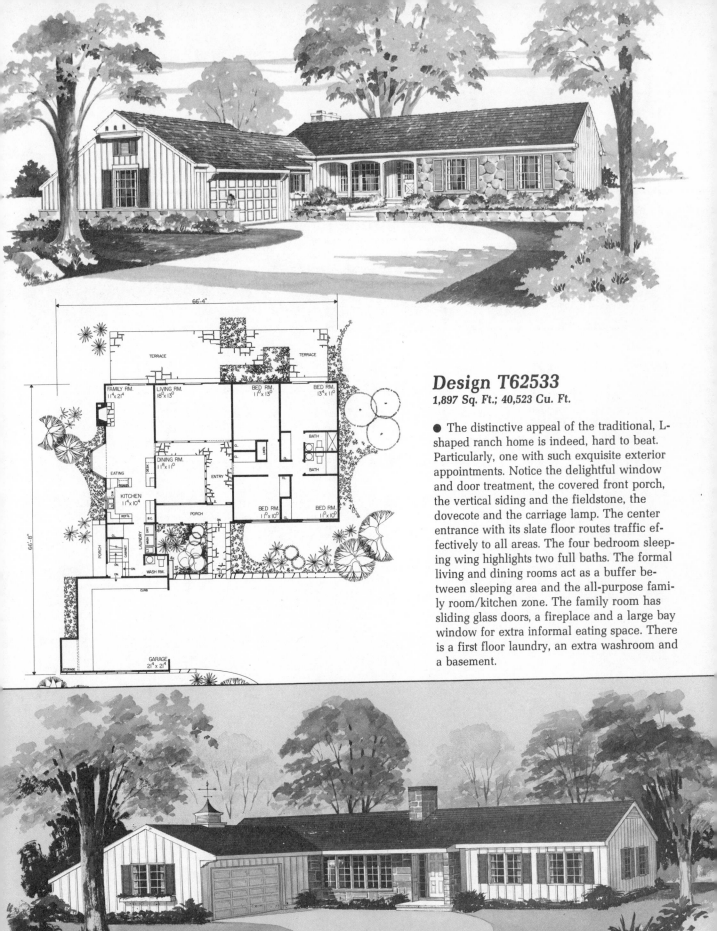

Design T62533
1,897 Sq. Ft.; 40,523 Cu. Ft.

● The distinctive appeal of the traditional, L-shaped ranch home is indeed, hard to beat. Particularly, one with such exquisite exterior appointments. Notice the delightful window and door treatment, the covered front porch, the vertical siding and the fieldstone, the dovecote and the carriage lamp. The center entrance with its slate floor routes traffic effectively to all areas. The four bedroom sleeping wing highlights two full baths. The formal living and dining rooms act as a buffer between sleeping area and the all-purpose family room/kitchen zone. The family room has sliding glass doors, a fireplace and a large bay window for extra informal eating space. There is a first floor laundry, an extra washroom and a basement.

Design T61186
1,872 Sq. Ft.; 31,680 Cu. Ft.

● This appealing home has an interesting and practical floor plan. It is cleverly zoned to cater to the living patterns of both the children and the parents. The children's bedroom wing projects to the rear and functions with their informal family room. The master bedroom is ideally isolated and is located in a part of the plan's quietly formal wing. The efficient kitchen looks out upon the rear terrace and functions conveniently with the dining area and family room. A full bath serves each of the two main living areas. A built-in vanity highlights each bath. The mud room features laundry equipment, storage unit and stairs to the basement. The blueprints show details for basement and non-basement construction.

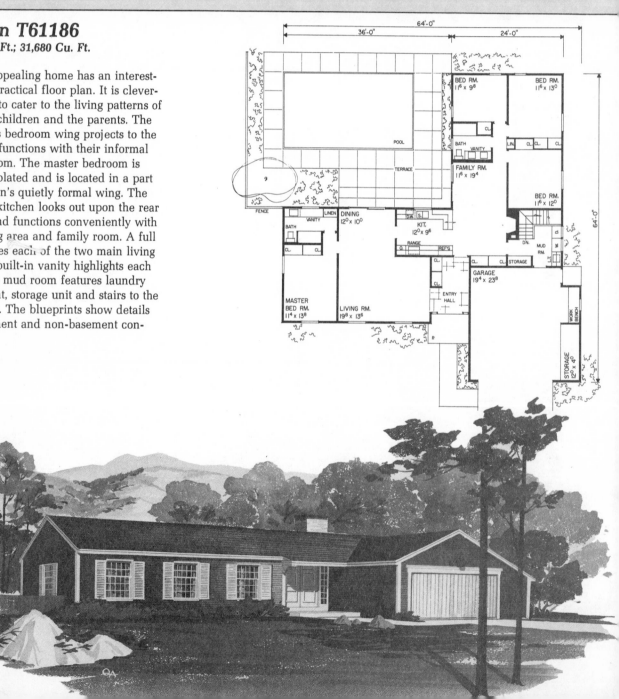

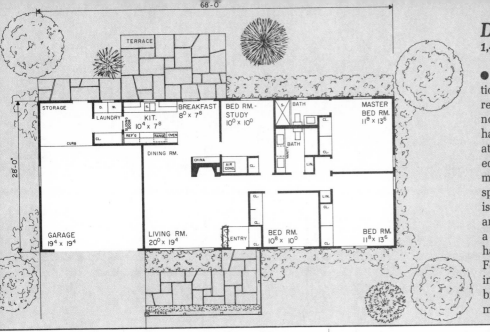

Design T61107
1,416 Sq. Ft.; 14,755 Cu. Ft.

● A smart looking traditional adaptation which, because of its perfectly rectangular shape, will be most economical to build. The low-pitched roof has a wide overhang which accentuates its low-slung qualities. The attached two-car garage is oversized to permit the location of extra bulk storage space. Further, its access to the house is through the handy separate laundry area. This house will function as either a four bedroom home, or as one that has three bedrooms, plus a quiet study. Features include a fireplace in the living room, built-in china cabinet in the breakfast room, sizable vanity in the main baths and more.

Design T62550
1,892 Sq. Ft.; 39,590 Cu. Ft.

● An enchanting low-slung traditional ranch with exceptional appeal. The low-pitched roof has a wide overhang and exposed beams. Stone and vertical siding offer a pleasing contrast. However, you may wish to substitute other materials of your choice. The diamond lite windows, the fence with its lamp post, the double front doors and the dovecote above the carriage lamp of the garage are among the interesting exterior features. Inside, there are four bedrooms and two full baths in the sleeping wing. The L-shaped living area is spacious and features a sloping ceiling for the gathering and dining rooms. The open stairwell to the basement recreation area is attractive. The pleasant kitchen is flanked by the nook and laundry.

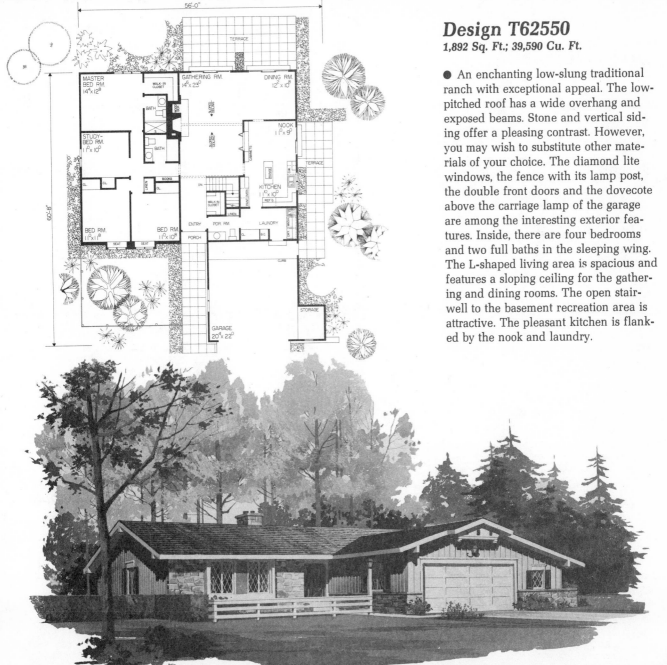

Design T62704

1,746 Sq. Ft.; 38,000 Cu. Ft.

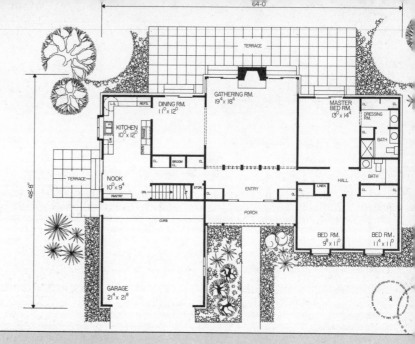

● This home's impressive entry hall is more than 19 feet long and offers double entry to a gathering room, notable for its size and design. A fireplace is flanked by sliding glass doors that lead to a terrace. There's a formal dining room and an efficient kitchen that makes meal preparation easier. There's also a bright dining nook with sliding doors to a second terrace. Three large bedrooms all are located to give family members privacy. A master bedroom suite includes a private dressing room, bath and sliding glass door to the main terrace.

Design T62603

1,949 Sq. Ft.; 41,128 Cu. Ft.

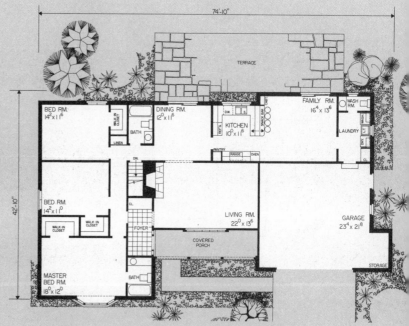

● Surely it would be difficult to beat the appeal of this traditional one-story home. Its slightly modified U-shape with the two front facing gables, the bay window, the covered front porch and the interesting use of exterior materials all add to the exterior charm. Besides, there are three large bedrooms serviced by two full baths and three walk-in closets. The excellent kitchen is flanked by the formal dining room and the informal family room. Don't miss the pantry, the built-in oven and the pass-thru to the snack bar. The handy first floor laundry is strategically located to act as a mud room. The extra washroom is but a few steps away. The sizable living room highlights a fireplace and a picture window. Note the location of the basement stairs.

Design T62672

1,717 Sq. Ft.; 37,167 Cu. Ft.

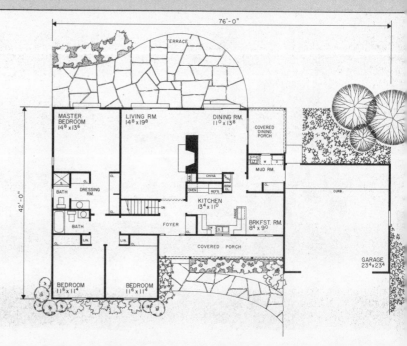

● The traditional appearance of this one-story is emphasized by its covered porch, multi-paned windows, narrow clapboard and vertical wood siding. The front U-shaped kitchen will work with the breakfast room and mud room, which houses the laundry facilities. An access to the garage is here. Outdoor dining can be enjoyed on the covered porch adjacent to the dining room. Both of these areas, the porch and dining room, are convenient to the kitchen. Sleeping facilities consist of three bedrooms and two full baths. Note the three sets of sliding glass doors leading to the terrace.

231

Shared Expense – Shared Livability

Design T62869
1,986 Sq. Ft.; 48,455 Cu. Ft.

● This traditional one-story design offers the economical benefits of shared living space without sacrificing privacy. The common area of this design is centrally located between the two private, sleeping wings. The common area, 680 square feet, is made up of the great room, dining room and kitchen. Sloping the ceiling in this area creates an open feeling as will the sliding glass doors on each side of the fireplace. These doors lead to a large covered porch with skylights above. Separate outdoor entrances lead to each of the sleeping wings. Two bedrooms, dressing area, full bath and space for an optional kitchenette occupy 653 square feet in each wing. Additional space will be found in the basement which is the full size of the common area. Don't miss the covered porch and garage with additional storage space.

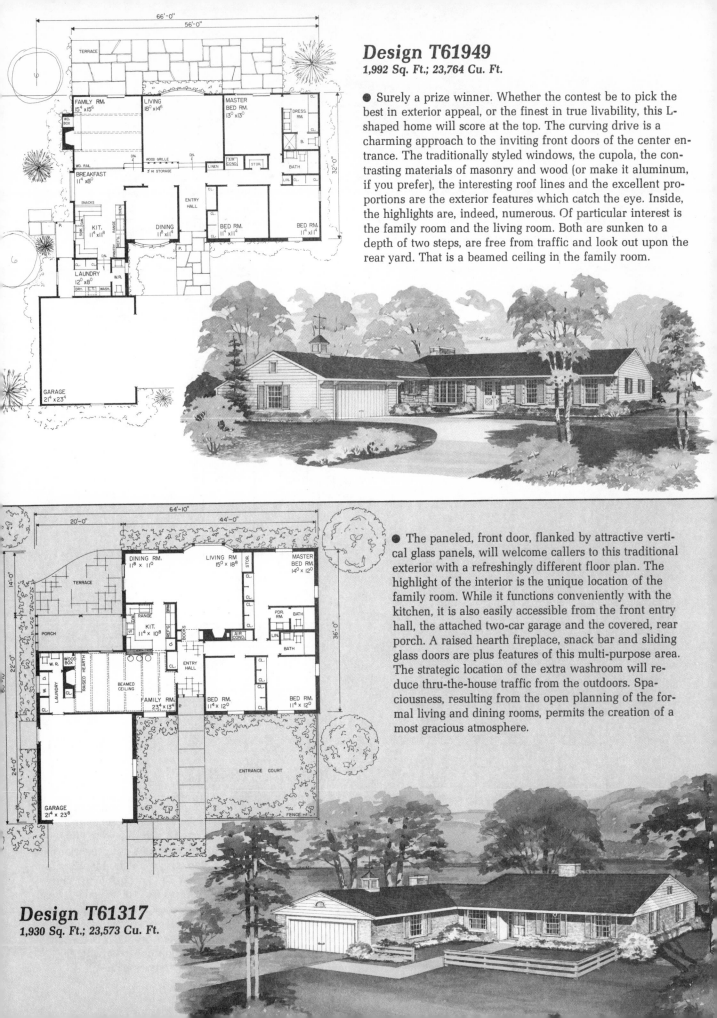

Design T61949
1,992 Sq. Ft.; 23,764 Cu. Ft.

● Surely a prize winner. Whether the contest be to pick the best in exterior appeal, or the finest in true livability, this L-shaped home will score at the top. The curving drive is a charming approach to the inviting front doors of the center entrance. The traditionally styled windows, the cupola, the contrasting materials of masonry and wood (or make it aluminum, if you prefer), the interesting roof lines and the excellent proportions are the exterior features which catch the eye. Inside, the highlights are, indeed, numerous. Of particular interest is the family room and the living room. Both are sunken to a depth of two steps, are free from traffic and look out upon the rear yard. That is a beamed ceiling in the family room.

● The paneled, front door, flanked by attractive vertical glass panels, will welcome callers to this traditional exterior with a refreshingly different floor plan. The highlight of the interior is the unique location of the family room. While it functions conveniently with the kitchen, it is also easily accessible from the front entry hall, the attached two-car garage and the covered, rear porch. A raised hearth fireplace, snack bar and sliding glass doors are plus features of this multi-purpose area. The strategic location of the extra washroom will reduce thru-the-house traffic from the outdoors. Spaciousness, resulting from the open planning of the formal living and dining rooms, permits the creation of a most gracious atmosphere.

Design T61317
1,930 Sq. Ft.; 23,573 Cu. Ft.

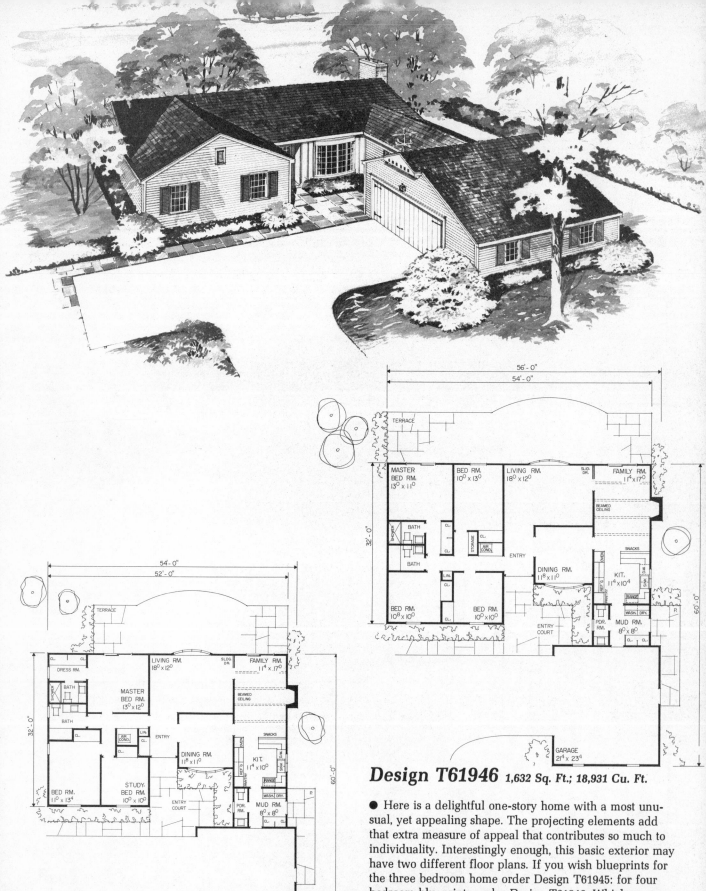

Design T61946 1,632 Sq. Ft.; 18,931 Cu. Ft.

● Here is a delightful one-story home with a most unusual, yet appealing shape. The projecting elements add that extra measure of appeal that contributes so much to individuality. Interestingly enough, this basic exterior may have two different floor plans. If you wish blueprints for the three bedroom home order Design T61945: for four bedroom blueprints, order Design T61946. Whichever you select, you will enjoy the efficiency of the remainder of the plan. There are formal living and dining rooms, an informal family room with a beamed ceiling, a U-shaped kitchen and a strategically placed mud room with an adjacent powder room for easy convenience.

Design T61945
1,568 Sq. Ft.; 18,188 Cu. Ft.

TRADITIONAL ADAPTATIONS OVER 2,000 SQ. FT.

These larger Early American homes offer plenty of comfort and livability for larger families who love the colonial charm of yesteryear. And while they offer plenty of usable space, everything in these homes is accessible on one floor, with no stairs to climb.

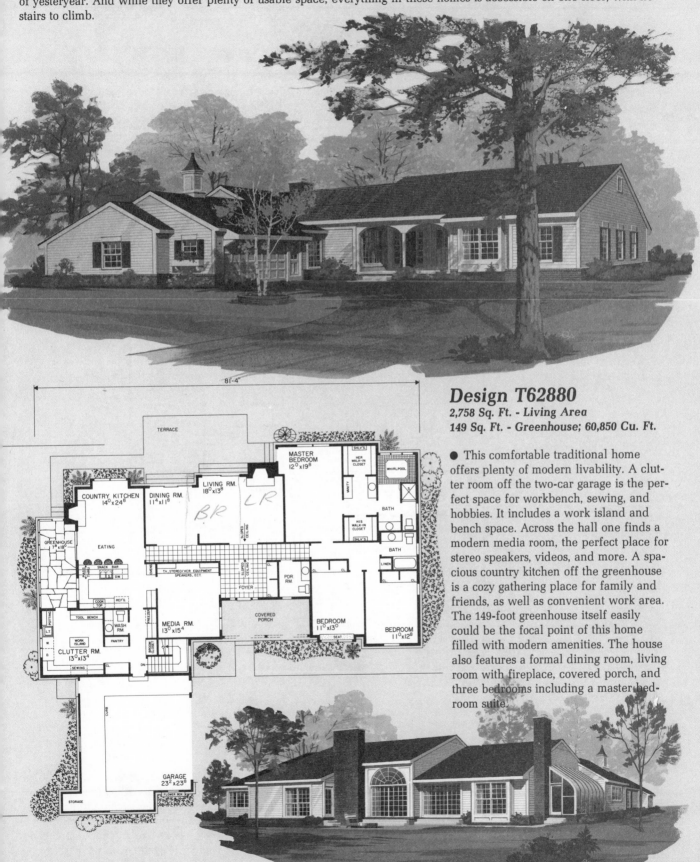

Design T62880
2,758 Sq. Ft. - Living Area
149 Sq. Ft. - Greenhouse; 60,850 Cu. Ft.

● This comfortable traditional home offers plenty of modern livability. A clutter room off the two-car garage is the perfect space for workbench, sewing, and hobbies. It includes a work island and bench space. Across the hall one finds a modern media room, the perfect place for stereo speakers, videos, and more. A spacious country kitchen off the greenhouse is a cozy gathering place for family and friends, as well as convenient work area. The 149-foot greenhouse itself easily could be the focal point of this home filled with modern amenities. The house also features a formal dining room, living room with fireplace, covered porch, and three bedrooms including a master bedroom suite.

Design T62527 *2,392 Sq. Ft.; 42,579 Cu. Ft.*

● Vertical boards and battens, field-stone, bay window, a dovecote, a gas lamp and a recessed front entrance are among the appealing exterior features of this U-shaped design. Through the double front doors, flanked by glass side lites, one enters the spacious foyer. Straight ahead is the cozy sunken gathering room with its sloping, beamed ceiling, raised hearth fireplace and two sets of sliding glass doors to the rear terrace. To the right of the foyer is the sleeping wing with its three bedrooms, study (make it the fourth bedroom if you wish) and two baths. To the left is the strategically located powder room and large kitchen with its delightful nook and bay window.

● What a pleasing, traditional exterior! And what a fine, convenient living interior! The configuration of this home leads to interesting roof planes and even functional, outdoor terrace areas. The front court and the covered porch strike an enchanting note. The gathering room will be just that. It will be the family's multi-purpose living area. Sunken to a level of two steps, its already spacious feeling is enhanced by its open planning with the dining room and study. This latter room may be closed off for more privacy if desired. Adjacent to the foyer, the open stairwell leads to the basement level. This area has the possibility of being developed into recreation space.

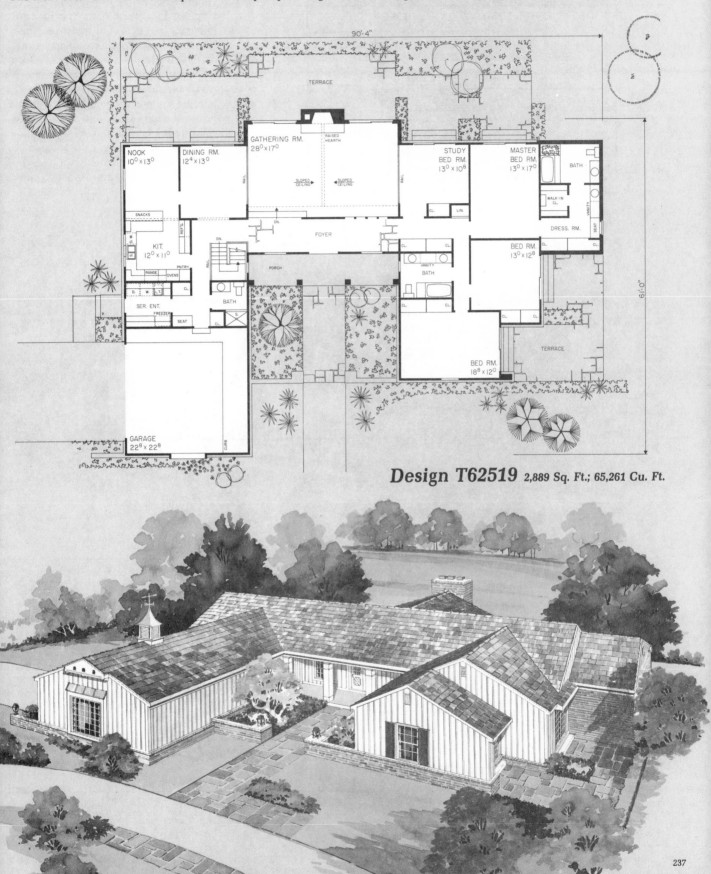

Design T62519 2,889 Sq. Ft.; 65,261 Cu. Ft.

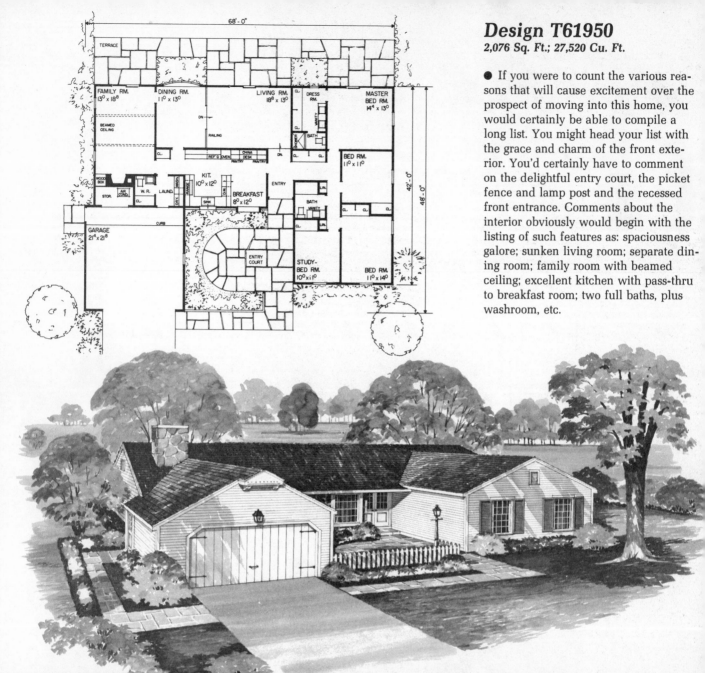

Design T61950
2,076 Sq. Ft.; 27,520 Cu. Ft.

● If you were to count the various reasons that will cause excitement over the prospect of moving into this home, you would certainly be able to compile a long list. You might head your list with the grace and charm of the front exterior. You'd certainly have to comment on the delightful entry court, the picket fence and lamp post and the recessed front entrance. Comments about the interior obviously would begin with the listing of such features as: spaciousness galore; sunken living room; separate dining room; family room with beamed ceiling; excellent kitchen with pass-thru to breakfast room; two full baths, plus washroom, etc.

Design T62544
2,527 Sq. Ft.; 61,943 Cu. Ft.

● Fieldstone masonry and horizontal siding give this four-bedroom home its Traditional good looks. Of course, you may substitute quarried stone or brick, if you wish. Also note the recessed front entrance, window treatment, and various projections and roof plans. Inside, this four-bedroom home features family room with sloped ceiling and raised-hearth fireplace. There's a breakfast nook off the kitchen, in addition to a dining room.

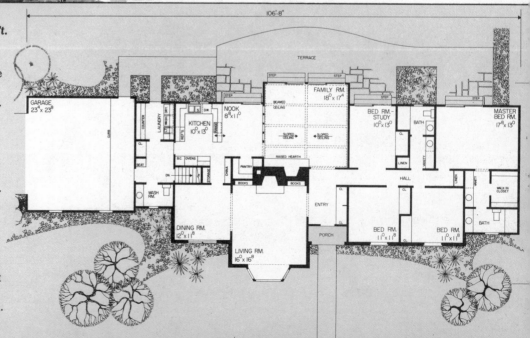

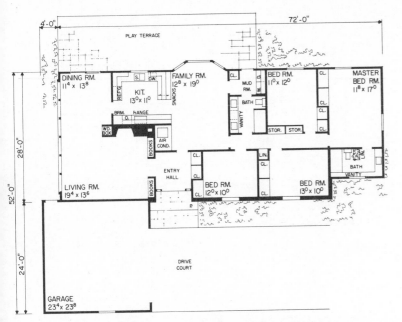

PLAY TERRACE

72'-0"

4'-0"

DINING RM.
11⁴ x 13⁸

FAMILY RM.
12⁸ x 19⁰

BED RM.
11⁰ x 12⁰

MASTER BED RM.
11⁸ x 17⁰

S.   DW

REF'G

KIT.
13⁰ x 11⁰

BRM. Q.
RANGE

SNACKS

CL.

MUD RM.

BATH

CL.

CL.

CL.

WD BOX

AIR COND.

BOOKS

VANITY

STOR. STOR.

28'-0"

52'-0"

LIVING RM.
19⁴ x 13⁶

ENTRY HALL

BOOKS

CL.

CL.

BED RM.
12⁰ x 10⁰

CL.

LIN.
CL.

CL.

BED RM.
13⁰ x 10⁰

BATH

VANITY

24'-0"

DRIVE COURT

GARAGE
23⁴ x 23⁸

Design T61170
2,000 Sq. Ft.; 24,840 Cu. Ft.

● Footnote to perfection! This L-shaped traditional design tells a fine story of excellent proportion. Its appeal is its delightful simplicity. The large family will find its living patterns admirably taken care of by this attractive home. A family with many members needs well-organized space in which to move around. Here, traffic circulation will be orderly. The double front doors are recessed and protected by the roof overhang. Traffic can flow directly to the living room, the family room-kitchen area or to the sleeping area from the formal entry hall. The kitchen serves both the dining and family rooms equally. The inside bath is conveniently accessible from the living areas and the bedrooms.

Design T62766
2,711 Sq. Ft.; 59,240 Cu. Ft.

● A sizable master bedroom has a dressing area featuring two walk-in closets, a twin lavatory and compartmented bath. The two-bedroom children's area has a spacious, full bath and supporting study. Formal living and dining zone is separated by a thru-fireplace. A spacious kitchen-nook is cheerfully informal with a sun room just a step away through sliding glass doors. The service area has a laundry, storage closet, washroom and stairs to basement. An array of sliding glass doors lead to outdoor living on the various terraces. These are but some of the highlights of this appealing, L-shaped traditional home. Be sure to note the large number of sizable closets for a variety of uses.

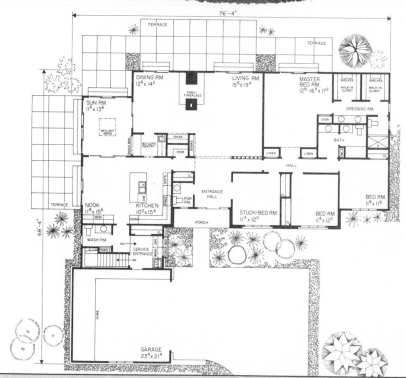

Design T62778
2,761 Sq. Ft.; 41,145 Cu. Ft.

● No matter what the occasion, family and friends alike will enjoy this sizable gathering room. A spacious 20' x 23', this room has a thru fireplace to the study and two sets of sliding glass doors to the large, rear terrace. Indoor-outdoor living also can be enjoyed from the dining room, study and master bedroom. There is also a covered porch accessible through sliding glass doors in the dining room and breakfast nook.

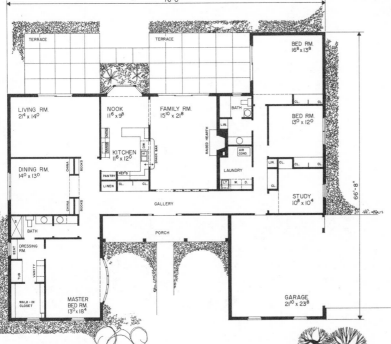

TERRACE

TERRACE

LIVING RM.
21⁴ x 14⁰

NOOK
11⁶ x 9⁸

FAMILY RM.
15¹⁰ x 21⁸

BED RM.
16⁸ x 13⁸

BATH

KITCHEN
11⁶ x 12⁰

BED RM.
13⁰ x 12⁰

DINING RM.
14⁰ x 13⁰

CHINA BOOKS

PANTRY REF'S

CHINA BOOKS

LINEN CL.

RAISED HEARTH

LIN.

AIR COND.

LAUNDRY

STUDY
10⁸ x 10⁴

BATH

GALLERY

DRESSING RM.

TUB VANITY

PORCH

WALK-IN CLOSET

MASTER BED RM.
13⁰ x 18⁴

GARAGE
21¹⁰ x 23⁸

76'-0"

66'-8"

Design T62784
2,980 Sq. Ft.; 41,580 Cu. Ft.

● The projection of the master bedroom and garage create an inviting U-shaped area leading to the covered porch of this delightful traditionally styled design. After entering through the double front doors, the gallery will lead to each of the three living areas: the sleeping wing of two bedrooms, full bath and study; the informal area of the family room with raised hearth fireplace and sliding glass doors to the terrace and the kitchen/nook area (the kitchen has a pass-thru snack bar to the family room); and the formal area consisting of a separate dining room with built-in china cabinets and the living room. Note the privacy of the master bedroom.

Design T61149
2,040 Sq. Ft.; 35,290 Cu. Ft.

● The very shape of this traditional adaptation seems to spell, "welcome". A study of the floor plan reflects excellent zoning. The sleeping area consists of four bedrooms and two full baths. The formal area, located to the front of the house, consists of a separate dining room with built-in china cabinet and living room with fireplace and accompanying woodbox. Study the work center of the kitchen, laundry and wash room. An informal family room. It is only a couple of steps from the kitchen and functions with the outdoor terrace.

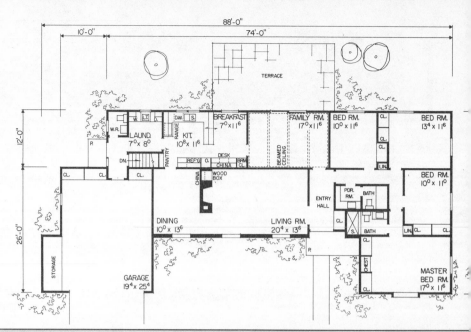

Design T62316
2,000 Sq. Ft.; 25,242 Cu. Ft.

● Here is a basic floor plan which is the favorite of many. It provides for the location, to the front of the plan, of the more formal areas (living and dining rooms); while the informal areas (family room and kitchen) are situated to the rear of the plan and function with the terrace. To the left of the center entrance is the four bedroom, two bath sleeping zone. Adjacent to the kitchen is the utility room with a wash room nearby. The garage features a storage room and work shop area with more storage.

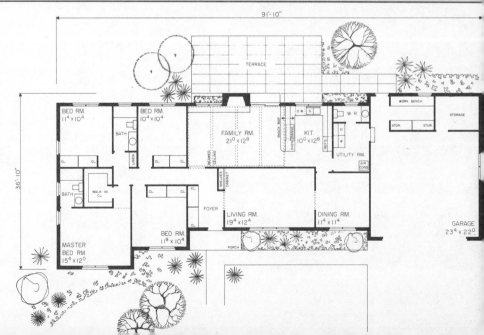

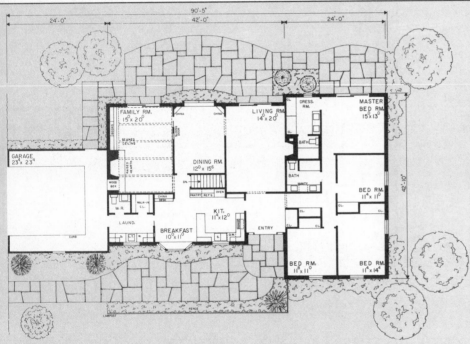

Design T62144
2,432 Sq. Ft.; 42,519 Cu. Ft.

● Have you ever wished you lived in a house in which the living, dining and family rooms all looked out upon the rear terrace? Further, have you ever wished your home had its kitchen located to the front so that you could see approaching callers? Or, have you ever wished for a house where traffic in from the garage was stopped right in the laundry so that wet, snowy, dirty and muddy apparel could be shed immediately? If these have been your wishes, this plan may be just for you.

Design T61835
2,144 Sq. Ft.; 33,310 Cu. Ft.

● Cedar shakes and quarried natural
stone are the exterior materials which
adorn this irregularly shaped traditional ranch home. Adding to the appeal of
the exterior are the cut-up windows,
the shutters, the pediment gable, the
cupola and the double front doors. The
detail of the garage door opening adds
further interest. Inside, this favorite
among floor plans, reflects all the features necessary to provide complete
livability for the large family. The
sleeping zone is a 24' x 40' rectangle
which contains four bedrooms and two
full baths. A dressing room with a vanity and a wall of wardrobe storage
highlights the master bedroom. Both
the informal family room and the formal living room have a fireplace.

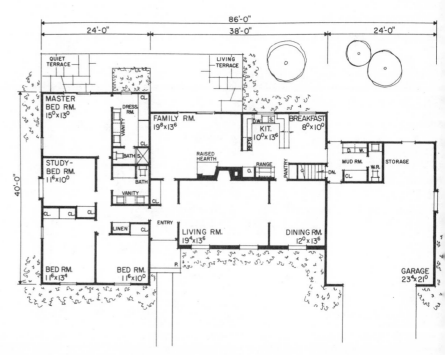

● Whatever the setting, here
is a traditional, one story
home that is truly impressive. Zoned in a most practical manner, the floor plan
features an isolated bedroom
wing, formal living and dining rooms and, across the
rear of the house, the informal living areas.

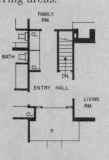

OPTIONAL BASEMENT

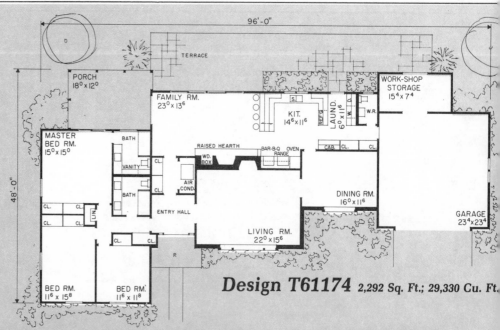

Design T61174 2,292 Sq. Ft.; 29,330 Cu. Ft.

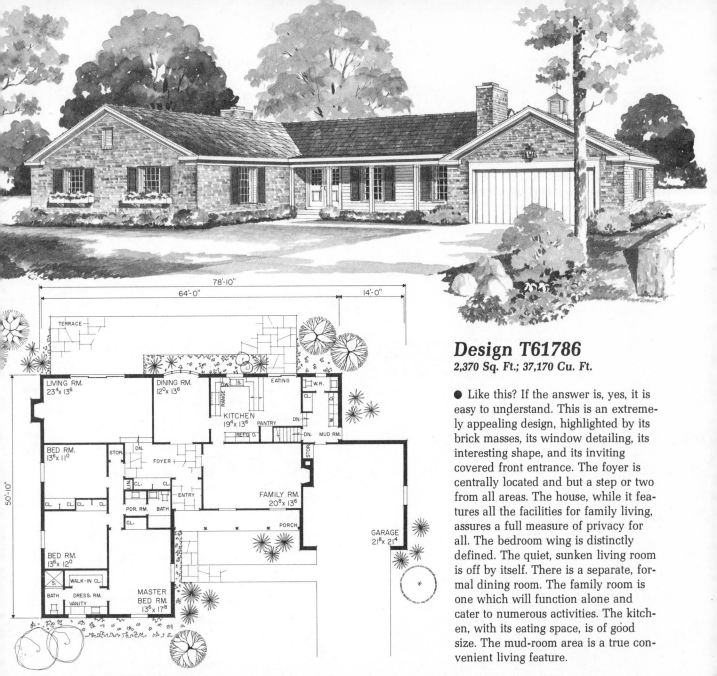

Design T61786
2,370 Sq. Ft.; 37,170 Cu. Ft.

● Like this? If the answer is, yes, it is easy to understand. This is an extremely appealing design, highlighted by its brick masses, its window detailing, its interesting shape, and its inviting covered front entrance. The foyer is centrally located and but a step or two from all areas. The house, while it features all the facilities for family living, assures a full measure of privacy for all. The bedroom wing is distinctly defined. The quiet, sunken living room is off by itself. There is a separate, formal dining room. The family room is one which will function alone and cater to numerous activities. The kitchen, with its eating space, is of good size. The mud-room area is a true convenient living feature.

Design T62209
2,659 Sq. Ft.; 45,240 Cu. Ft.

● Such an impressive home would, indeed, be difficult to top. And little wonder when you consider the myriad of features this one-story Colonial possesses. Consider the exquisite detailing, the fine proportions, and the symmetry of the projecting wings. The gracious and inviting double front doors are a prelude to the exceptional interior. Consider the four bedroom, two-bath sleeping wing. Formal entertaining can be enjoyed in the front living and dining rooms. For informal living there is the rear family room.

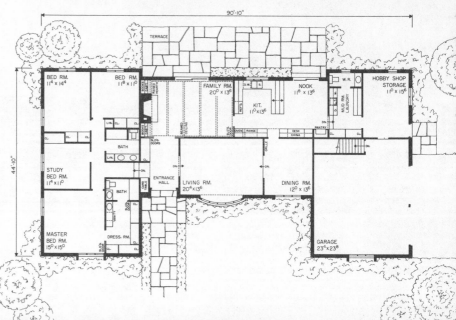

Design T62264
2,352 Sq. Ft.; 33,924 Cu. Ft.

● This U-shaped traditional will be a welcomed addition on any site. It has living facilities which will provide your family with years of delightful livability. The two living areas are located to the rear and function with the outdoor terrace. The outstanding kitchen is strategically located handy to the family room and the eating areas. A separate laundry area with fine storage and nearby powder room is a favorite feature. Note garage size and storage potential. Also notice stairway to attic.

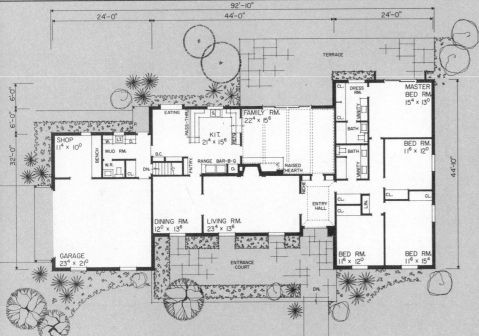

Design T61761
2,548 Sq. Ft.; 43,870 Cu. Ft.

● Low, strong roof lines and solid, enduring qualities of brick give this house a permanent, here-to-stay appearance. Bedroom wing is isolated, and the baths and closets deaden noise from the rest of the house. Center fireplaces in family and living rooms make furniture arrangement easy. There are a number of extras – a workshop, an unusually large garage, and an indoor barbecue. Garage has easy access to both basement and kitchen area. There are two eating areas – a formal dining room and a breakfast nook next to the delightful kitchen.

Design T61924 2,504 Sq. Ft.; 42,498 Cu. Ft.

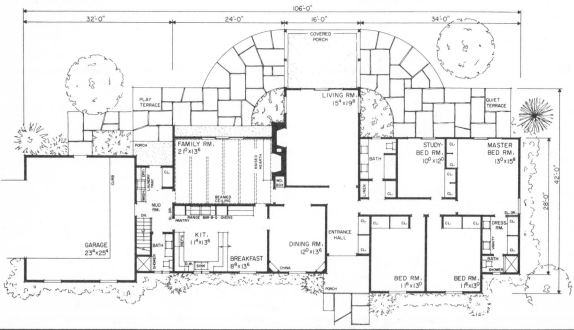

Design T61851
2,450 Sq. Ft.; 42,052 Cu. Ft.

248

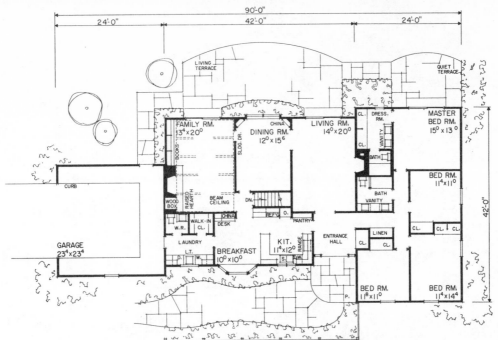

Design T61886 2,352 Sq. Ft.; 41,244 Cu. Ft.

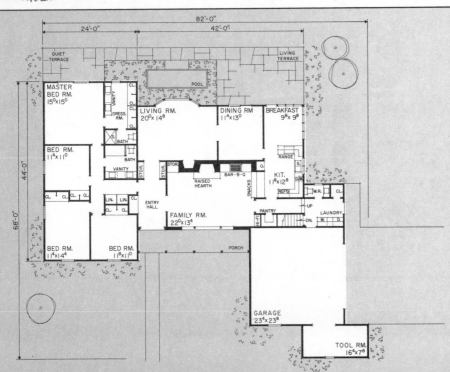

● Here are three designs each featuring four bedrooms and two plus baths. While each home has a basement, it also highlights a first floor laundry. The differing arrangements of the living, dining, and family rooms are most interesting. The kitchens function directly with the breakfast rooms, yet again, their locations vary. Raised hearth fireplaces are a focal point of the family rooms, while a second fireplace can be found in the living rooms. Note the side opening garages. Design T61851 has a handy tool room for heavy equipment.

Design T62777
2,006 Sq. Ft.; 44,580 Cu. Ft.

● Many years of delightful living will be enjoyed in this one-story traditional home. The covered, front porch adds a charm to the exterior as do the paned windows and winding drive. Inside, there is livability galore. An efficient kitchen with island range and adjacent laundry make this work area very pleasing. A breakfast nook with bay window and built-in desk will serve the family when informal dining is called upon. A formal dining room with sliding glass doors leads to the rear terrace. The large gathering room with raised hearth fireplace can serve the family on any occasion gracefully. The sleeping wing consists of two bedrooms and a study (or make it three bedrooms). The master bedroom includes all of the fine features one would expect: a huge walk-in closet, a vanity, a bath and sliding glass doors to a private terrace.

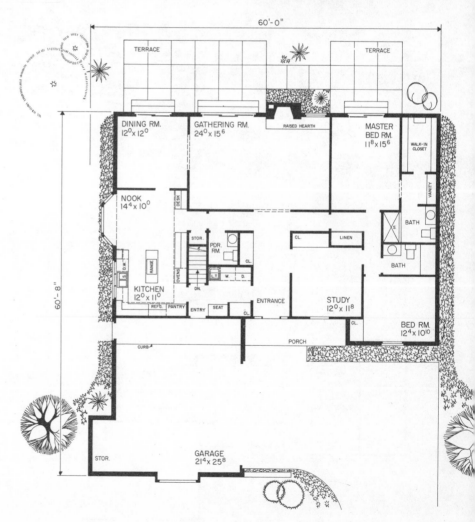

Design T62867 2,388 Sq. Ft.; 49,535 Cu. Ft.

● A live-in relative would be very comfortable in this home. This design features a self-contained suite (473 sq. ft.) consisting of a bedroom, bath, living room and kitchenette with dining area. This suite is nestled behind the garage away from the main areas of the house. The rest of this traditional, one-story house, faced with fieldstone and vertical wood siding, is also very livable. One whole wing houses the four family bedrooms and bath facilities. The center of the plan has a front, U-shaped kitchen and breakfast room. The formal dining room and large gathering room will enjoy the view, and access to, the backyard. The large, covered porch will receive much use.

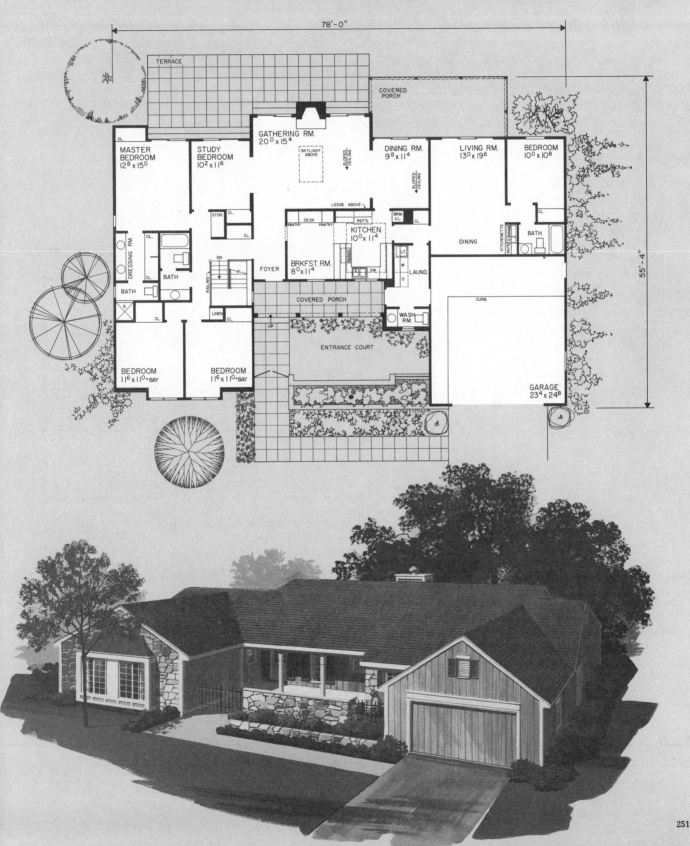

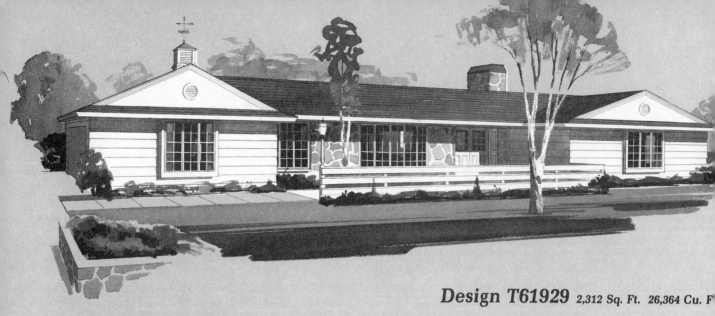

Design T61929 2,312 Sq. Ft. 26,364 Cu. F

● There's more to this U-shaped, traditional adaptation than meets the eye. Much more! And, yet, what does meet the eye is positively captivating. The symmetry of the pediment gables, the window styling, the projecting garden wall, the iron gates, and the double front doors, are extremely pleasing. Once inside, a quick tour reveals plenty of space and a super-abundance of features. Each of the rooms is extra large and allows for fine furniture placement. In addition to the raised hearth fireplace, the family room highlights built-in book shelves, sliding glass doors and beamed ceilings.

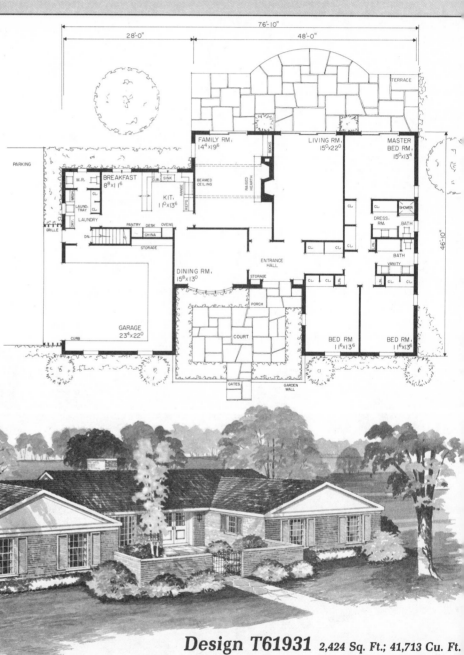

Design T61931 2,424 Sq. Ft.; 41,713 Cu. Ft.

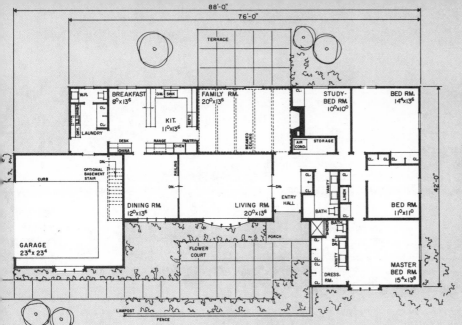

● This home will lead the hit parade in your new subdivision. Its sparkling, traditionally styled exterior will be the favorite of all that pass. And, once inside, friends will marvel at how the plan just seems to cater to your family's every activity. When it comes to eating, you can eat in the informal breakfast room or the formal dining room. As you come in the front door you may sit down and relax in the sunken living room or the beamed ceiling family room. Two full baths with built-in vanities, plus the extra washroom will more than adequately serve the family.

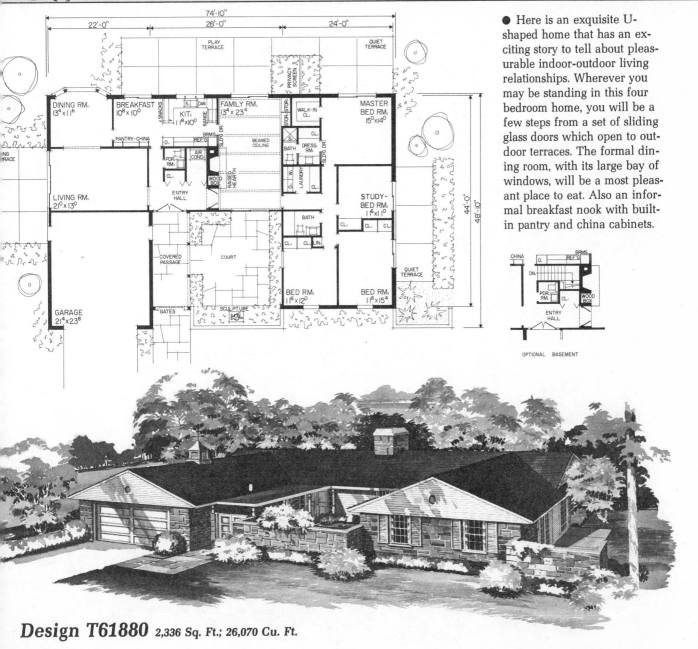

● Here is an exquisite U-shaped home that has an exciting story to tell about pleasurable indoor-outdoor living relationships. Wherever you may be standing in this four bedroom home, you will be a few steps from a set of sliding glass doors which open to outdoor terraces. The formal dining room, with its large bay of windows, will be a most pleasant place to eat. Also an informal breakfast nook with built-in pantry and china cabinets.

OPTIONAL BASEMENT

Design T61880 2,336 Sq. Ft.; 26,070 Cu. Ft.

Design T62259
2,016 Sq. Ft.; 43,337 Cu. Ft.

● Here is a 28 x 72 foot basic rectangle which houses 2,016 square feet of livability. Because of its rectangular shape it will be most economical to build. The projecting garage adds delightfully to the overall appeal and permits the utilization of a smaller building site. The covered front porch provides sheltered passage between the house and the garage. Inside there is a whale of a lot of livability. There are four bedrooms, two baths, laundry area, family room, large kitchen, spacious living and dining area. There is a fireplace flanked by bookshelves and sliding glass doors to terraces.

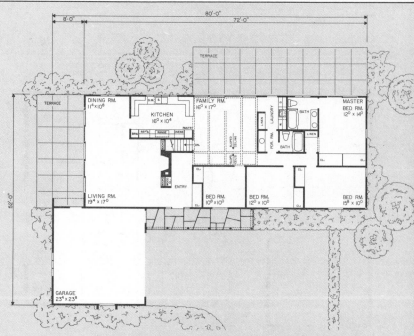

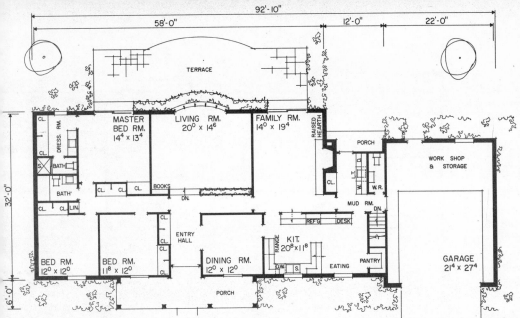

Design T61788
2,218 Sq. Ft.; 36,002 Cu. Ft.

● "Charm" is one of the many words which may be used to correctly describe this fine design. In addition to its eye-appeal, it has a practical and smoothly functioning floor plan. The detail of the front entrance, highlighted by columns supporting the projecting pediment gable, is outstanding. Observe the window treatment and the double, front doors. Perhaps the focal point of the interior will be the formal living room. It is, indeed, dramatic with its bay window overlooking the backyard. Three bedrooms and two baths are in the private area.

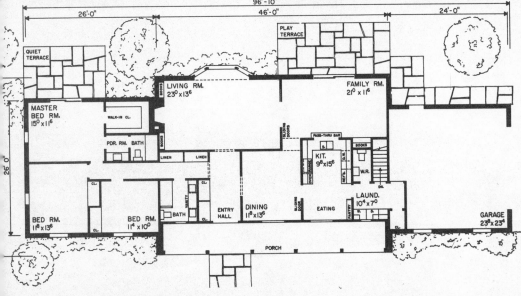

Design T62109
2,054 Sq. Ft.; 38,392 Cu. Ft.

● Long and low are characteristics of this traditional one-story. The main portion of the house is highlighted by the porch with its columns. The shuttered windows and doors add their note of distinction. The breadth of this design is emphasized by the addition of the two wings. One comprises the attached two-car garage. The other, the sleeping area made up of three bedrooms and two full baths. The master bedroom has its own compartmented bath, the huge walk-in closet, and sliding glass doors to its quiet terrace.

Design T62181
2,612 Sq. Ft.; 45,230 Cu. Ft.

● It is hard to imagine a home with any more eye-appeal than this one. It is the complete picture of charm. The interior is just as outstanding. Sliding glass doors permit the large, master bedroom, quiet, living room and all-purpose family room to function directly with the outdoors. Two fireplaces, built-in china cabinets, bookshelves, complete laundry and kitchen pass-thru to breakfast room are extra features. Although the illustration of this home shows natural quarried stone, you may wish to substitute brick or even siding.

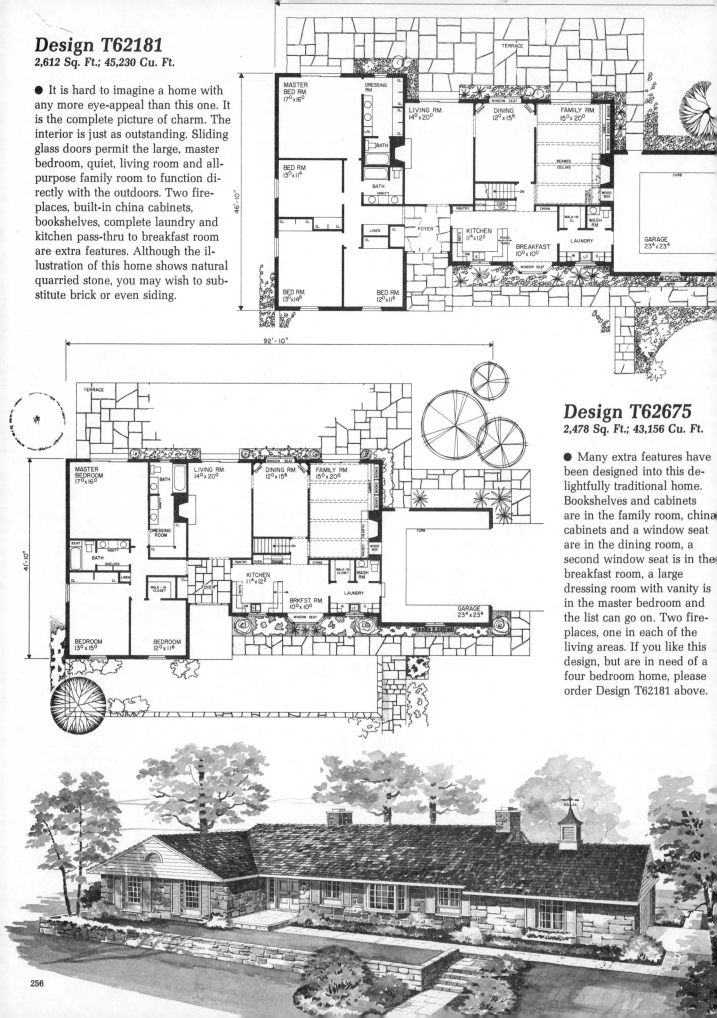

Design T62675
2,478 Sq. Ft.; 43,156 Cu. Ft.

● Many extra features have been designed into this delightfully traditional home. Bookshelves and cabinets are in the family room, china cabinets and a window seat are in the dining room, a second window seat is in the breakfast room, a large dressing room with vanity is in the master bedroom and the list can go on. Two fireplaces, one in each of the living areas. If you like this design, but are in need of a four bedroom home, please order Design T62181 above.

ONE-STORY
COUNTRY ESTATE AMBIENCE

Many delightful Early American designs offer Country Estate comfort and styling all on one floor. These designs feature estate exterior detailing plus many built-in luxuries of space. These may include master bedroom suites, libraries, formal and informal dining areas, breakfast rooms, separate dining rooms, porches, efficient kitchens, and fireplaces.

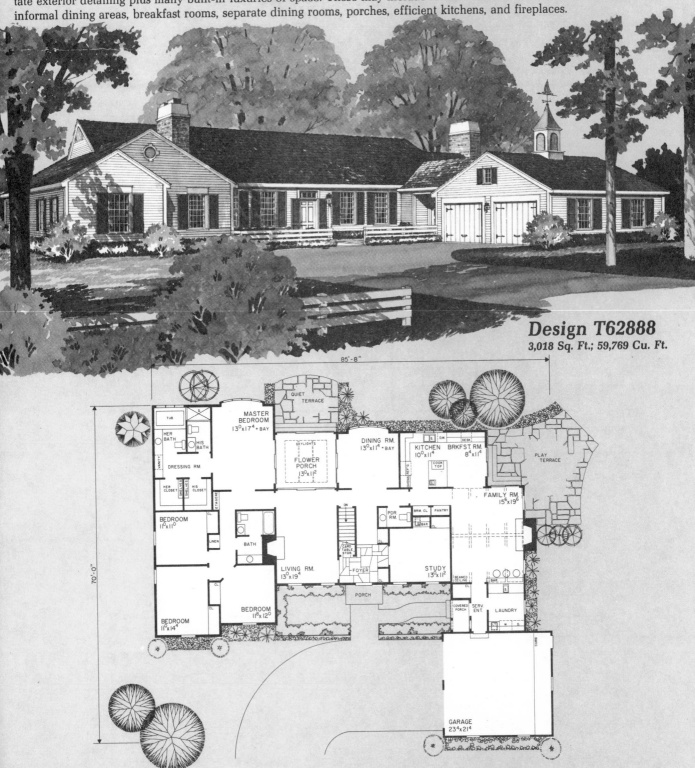

Design T62888
3,018 Sq. Ft.; 59,769 Cu. Ft.

● This is an outstanding Early American design for the 20th-Century. The exterior detailing with narrow clapboards, multi-paned windows and cupola are the features of yesteryear. Interior planning, though, is for today's active family. Formal living room, informal family room plus a study are present. Every activity will have its place in this home. Picture yourself working in the kitchen. There's enough counter space for two or three helpers. Four bedrooms are in the private area. Stop and imagine your daily routine if you occupied the master bedroom. Both you and your spouse would have plenty of space and privacy. The flower porch, accessible from the master bedroom, living and dining rooms, is a very delightful "plus" feature. Study this design's every detail.

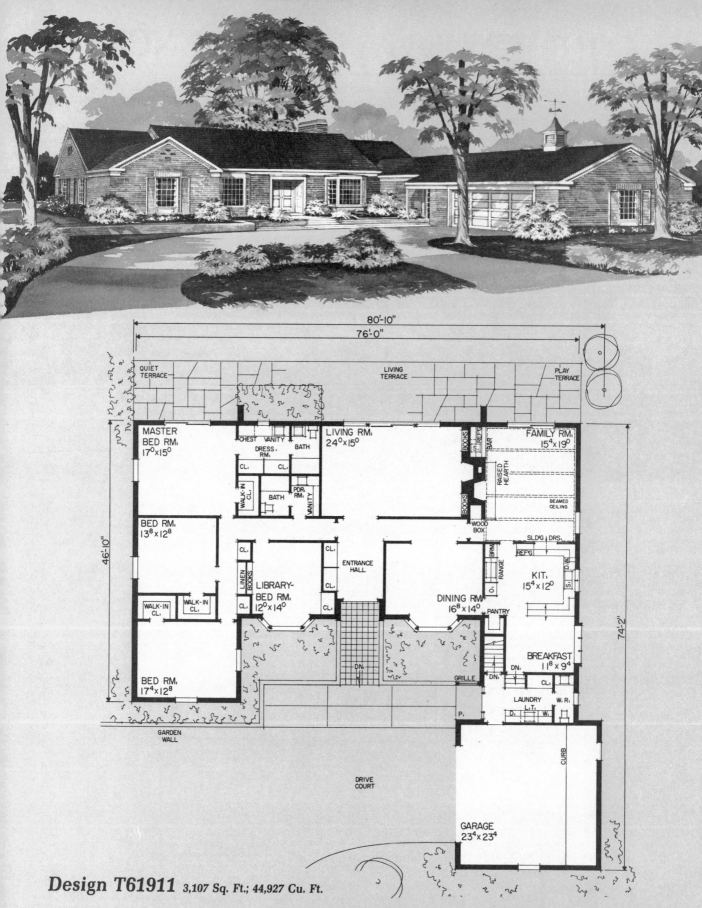

Design T61911 3,107 Sq. Ft.; 44,927 Cu. Ft.

● For luxurious, country-estate living it would be difficult to beat the livability offered by these two impressive traditional designs. To begin with, their exterior appeal is, indeed, gracious. Their floor plans highlight plenty of space, excellent room arrangements, fine traffic circulation, and an abundance of convenient living features. It is interesting to note that each design features similar livability facilities. Both may function as four bedroom homes . . .

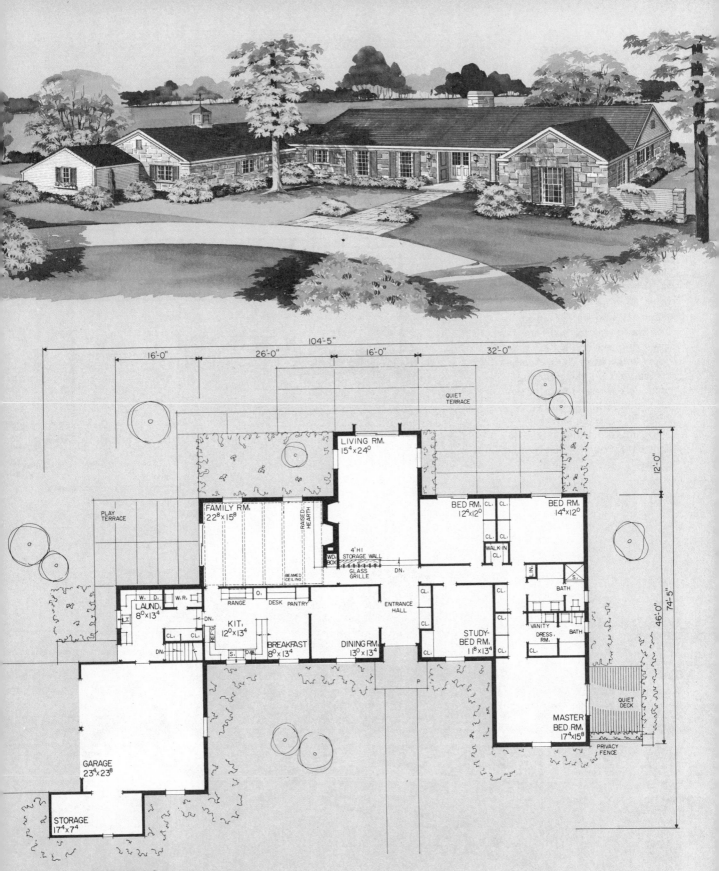

Design T61916   3,024 Sq. Ft.; 46,470 Cu. Ft.

● . . . or three bedroom with a study or library. There are first floor laundries, two fireplaces, formal and informal living and dining areas, fine storage potential, and delightful indoor-outdoor living relationships. You'll have fun listing the built-in features. The two family rooms have beamed ceilings and sliding glass doors to the play terraces. The two living rooms are spacious and enjoy a full measure of privacy. They are but a step from outdoor living.

Design T62783

3,210 Sq. Ft.; 57,595 Cu. Ft.

● The configuration of this traditional design is outstanding indeed. The garage-bedroom wing on one side and the master bedroom on the other create an inviting, U-shaped entry court. This area is raised two steps from the driveway and has a 6 foot high masonry wall with coach lamps for an added attraction. Upon entrance through the double front doors, one will begin to enjoy the livability that this design has to offer. Each room is well planned and deserves praise. The sizable master bedroom has a fireplace and sliding glass doors to the entry court. Another sizable room, the gathering room, has access to the rear terrace, along with the dining room, family room and rear bedroom. An interior kitchen is adjacent to each of the major rooms.

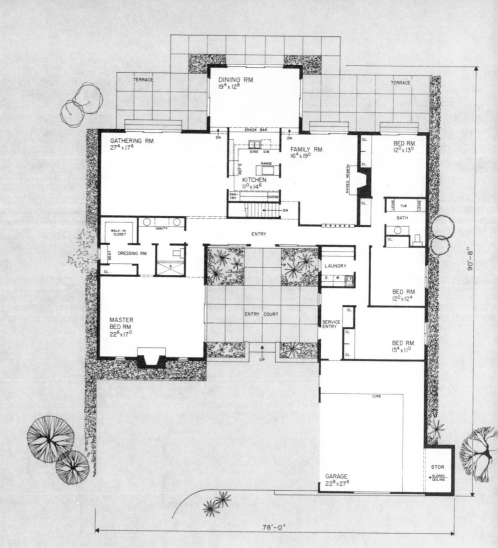

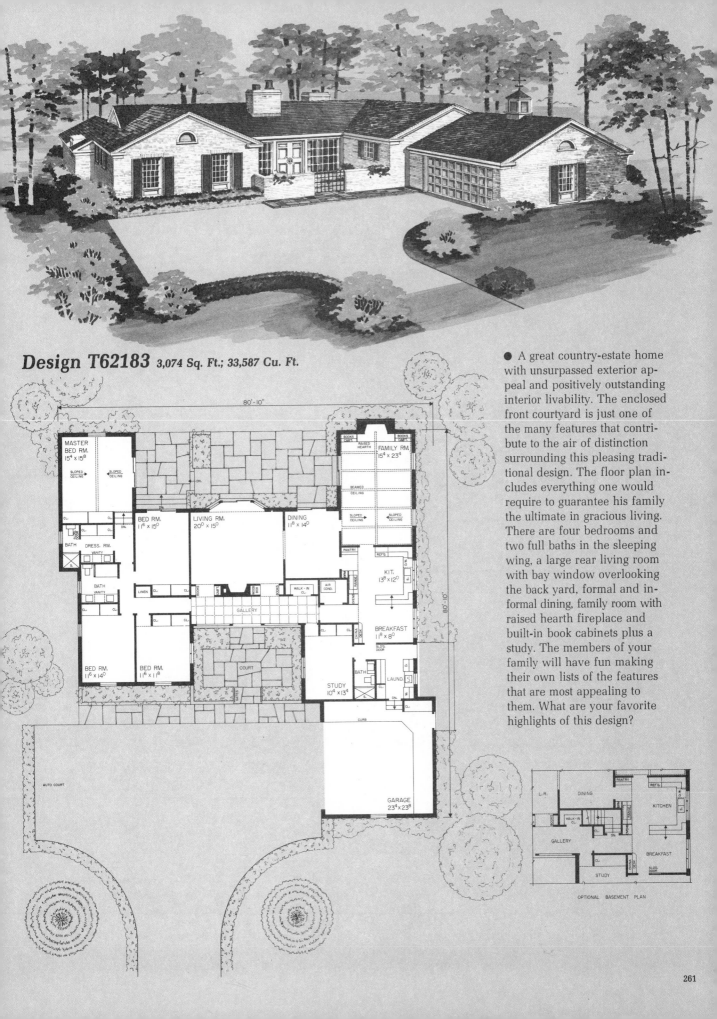

Design T62183 3,074 Sq. Ft.; 33,587 Cu. Ft.

● A great country-estate home with unsurpassed exterior appeal and positively outstanding interior livability. The enclosed front courtyard is just one of the many features that contribute to the air of distinction surrounding this pleasing traditional design. The floor plan includes everything one would require to guarantee his family the ultimate in gracious living. There are four bedrooms and two full baths in the sleeping wing, a large rear living room with bay window overlooking the back yard, formal and informal dining, family room with raised hearth fireplace and built-in book cabinets plus a study. The members of your family will have fun making their own lists of the features that are most appealing to them. What are your favorite highlights of this design?

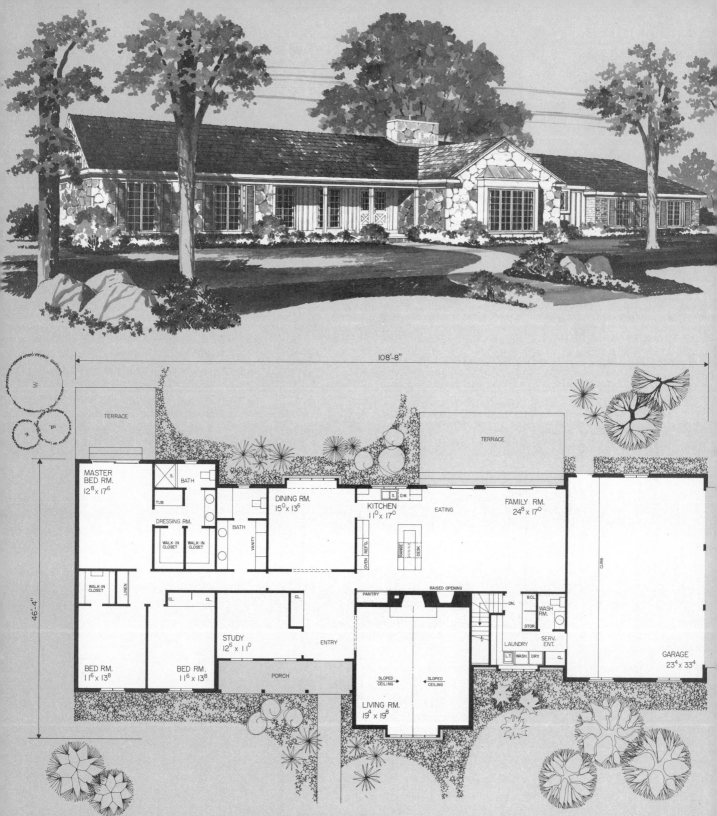

Design T62767 *3,000 Sq. Ft.; 58,460 Cu. Ft.*

● What a sound investment this impressive home will be. And while its value withstands the inflationary pressures of ensuing years, it will serve your family well. It has all the amenities to assure truly pleasurable living. The charming exterior will lend itself to treatment other than the appealing fieldstone, brick and frame shown. Inside, the plan will impress you with large, spacious living areas, formal and informal dining areas, three large bedrooms, two full baths with twin lavatories, walk-in closets and a fine study. The kitchen features an island work center with range and desk. The two fireplaces will warm their surroundings in both areas. Two separate terraces for a variety of uses. Note laundry, washroom and three-car garage with extra curb area.

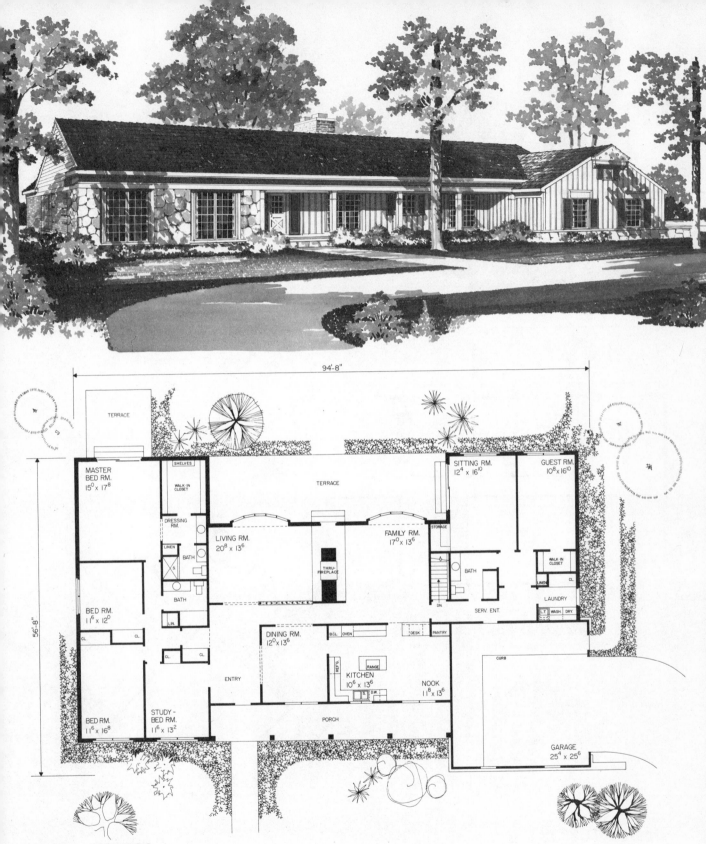

Design T62768 3,436 Sq. Ft.; 65,450 Cu. Ft.

● Besides its elegant traditionally styled exterior with its delightfully long covered front porch, this home has an exceptionally livable interior. There is the outstanding four bedroom and two-bath sleeping wing. Then, the efficient front kitchen with island range flanked by the formal dining room and the informal breakfast nook. Separated by the two-way, thru fireplace are the living and family rooms which look out on the rear yard. Worthy of particular note is the development of a potential live-in relative facility. These two rooms would also serve the large family well as a hobby room and library or additional bedrooms. A full bath is adjacent as well as the laundry. Note curb area in the garage for the storage of outdoor equipment.

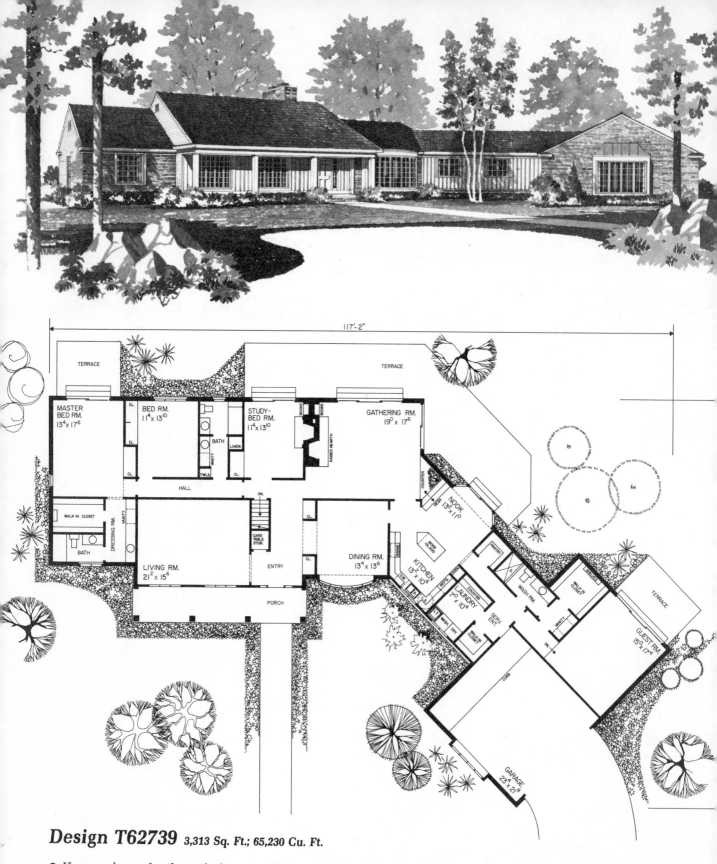

Design T62739 3,313 Sq. Ft.; 65,230 Cu. Ft.

● If you and your family are looking for new living patterns, try to envision your days spent in this traditionally styled home. Its Early American flavor is captured by effective window and door treatment, cornice work and porch pillars. Its zoning is interesting.

The spacious interior leaves nothing to be desired. There are three bedrooms and two full baths in the sleeping area. A quiet, formal living room is separated from the other living areas. The gathering and dining rooms are adjacent to each other and function with

the excellent kitchen and its breakfast eating area. Note work island, pantry and pass-thru. Then, there is an extra guest room sunken one step. A live-in relative would enjoy the privacy of this room. Full bath is nearby. This is definitely a home for all to enjoy.

MULTI-LEVEL DESIGNS

The detailing of Early American architecture lends itself in a most pleasing manner to various multi-level configurations. Bi-level and split-level designs offer interesting zoning of areas within a household or conformity to building sites. Floor relationships in split-levels generally run side to side or front to back, while bi-levels generally are split-foyer type with a short flight of stairs at the entrance.

Design T61850
1,456 Sq. Ft. - Upper Level
728 Sq. Ft. - Lower Level
23,850 Cu. Ft.

● This attractive, traditional bi-level house surely will prove to be an outstanding investment. While it is a perfect rectangle—which leads to economical construction—it has a full measure of eye-appeal. Setting the character of the exterior is the effective window treatment, plus the unique design of the recessed front entrance. Opening at the end of the house is the two-car garage which features a delightful, protective roof projection. From the front entry you go up a short flight of stairs to the upper level. This is the main level which offers complete livability. There are three bedrooms, two baths, an efficient kitchen, a breakfast room, a separate dining room and a sizable living room. A wood deck functions with the eating areas. It creates good indoor-outdoor access to the rear yard.

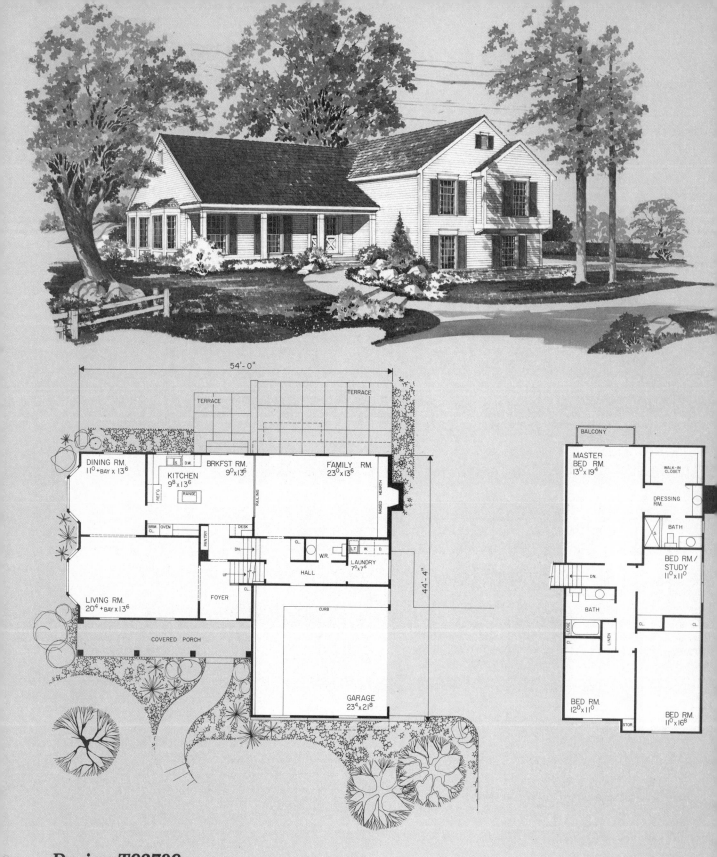

TERRACE

TERRACE

54'-0"

DINING RM.
11⁰+BAY x 13⁶

KITCHEN
9⁸x13⁶

BRKFST RM.
9⁰x13⁶

FAMILY RM.
23⁰x13⁶

REF'G

RANGE

S. D.W.

BRM. CL.

OVEN

PANTRY

DESK

DN.

CL.

RAISED HEARTH

RAILING

44'-4"

LIVING RM.
20⁴+BAY x 13⁶

UP

FOYER

CL.

HALL

W.R.

LT. W.
D.

LAUNDRY
7⁰x7⁶

COVERED PORCH

CURB

GARAGE
23⁴x21⁸

BALCONY

MASTER BED RM.
13⁰x19⁴

WALK-IN CLOSET

DRESSING RM.

BATH

S.

BED RM./STUDY
11⁰x11⁰

DN.

BATH

LEDGE

CL.

LINEN

CL.

CL.

BED RM.
12⁰x11⁰

STOR.

BED RM.
11⁰x16⁸

Design T62786 *871 Sq. Ft. - Main Level; 1,132 Sq. Ft. - Upper Level; 528 Sq. Ft. - Lower Level; 44,000 Cu. Ft.*

● A bay window in each the formal living room and dining room. A great interior and exterior design feature to attract attention to this tri-level home. The exterior also is enhanced by a covered front porch to further the Colonial charm. The interior livability is outstanding, too. An abundance of built-ins in the kitchen create an efficient work center. Features include an island range, pantry, broom closet, desk and breakfast room with sliding glass doors to the rear terrace. The lower level houses the informal family room, washroom and laundry. Further access is available to the outdoors by the family room to the terrace and laundry room to the side yard.

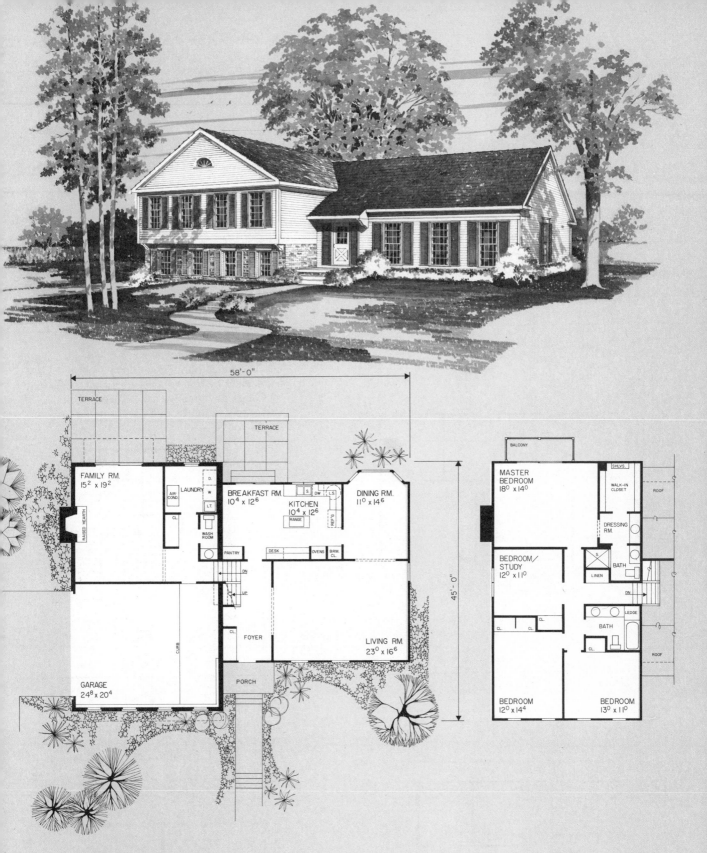

TERRACE

TERRACE

FAMILY RM.
15² x 19²

LAUNDRY

AIR-
COND.

BREAKFAST RM.
10⁴ x 12⁶

KITCHEN
10⁴ x 12⁶

RANGE

DINING RM.
11⁰ x 14⁶

RAISED HEARTH

CL

WASH
ROOM

PANTRY

DESK

OVENS

BRM.
CL.

REF'G

DN

UP

CL

FOYER

LIVING RM.
23⁰ x 16⁶

GARAGE
24⁸ x 20⁴

CURB

PORCH

58'-0"

45'-0"

BALCONY

MASTER
BEDROOM
18⁰ x 14⁰

SHLVS.

WALK-IN
CLOSET

ROOF

DRESSING
RM.

BEDROOM/
STUDY
12⁰ x 11⁰

BATH

LINEN

DN

BATH

LEDGE

CL

CL

CL

ROOF

BEDROOM
12⁰ x 14⁴

BEDROOM
13⁰ x 11⁰

Design T62787 *976 Sq. Ft. - Main Level; 1,118 Sq. Ft. - Upper Level; 524 Sq. Ft. - Lower Level; 36,110 Cu. Ft.*

● Three level living! Main, upper and lower levels to serve you and your family with great ease. Start from the bottom and work your way up. Family room with raised hearth fireplace, laundry and washroom on the lower level. Formal living and dining rooms, kitchen and breakfast room on the main level. Stop and take note at the efficiency of the kitchen with its many outstanding extras. The upper level houses the three bedrooms, study (or fourth bedroom if you prefer) and two baths. This design has really stacked up its livability to serve its occupants to their best advantage. This design has great interior livability and exterior charm.

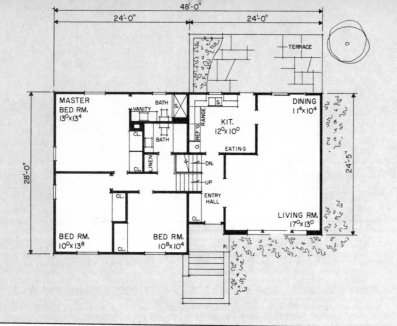

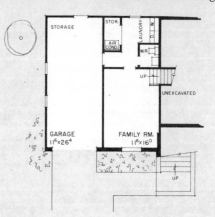

Here are three charming split-levels designed for the modest budget. They will not require a large, expensive piece of property. Nevertheless, each is long on livability and offers all the features necessary to guarantee years of convenient living.

Charming? It certainly is. And with good reason, too. This delightfully proportioned split level is highlighted by fine window treatment, interesting roof lines, an attractive use of materials and an inviting front entrance with double doors.

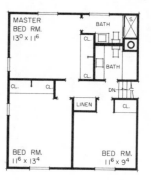

Four level livability. And what livability it will be! This home will be most economical to build. As the house begins to take form you'll appreciate even more all the livable space you and your family will enjoy. List features that appeal to you.

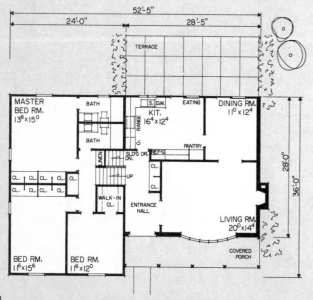

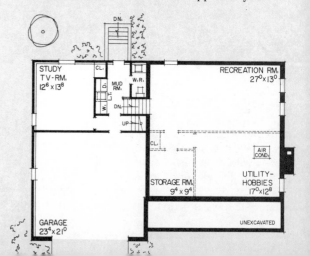

Design T61358 576 Sq. Ft. - Main Level; 672 Sq. Ft. - Upper Level; 328 Sq. Ft. - Lower Level; 20,784 Cu. Ft.

Design T61770 636 Sq. Ft. - Main Level; 672 Sq. Ft. - Upper Level; 528 Sq. Ft. - Lower Level; 19,980 Cu. Ft.

Design T61882 800 Sq. Ft. - Main Level; 864 Sq. Ft. - Upper Level; 344 Sq. Ft. - Lower Level; 28,600 Cu. Ft.

269

● Projecting over the lower level in Garrison Colonial style is the upper level containing three bedrooms a compartmented bath with twin lavatories and two handy linen closets. The main level consists of an L-shaped kitchen with convenient eating space, a formal dining room with sliding glass doors to the terrace and a sizable living room. On the lower level there is access to the outdoors, a spacious family room and a laundry-wash room area.

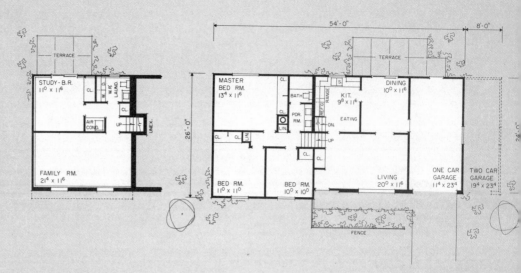

● Here are four levels just waiting for the opportunity to serve the living requirements of the active family. The traditional appeal of the exterior will be difficult to beat. Observe the window treatment, the double front doors, the covered front porch and the wrought iron work.

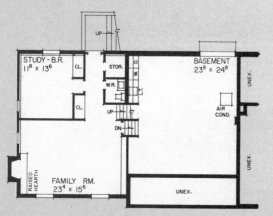

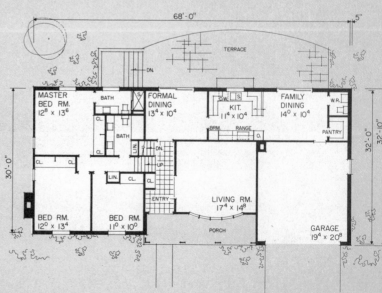

Design T61308 496 Sq. Ft. - Main Level; 572 Sq. Ft. - Upper Level; 537 Sq. Ft. - Lower Level; 16,024 Cu. Ft.

Design T61981

784 Sq. Ft. - Main Level; 912 Sq. Ft. - Upper Level
336 Sq. Ft. - Lower Level; 26,618 Cu. Ft.

● Here are three multi-level designs which are ideal for those who wish to build on a relatively narrow site. These split-levels have delightful exteriors and each offers exceptional family livability. Formal and informal areas are in each along with efficiently planned work centers. Outdoor areas are easily accessible from various rooms in these plans. Note that two of the upper level plans even have balconies.

Design T61768 844 Sq. Ft. - Main Level; 740 Sq. Ft. - Upper Level; 740 Sq. Ft. - Lower Level; 29,455 Cu. Ft.

Design T61935 904 Sq. Ft. - Main Level; 864 Sq. Ft. - Upper Level; 840 Sq. Ft. - Lower Level; 26,745 Cu. Ft.

● This design will adapt equally well to a flat or sloping site. There would be no question about the family's ability to adapt to what the interior has to offer. Everything is present to satisfy the family's desire to "live a little". There are features such as the covered porch, balcony, two fireplaces, extra study, family room with beamed ceiling, complete laundry and a basement level for added recreational and storage space. Blueprints for this design include optional non-basement details.

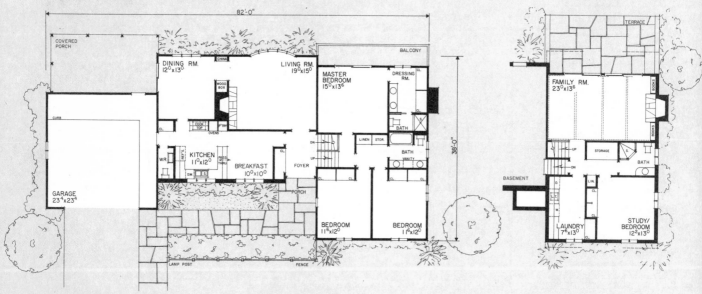

Design T61927 1,272 Sq. Ft. - Main Level; 960 Sq. Ft. - Upper Level; 936 Sq. Ft. - Lower Level; 36,815 Cu. Ft.

● This traditional split-level home features four bedrooms, three full baths, beamed ceiling family room, sunken living room, formal dining room, informal breakfast room, extra washroom, outstanding kitchen, two fireplaces and a covered porch that shelters a bowed window and inviting double front doors.

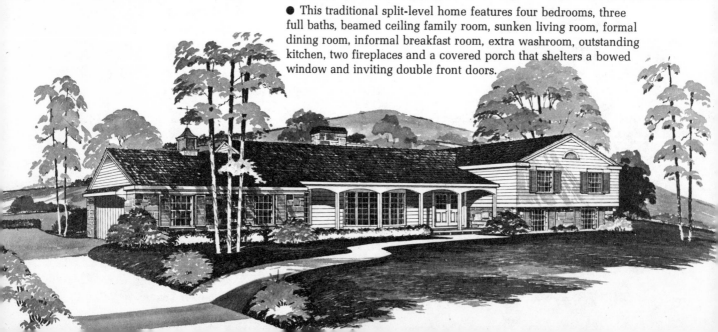

Design T61265 *1,298 Sq. Ft. - Main Level; 964 Sq. Ft. - Upper Level; 964 Sq. Ft. - Lower Level; 48,588 Cu. Ft.*

● Impressive, may be just the word to describe this appealingly formal, traditional tri-level. Changes in level add interest to its plan and make this already spacious house seem even larger. A glamorous living room, two steps below entry level, features a handsome fireplace and a broad, bay window. Raised two additional steps to emphasize the sunken area, the formal dining room is partitioned from the living room by a built-in planter. Up a few stairs from the entry hall, the sleeping level houses three bedrooms and two baths. The lower level has areas which will lend themselves to flexible living patterns.

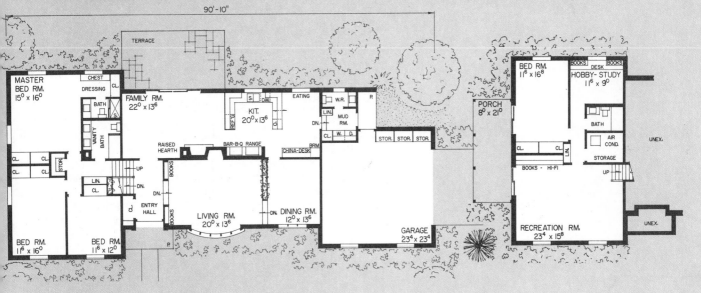

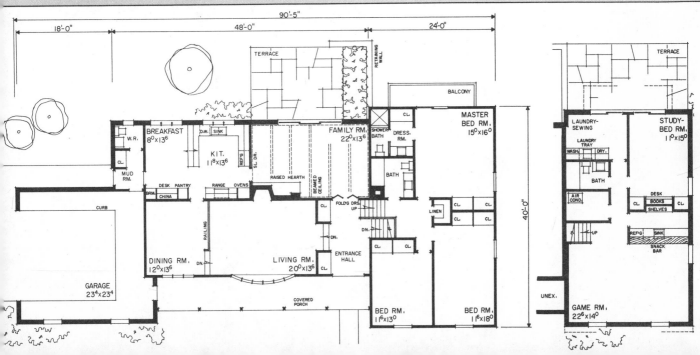

Design T61822 *1,836 Sq. Ft. - Upper Level; 1,150 Sq. Ft. - Lower Level; 33,280 Cu. Ft.*

● Here is a unique bi-level. Not only in its delightful exterior appeal, but in its practical planning. The covered porch with its impressive columns, the contrasting use of materials and the traditional window and door detailing are all features which will provoke comment from passers-by. The upper level is a complete living unit of three bedrooms, two baths, separate living, dining and family rooms, a kitchen with an eating area, two fireplaces and an outdoor balcony. The lower level represents extra living space which is bright and cheerful.

Design T62514 1,713 Sq. Ft. - Upper Level; 916 Sq. Ft. - Lower Level; 32,000 Cu. Ft.

● This efficient multi-level traditional home sports classic good looks outside to match its comfort inside. Note the Southern Colonial columns, reminiscent of Greco-Roman styling. The porch is covered. The interior zoning of this bi-level home allows for quiet bedrooms all on one floor, plus spacious dining room, breakfast nook and kitchen also on the upper level. Note the luxurious space of the master bedroom suite. Downstairs, the living area of the house includes a large activities room, a utility room, and a study. Both the activity room and the study open to a terrace. Balconies upstairs are accessible to residents in the dining room, breakfast nook, kitchen, or master bedroom. This lovely three-bedroom home is built for comfort! Study the floor plans carefully.

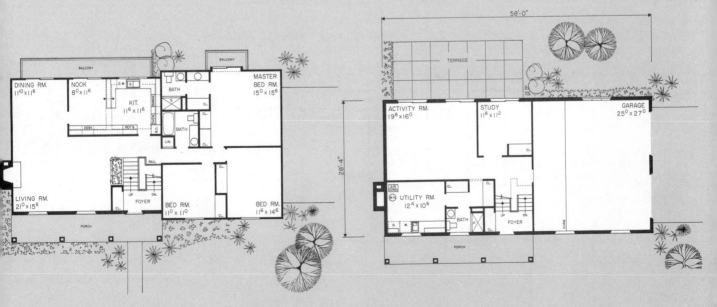

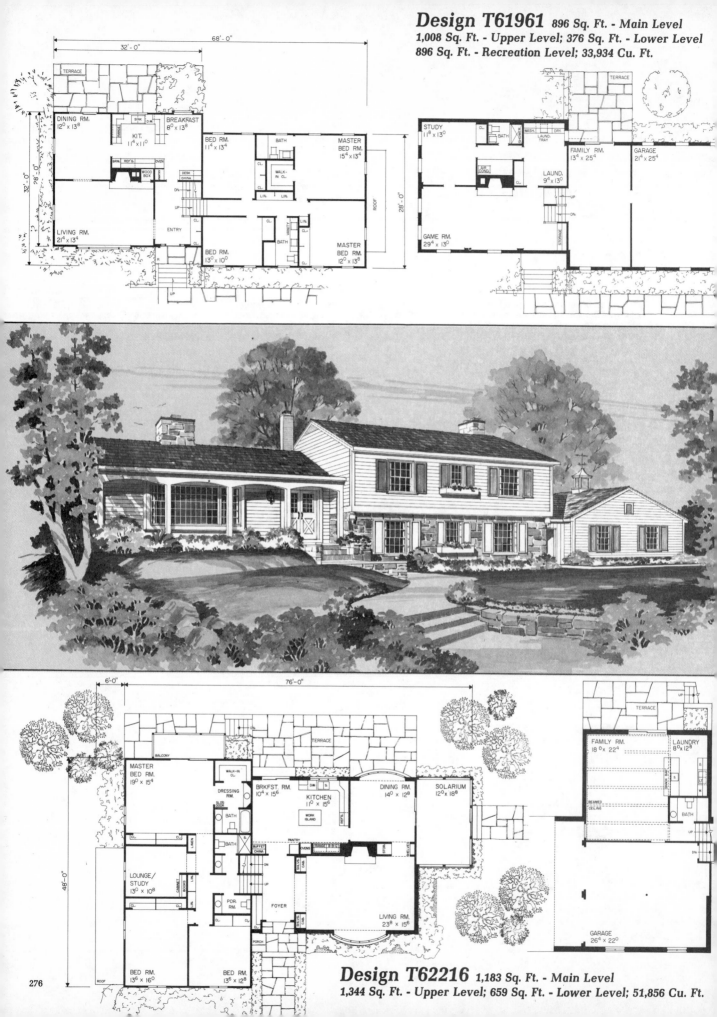

Design T61961
896 Sq. Ft. - Main Level
1,008 Sq. Ft. - Upper Level; 376 Sq. Ft. - Lower Level
896 Sq. Ft. - Recreation Level; 33,934 Cu. Ft.

68'-0"
32'-0"
32'-0"
28'-0"
28'-0"

TERRACE

DINING RM.
12⁰ x 13⁸

SINK   D.W.

KIT.
11⁴ x 11⁰

BREAKFAST
8⁰ x 13⁸

BED RM.
11⁴ x 13⁴

BATH

MASTER
BED RM.
15⁴ x 13⁴

BRN. REF'S.

OVEN

WOOD
BOX

PANTRY

DESK

CHINA

WALK-IN CL.

DN.

UP

LIN.   LIN.

ROOF

LIVING RM.
21⁴ x 13⁴

ENTRY

CL.

CL.

BATH

VANITY

LIN.
CL.

BED RM.
13⁰ x 10⁰

BATH

MASTER
BED RM.
12⁰ x 13⁸

UP

STUDY
11⁸ x 13⁰

CL.

BATH

SHOWER

WASH.   DRY

LAUND.
TRAY

TERRACE

FAMILY RM.
13⁴ x 25⁴

GARAGE
21⁴ x 25⁴

AIR COND.

LAUND.
9⁴ x 13⁰

CL.

UP

DN.

STORAGE

GAME RM.
29⁴ x 13⁰

Design T62216
1,183 Sq. Ft. - Main Level
1,344 Sq. Ft. - Upper Level; 659 Sq. Ft. - Lower Level; 51,856 Cu. Ft.

6'-0"
76'-0"
48'-0"

BALCONY

MASTER
BED RM.
19⁰ x 15⁴

WALK-IN CL.

DRESSING RM.

TERRACE

BRKFST. RM.
10⁴ x 15⁶

KITCHEN
11⁰ x 15⁶

DINING RM.
14⁰ x 12⁸

SOLARIUM
12⁰ x 18⁸

FAMILY RM.
18⁰ x 22⁴

LAUNDRY
8⁰ x 12⁸

SLID.
DOOR

BATH

WORK
ISLAND

REF'S.

BEAMED
CEILING

BATH

CL.   CL.

LINEN

BATH

BUFFET

CHINA

PANTRY

OVENS

CAB.   B-B-Q

STG.

SHELVES

LOUNGE/
STUDY
13⁰ x 10⁸

CABINET

BOOKS

DN.

UP

DN.

PDR.
RM.

FOYER

LIVING RM.
23⁸ x 15⁶

GARAGE
26⁴ x 22⁰

BED RM.
13⁶ x 16⁰

BED RM.
13⁶ x 12⁸

ROOF

PORCH

276

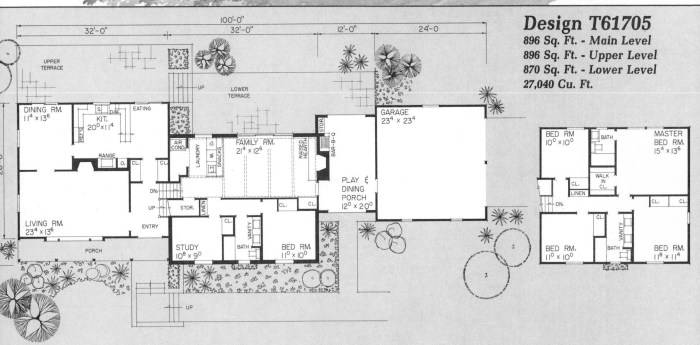

Design T61705

896 Sq. Ft. - Main Level
896 Sq. Ft. - Upper Level
870 Sq. Ft. - Lower Level
27,040 Cu. Ft.

DINING RM. 11⁴ × 13⁶

KIT. 20⁰ × 11⁴

EATING

REFG

RANGE

O.

CL.

DN.

UP

LIVING RM. 23⁴ × 13⁶

ENTRY

STOR.

LINEN

PORCH

UP

STUDY 10⁸ × 9⁰

VANITY

BATH

CL.

BED RM. 11⁰ × 10⁰

UP

LOWER TERRACE

UPPER TERRACE

AIR COND.

LAUNDRY

W. D.

SNACKS

FAMILY RM. 21⁴ × 12⁶

RAISED HEARTH

STOR.

BAR-B-Q

CL.

CL.

GARAGE 23⁴ × 23⁴

PLAY & DINING PORCH 12⁰ × 20⁰

100'-0"

32'-0"   32'-0"   12'-0"   24'-0"

BED RM. 10⁰ × 10⁰

BATH

WALK IN CL.

MASTER BED RM. 15⁴ × 13⁶

CL.

LINEN

DN.

CL.

CL.

BED RM. 11⁰ × 10⁰

CL.

VANITY

BATH

BED RM. 11⁸ × 11⁴

Design T61977 *896 Sq. Ft. - Main Level; 884 Sq. Ft. - Upper Level; 896 Sq. Ft. - Lower Level; 36,718 Cu. Ft.*

● This split-level is impressive. It has a two-story center portion, flanked by a projecting living wing on one side and a garage on the other side, yet it still maintains that ground-hugging quality. There is an orderly flow of traffic. You will go up to the sleeping zone; down to the hobby/recreation level; straight ahead to the kitchen and breakfast room; left to the living room.

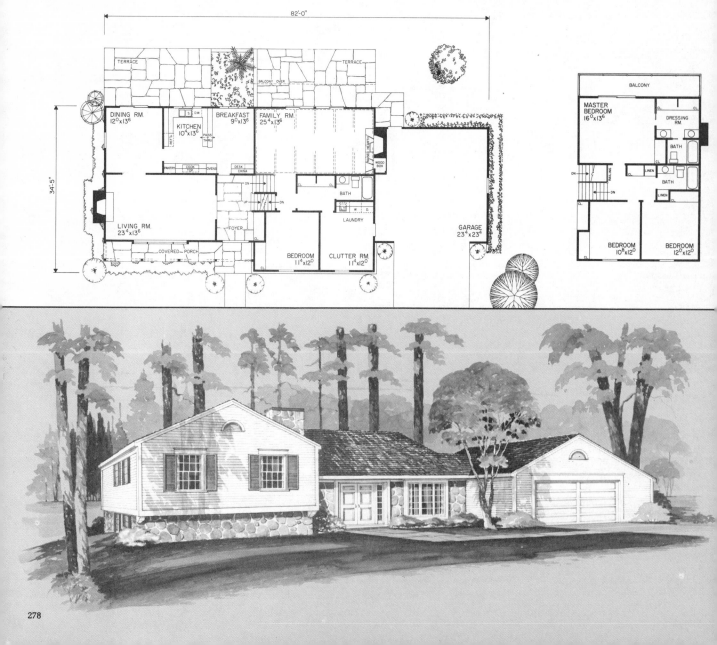

Design T62125 728 Sq. Ft. - Main Level; 672 Sq. Ft. - Upper Level; 656 Sq. Ft. - Lower Level; 28,315 Cu. Ft.

● A long list of features are available to recommend this four level, traditional home. First of all, it is a real beauty. The windows, shutters, doorway, horizontal siding and stone all go together with great proportion to project an image of design excellence. Inside, the livability is outstanding. There are three bedrooms, plus a study (make it the fourth bedroom if you wish); two full baths and a washroom; a fine kitchen with eating space; formal living and dining areas and an all-purpose family room.

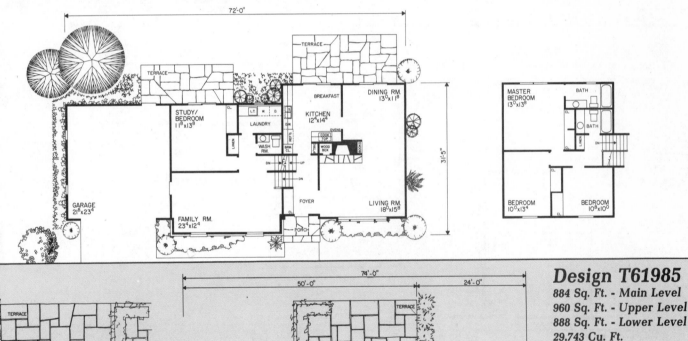

Design T61985

884 Sq. Ft. - Main Level
960 Sq. Ft. - Upper Level
888 Sq. Ft. - Lower Level
29,743 Cu. Ft.

● Here is a split-level that expresses all that is warm and inviting in the traditional vein. Delightfully proportioned, the projecting wings add that desired look of distinction. The double front doors open into a spacious entry hall. Straight ahead is the living room with the dining room but a step away. The kitchen is strategically located with a pass-thru to the breakfast room.

279

Design T62849 1,003 Sq. Ft. - Main Level
936 Sq. Ft. - Upper Level; 832 Sq. Ft. - Lower Level; 36,250 Cu. Ft.

● Enter into the front foyer of this traditional design and you will be impressed by the dramatic sloped ceiling. Sunken two steps, the formal living room is to the right. This room is high-lighted by a fireplace with adjacent wood box, sloped ceiling and a multi-paned bay window. Formal and informal dining, kitchen, laundry and washroom also share the main level with the living room and foyer. The lower level houses the family room, bedroom/study, full bath and mechanical room; the upper level, three bedrooms and two more full baths. Notice the excellent indoor-outdoor living relationships. There is a side terrace accessible from each of the dining areas plus a rear ter-race. The front projecting garage reduces the size of the lot re-quired for this home.

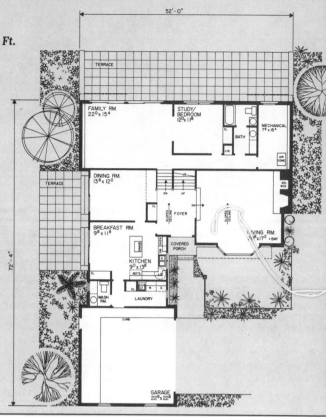

Design T61930 947 Sq. Ft. - Main Level; 768 Sq. Ft. - Upper Level; 740 Sq. Ft. - Lower Level; 25,906 Cu. Ft.

● The warmth of this inspiring Colonial adapta-tion is not restricted to the exterior. Its charm is readily apparent upon stepping through the double front doors. The sunken living room and family room will be in great demand.

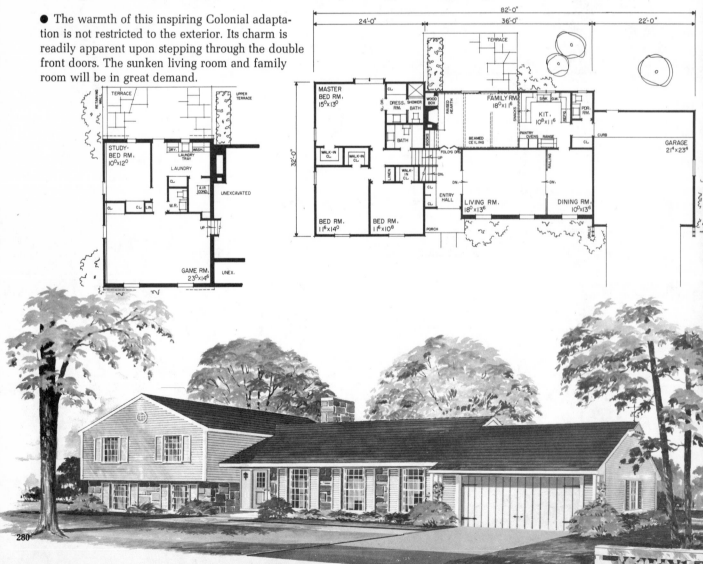

Design T61348 750 Sq. Ft. - Main Level; 672 Sq. Ft. - Upper Level; 664 Sq. Ft. - Lower Level; 22,143 Cu. Ft.

● The massive center section with its pediment gable and flanking wings highlights the exterior of this design. U-shaped, the kitchen is flanked by the separate dining room and the breakfast eating area.

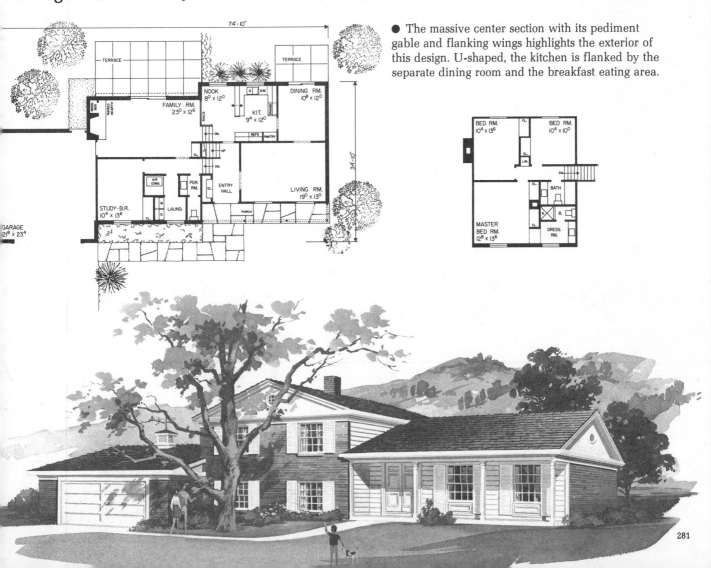

Design T62842
156 Sq. Ft. - Entrance Level; 1,038 Sq. Ft. - Upper Level
1,022 Sq. Ft. - Lower Level; 25,630 Cu. Ft.

● This narrow, 42 foot width, house can be built on a narrow lot to cut down overall costs. Yet its dramatic appeal surely is worth a million. The projecting front garage creates a pleasing curved drive. One enters this house through the covered porch to the entrance level foyer. At this point the stairs lead down to the living area consisting of formal living room, family room, kitchen and dining area then up the stairs to the four bedroom-two bath sleeping area. The indoor-outdoor living relationship at the rear is outstanding.

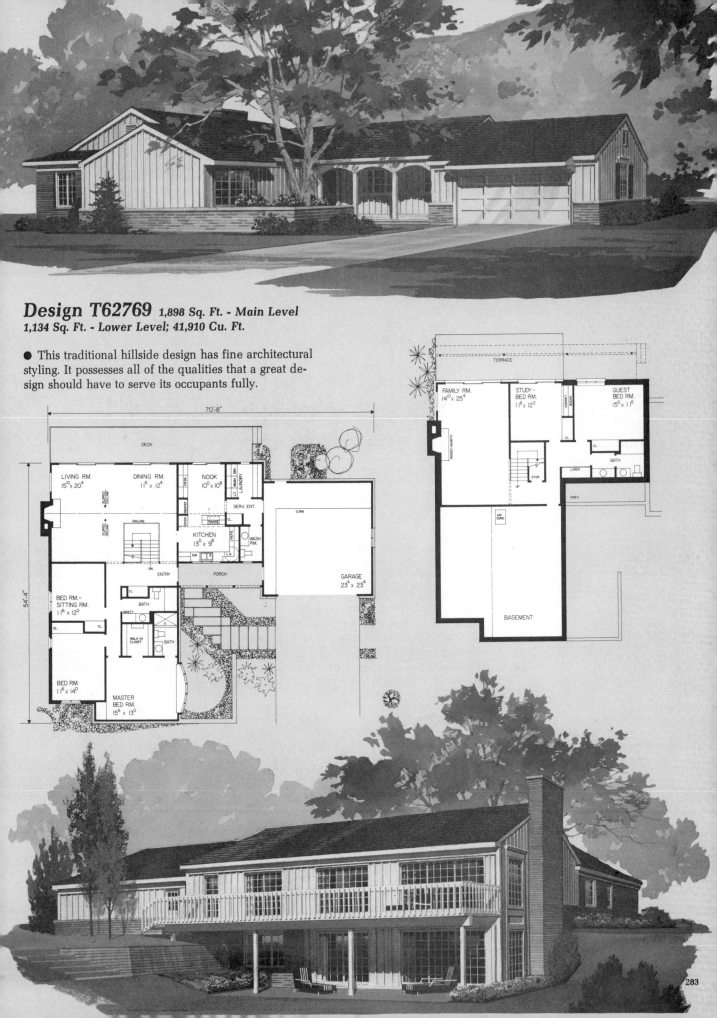

Design T62769 1,898 Sq. Ft. - Main Level
1,134 Sq. Ft. - Lower Level; 41,910 Cu. Ft.

● This traditional hillside design has fine architectural styling. It possesses all of the qualities that a great design should have to serve its occupants fully.

Main Level (70'-8" × 54'-4")

- DECK
- LIVING RM. 15⁰ x 20⁴
- DINING RM. 11⁶ x 12⁴
- NOOK 10⁰ x 10⁸
- LAUNDRY / LT. / WASH. / DRY.
- SLOPED CEILING
- SERV. ENT.
- OVEN / PANTRY / DESK
- RANGE
- KITCHEN 13⁰ x 9⁸
- DW.
- REF.
- WASH RM.
- RAILING
- DN.
- ENTRY
- PORCH
- CURB
- GARAGE 23⁴ x 23⁴
- BED RM.- SITTING RM. 11⁶ x 12⁰
- CL. / CL.
- BATH
- VANITY
- WALK IN CLOSET
- BATH
- BED RM. 11⁶ x 14⁰
- MASTER BED RM. 15⁶ x 13⁰

Lower Level

- TERRACE
- FAMILY RM. 14¹⁰ x 25⁴
- STUDY - BED RM. 11⁶ x 12⁰
- CABINET / BOOKS
- GUEST BED RM. 15⁰ x 11⁶
- RAISED HEARTH
- CL.
- BATH
- UP / STOR.
- LINEN
- UNEX.
- AIR COND.
- BASEMENT

Design T61974 1,680 Sq. Ft. - Main Level; 1,344 Sq. Ft. - Lower Level; 34,186 Cu. Ft.

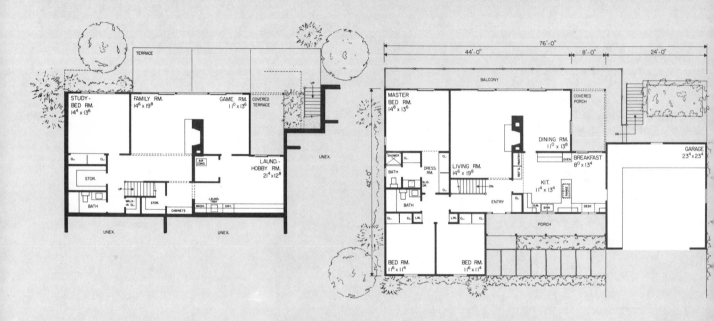

● You would never guess from looking at the front of this traditional design that it possessed such a strikingly different rear. From the front, you would guess that all of its livability is on one floor. Yet, just imagine the tremendous amount of livability that is added to the plan as a result of exposing the lower level - 1,344 square feet of it. Living in this hillside house will mean fun. Obviously, the most popular spot will be the balcony. Then again, maybe it could be the terrace adjacent to the family room. Both the terrace and the balcony have a covered area to provide protection against unfavorable weather. The interior of the plan also will serve the family with ease.

Design T61739   1,281 Sq. Ft. - Main Level; 857 Sq. Ft. - Sleeping Level; 687 Sq. Ft. - Lower Level; 37,624 Cu. Ft.

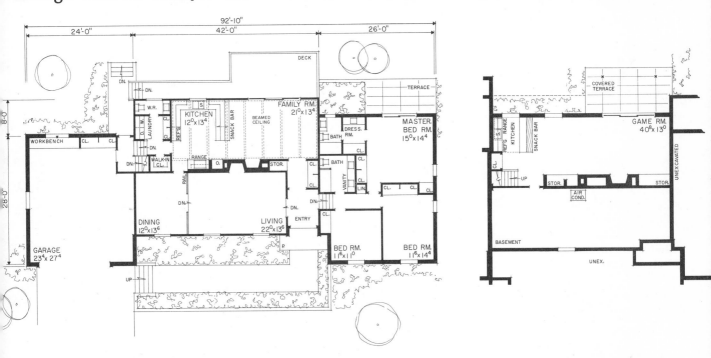

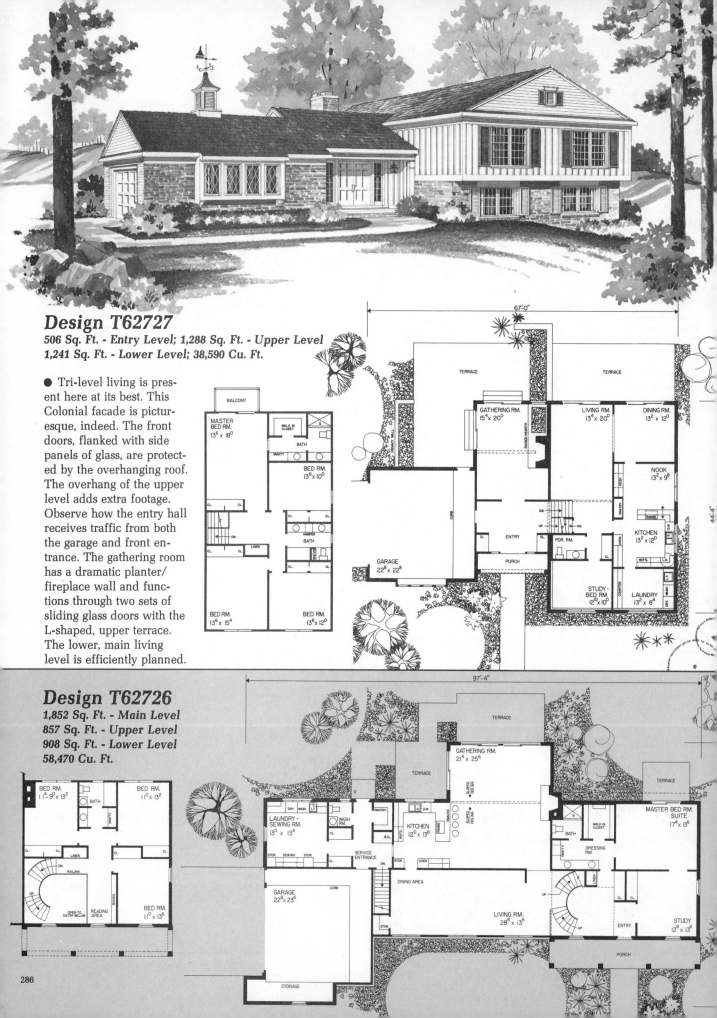

Design T62727

506 Sq. Ft. - Entry Level; 1,288 Sq. Ft. - Upper Level
1,241 Sq. Ft. - Lower Level; 38,590 Cu. Ft.

● Tri-level living is present here at its best. This Colonial facade is picturesque, indeed. The front doors, flanked with side panels of glass, are protected by the overhanging roof. The overhang of the upper level adds extra footage. Observe how the entry hall receives traffic from both the garage and front entrance. The gathering room has a dramatic planter/fireplace wall and functions through two sets of sliding glass doors with the L-shaped, upper terrace. The lower, main living level is efficiently planned.

Design T62726

1,852 Sq. Ft. - Main Level
857 Sq. Ft. - Upper Level
908 Sq. Ft. - Lower Level
58,470 Cu. Ft.

286

TERRACE

DINING RM.
13⁰ x 12⁰

LIVING RM.
14⁴ x 20⁰

CL. CL.

DRESS.
RM.

MASTER
BED RM.
15⁰ x 13⁰

BATH

BRM.
REFG

RANGE

KIT.
13⁰ x 11⁰

CL.

DW

S

RAISED
HEARTH

WOOD
BOX

BATH

BED RM.
11⁶ x 10⁰

SNACKS

DN.

UP

CL. CL. CL.

R

BREAKFAST
13⁰ x 8⁰

PANTRY

W.R.

ENTRY

CL.

LIN.

PORCH

BED RM.
11⁶ x 10⁰

BED RM.
11⁶ x 13⁴

DN.

GARAGE
23⁴ x 23⁸

56'-5"
52'-0"
40'-0"
64'-5"
24'-0"

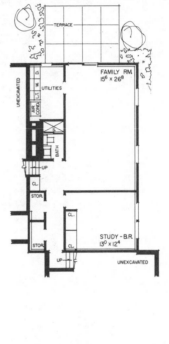

TERRACE

UNEXCAVATED

W
D

UTILITIES

L.T.

AIR
COND.

BATH

FAMILY RM.
15⁶ x 26⁸

UP

CL.

STOR.

CL.

STOR.

UP

CL.

STUDY - B.R.
13⁰ x 12⁴

UNEXCAVATED

Design T61721

896 Sq. Ft. - Main Level
960 Sq. Ft. - Upper Level
960 Sq. Ft. - Lower Level
32,595 Cu. Ft.

● Ideal for a relatively narrow site, this L-shaped tri-level will serve the large family wonderfully. The double doors of the front entry are sheltered by the long, covered porch and lead to the spacious hall which routes traffic efficiently to all areas. The kitchen, flanked by the informal breakfast room and the separate dining room, has an abundance of counter and cupboard space. Four bedrooms and two baths comprise the quiet, upper level sleeping area. An abundance of dual-use space is found on the lower level, accessible from the garage. Note utility room, bath with stall shower, study/bedroom, large, family room and two storage closets which are all features of the lower level.

Hillside Design Loaded with Comfort

Design T62841 1,044 Sq. Ft. - Main Level
851 Sq. Ft. - Upper Level; 753 Sq. Ft. - Lower Level; 30,785 Cu. Ft.

● This charming Traditional tri-level home offers loads of comfort for today's lifestyle on all levels. Notice the balconies and deck in the rear. The rear deck forms a covered patio below on the lower level. The patio/terrace opens to an activities room with its own raised hearth fireplace, a basement, and optional bunk room with its own bath. The main level of this stone house includes a convenient kitchen with snack bar, dining room, a study (which can double as another bedroom), and a large gathering room with fireplace. That gathering room is continued above with an upper-level gathering room. There's also an upper level lounge and upper foyer, in addition to a bedroom and long bunk room. A wide garage offers plenty of storage space. The large rear deck angles off the kitchen, dining room, and main-level gathering room for plenty of view areas. This comfortable home with dashing good looks is convertible! Spare rooms convert to extra bedrooms with expanding families. Or, bedrooms convert to other functions when the children grow older and leave the nest.

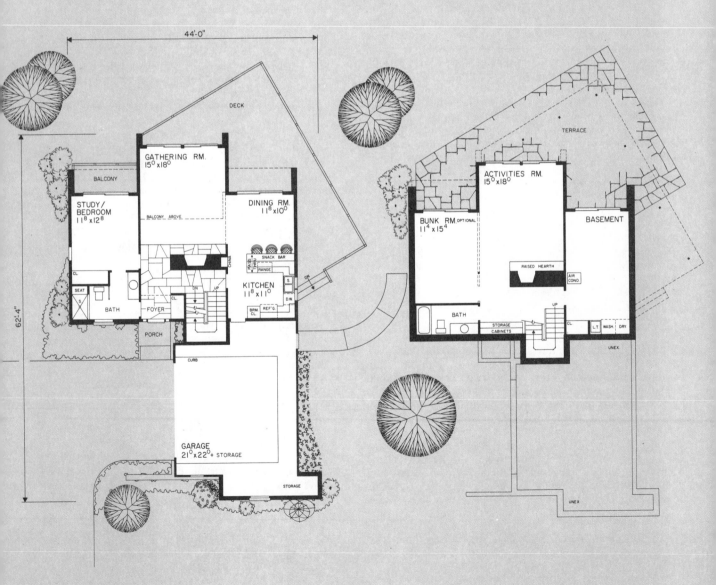

How To Read Floor Plans and Blueprints

Selecting the most suitable house plan for your family is a matter of matching your needs, tastes, and life-style against the many designs we offer. When you study the floor plans in this issue, and the blueprints that you may subsequently order, remember that they are simply a two-dimensional representation of what will eventually be a three-dimensional reality.

Floor plans are easy to read. Rooms are clearly labeled, with dimensions given in feet and inches. Most symbols are logical and self-explanatory: The location of bathroom fixtures, planters, fireplaces, tile floors, cabinets and counters, sinks, appliances, closets, sloped or beamed ceilings will be obvious.

A blueprint, although much more detailed, is also easy to read; all it demands is concentration. The blueprints that we offer come in many large sheets, each one of which contains a different kind of information. One sheet contains foundation and excavation drawings, another has a precise plot plan. An elevations sheet deals with the exterior walls of the house; section drawings show precise dimensions, fittings, doors, windows, and roof structures. Our detailed floor plans give the construction information needed by your contractor. And each set of blueprints contains a lengthy materials list with size and quantities of all necessary components. Using this list, a contractor and suppliers can make a start at calculating costs for you.

When you first study a floor plan or blueprint, imagine that you are walking through the house. By mentally visualizing each room in three dimensions, you can transform the technical data and symbols into something more real.

Start at the front door. It's preferable to have a foyer or entrance hall in which to receive guests. A closet here is desirable; a powder room is a plus.

Look for good traffic circulation as you study the floor plan. You should not have to pass all the way through one main room to reach another. From the entrance area you should have direct access to the three principal areas of a house—the living, work, and sleeping zones. For example, a foyer might provide separate entrances to the living room, kitchen, patio, and a hallway or staircase leading to the bedrooms.

Study the layout of each zone. Most people expect the living room to be protected from cross traffic. The kitchen, on the other hand, should connect with the dining room—and perhaps also the utility room, basement, garage, patio or deck, or a secondary entrance. A homemaker whose workday centers in the kitchen may have special requirements: a window that faces the backyard; a clear view of the family room where children play; a garage or driveway entrance that allows for a short trip with groceries; laundry facilities close at hand. Check for efficient placement of kitchen cabinets, counters, and appliances. Is there enough room in the kitchen for additional appliances, for eating in? Is there a dining nook?

Perhaps this part of the house contains a family room or a den/bedroom/office. It's advantageous to have a bathroom or powder room in this section.

As you study the plan, you may encounter a staircase, indicated by a group of parallel lines, the number of lines equaling the number of steps. Arrows labeled "up" mean that the staircase leads to a higher level, and those pointing down mean it leads to a lower one. Staircases in a split-level will have both up and down arrows on one staircase because two levels are depicted in one drawing and an extra level in another.

Notice the location of the stairways. Is too much floor space lost to them? Will you find yourself making too many trips?

Study the sleeping quarters. Are the bedrooms situated as you like? You may want the master bedroom near the kids, or you may want it as far away as possible. Is there at least one closet per person in each bedroom or a double one for a couple? Bathrooms should be convenient to each bedroom—if not adjoining, then with hallway access and on the same floor.

Once you are familiar with the relative positions of the rooms, look for such structural details as:

• Sufficient uninterrupted wall space for furniture arrangement.

• Adequate room dimensions.

• Potential heating or cooling problems—i.e., a room over a garage or next to the laundry.

• Window and door placement for good ventilation and natural light.

• Location of doorways—avoid having a basement staircase or a bathroom in view of the dining room.

• Adequate auxiliary space—closets, storage, bathrooms, countertops.

• Separation of activity areas. (Will noise from the recreation room disturb sleeping children or a parent at work?)

As you complete your mental walk through the house, bear in mind your family's long-range needs. A good house plan will allow for some adjustments now and additions in the future.

Each member of your family may find the listing of his, or her, favorite features a most helpful exercise. Why not try it?

All The "TOOLS" You And Your Builder Need...

1. THE PLAN BOOKS

Home Planners' unique Design Category Series makes it easy to look at and study only the types of designs for which you and your family have an interest. Each of six plan books features a specific type of home, namely: Two-Story, 1½ Story, One-Story Over 2000 Sq. Ft., One-Story Under 2000 Sq. Ft., Multi-Levels and Vacation Homes. In addition to the convenient Design Category Series, there is an impressive selection of other current titles. While the home plans featured in these books are also to be found in the Design Category Series, they, too, are edited for those with special tastes and requirements. Your family will spend many enjoyable hours reviewing the delightfully designed exteriors and the practical floor plans. Surely your home or office library should include a selection of these popular plan books. Your complete satisfaction is guaranteed.

2. THE CONSTRUCTION BLUEPRINTS

There are blueprints available for each of the designs published in Home Planners' current plan books. Depending upon the size, the style and the type of home, each set of blueprints consists of from five to ten large sheets. Only by studying the blueprints is it possible to give complete and final consideration to the proper selection of a design for your next home. The blueprints provide the opportunity for all family members to familiarize themselves with the features of all exterior elevations, interior elevations and details, all dimensions, special built-in features and effects. They also provide a full understanding of the materials to be used and/or selected. The low-cost of our blueprints makes it possible and indeed, practical, to study in detail a number of different sets of blueprints before deciding upon which design to build.

3. THE MATERIALS LIST

A separate list of materials, available for a small fee, is an important part of the plan package. It comprises the last sheet of each set of blueprints and serves as a handy reference during the period of construction. Of course, at the pricing and the material ordering stages, it is indispensable.

4. THE SPECIFICATION OUTLINE

Each order for blueprints is accompanied by one Specification Outline. You and your builder will find this a time-saving tool when deciding upon your own individual specifications. An important reference document should you wish to write your own specifications.

5. THE PLUMBING & ELECTRICAL PACKAGE

The construction blueprints you order from Home Planners, Inc. include locations for all plumbing fixtures — sinks, lavatories, tubs, showers, water closets, laundry trays, hot water heaters, etc. The blueprints also show the locations of all electrical switches, plugs, and outlets. These plumbing and electrical details are sufficient to present to your local contractor for discussions about your individual specifications and subsequent installations in conformance with local codes. However, for those who wish to acquaint themselves with many of the intricacies of residential plumbing and electrical details and installations, Home Planners, Inc. has made available this package. We do not recommend that the layman attempt to do his own plumbing and electrical work. It is, nevertheless, advisable that owners be as knowledgeable as possible about each of these disciplines. The entire family will appreciate the educational value of these low-cost, easy-to-understand details.

THE DESIGN CATEGORY SERIES

210 ONE STORY HOMES OVER 2,000 SQUARE FEET
Spacious homes for gracious living. Includes all popular styles—Spanish, Western, Tudor, French, Contemporary, and others. Amenity-filled plans feature master bedroom suites, atriums, courtyards, and pools.

1. 192 pages. $4.95 ($5.95 Canada)

315 ONE STORY HOMES UNDER 2,000 SQUARE FEET
Economical homes in a variety of styles. Efficient floor plans contain plenty of attractive features—gathering rooms, formal and informal living and dining rooms, mudrooms, outdoor living spaces, and more. Many plans are expandable.

2. 192 pages. $4.95 ($5.95 Canada)

150 1½ STORY HOMES
From starter homes to country estates. Includes classic story-and-a-half styles: Contemporary, Williamsburg, Georgian, Tudor, and Cape Cod. Outstanding outdoor livability. Many expandable plans.

3. 128 pages. $3.95 ($4.95 Canada)

360 TWO STORY HOMES
Plans for all budgets and all families—in a wide range of styles: Tudors, Saltboxes, Farmhouses, Southern Colonials, Georgians, Contemporaries, and more. Many plans have extra-large kitchens, extra bedrooms, and extra baths.

4. 288 pages. $6.95 ($8.95 Canada)

215 MULTI-LEVEL HOMES
Distinctive styles for both flat and sloping sites. Tailor-made for great outdoor living. Features include exposed lower levels, upper-level lounges, balconies, decks, and terraces. Includes plans for all building budgets.

5. 192 pages. $4.95 ($5.95 Canada)

223 VACATION HOMES
Full-color volume features A-frames, chalets, lodges, hexagons, cottages, and other attractive styles in one-story, two-story, and multi-level plans ranging from 480 to 3,238 square feet. Perfect for woodland, lakeside, or seashore.

6. 176 pages. $4.95 ($5.95 Canada)

THE EXTERIOR STYLE SERIES

7.

8.

9.

10.

330 EARLY AMERICAN HOME PLANS
A heart-warming collection of the best in Early American architecture. Traces the style from colonial structures to popular Traditional versions. Includes a history of different styles.

304 pages. $9.95 ($11.95 Canada)

335 CONTEMPORARY HOME PLANS
Required reading for anyone interested in the clean-lined elegance of Contemporary design. Features plans of all sizes and types, as well as a fascinating look at the history of this style.

304 pages. $9.95 ($11.95 Canada)

135 ENGLISH TUDOR HOMES Tudor architecture may well be America's favorite style. This book is packed with Tudor and English-style homes of all types and sizes, ranging from mansions to truly affordable designs. Must reading for the Tudor lover.

104 pages. $3.95 ($4.95 Canada)

136 SPANISH & WESTERN HOME DESIGNS Includes an array of sun-filled plans that emphasize indoor-outdoor livability. Key architectural features include stucco exteriors, arches, tile roofs, terraces, patios, and more.

120 pages. $3.95 ($4.95 Canada)

PLAN PORTFOLIOS

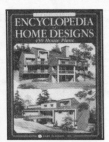

ENCYCLOPEDIA OF HOME DESIGNS (450 PLANS) The largest book of its kind—450 plans in a complete range of housing types, styles, and sizes. Includes plans for all building budgets, families, and styles of living.

11. 320 pages. $9.95 ($11.95 Canada)

MOST POPULAR HOME DESIGNS (360 PLANS) Our customers' favorite plans, including one-story, 1½-story, two-story, and multi-level homes in a variety of styles. For families large and small. Designs feature many of today's most popular amenities: lounges, clutter rooms, sunspaces, media rooms, and more.

12. 272 pages. $8.95 ($10.95 Canada)

COLOR PORTFOLIO OF HOUSES & PLANS (310 PLANS) A beautiful full-color guide to Home Planners' best plans, including Early American, Spanish, French, Tudor, Contemporary, and our own Trend Home styles. One-story, 1½-story, two-story, and multi-level designs for all budgets.

13. 288 pages. $12.95 ($14.95 Canada)

Frontal Sheet

Foundation Plans

Detailed Floor Plans

House Cross-Sections

Interior Elevations

Exterior Elevations

Materials List

What Our Plans Include

The Blueprints

1. FRONTAL SHEET.
Artist's landscaped sketch of the exterior and ink-line floor plans are on the frontal sheet of each set of blueprints.

2. FOUNDATION PLAN.
¼" Scale basement and foundation plan. All necessary notations and dimensions. Plot plan diagram for locating house on building site.

3. DETAILED FLOOR PLAN.
¼" Scale first and second floor plans with complete dimensions. Cross-section detail keys. Diagrammatic layout of electrical outlets and switches.

4. HOUSE CROSS-SECTIONS.
Large scale sections of foundation, interior and exterior walls, floors and roof details for design and construction control.

5. INTERIOR ELEVATIONS.
Large scale interior details of the complete kitchen cabinet design, bathrooms, powder room, laundry, fireplaces, paneling, beam ceilings, built-in cabinets, etc.

6. EXTERIOR ELEVATIONS.
¼" Scale exterior elevation drawings of front, rear, and both sides of the house. All exterior materials and details are shown to indicate the complete design and proportions of the house.

7. MATERIALS LIST.
For a small additional fee, complete lists of all materials required for the construction of the house as designed are included in each set of blueprints (one charge for any size order).

THIS BLUEPRINT PACKAGE
will help you and your family take a major step forward in the final appraisal and planning of your new home. Only by spending many enjoyable and informative hours studying the numerous details included in the complete package will you feel sure of, and comfortable with, your commitment to build your new home. To assure successful and productive consultation with your builder and/or architect, reference to the various elements of the blueprint package is a must. The blueprints, materials list and specification outline will save much consultation time and expense. Don't be without them.

The Materials List

For a small extra charge, you will receive a materials list with each set of blueprints you order (one fee for any size order). Each list shows you the quantity, type and size of the non-mechanical materials required to build your home. It also tells you where these materials are used. This makes the blueprints easy to understand.

Influencing the mechanical requirements are geographical differences in availability of materials, local codes, methods of installation and individual preferences. Because of these factors, your local heating, plumbing and electrical contractors can supply you with necessary material take-offs for their particular trades.

Materials lists simplify your material ordering and enable you to get quicker price quotations from your builder and material dealer. Because the materials list is an integral part of each set of blueprints, it is not available separately.

Among the materials listed:

• Masonry, Veneer & Fireplace • Framing Lumber • Roofing & Sheet Metal • Windows & Door Frames • Exterior Trim & Insulation • Tile Work, Finish Floors • Interior Trim, Kitchen Cabinets • Rough & Finish Hardware

The Specification Outline

This fill-in type specification lists over 150 phases of home construction from excavating to painting and includes wiring, plumbing, heating and air-conditioning. It consists of 16 pages and will prove invaluable for specifying to your builder the exact materials, equipment and methods of construction you want in your new home. One Specification Outline is included free with each order for blueprints. Additional Specification Outlines are available at $5.00 each.

CONTENTS
• General Instructions, Suggestions and Information • Excavating and Grading • Masonry and Concrete Work • Sheet Metal Work • Carpentry, Millwork, Roofing, and Miscellaneous Items • Lath and Plaster or Drywall Wallboard • Schedule for Room Finishes • Painting and Finishing • Tile Work • Electrical Work • Plumbing • Heating and Air-Conditioning

More Products from Home Planners To Help You Plan Your Home

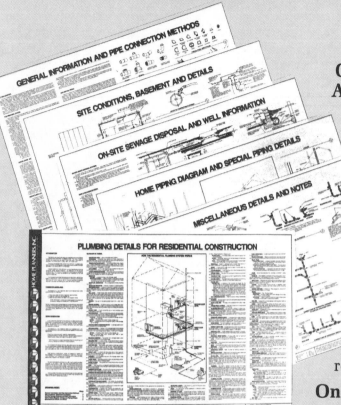

Comprehensive Plumbing Details for All Types of Residential Construction

If you want to find out more about the intricacies of household plumbing, these 24x36-inch drawings– six individual, fact-packed sheets– will prove to be remarkably useful tools. Prepared to meet requirements of the National Plumbing Code, they show pipe schedules, fittings, sump-pump details, water-softener hookups, septic-system details, and many more. Sheets are bound together and color coded for easy reference. Glossary of terms included.

Only $14.95

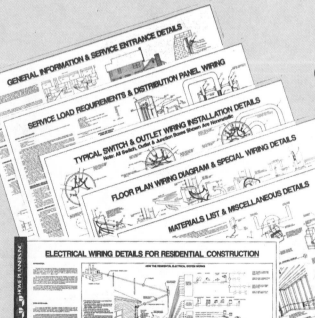

Complete Electrical Wiring Details for All Types of Residential Construction

Designed to take the mystery out of household electrical systems, these comprehensive 24x36-inch drawings come packed with details. Prepared to meet requirements of the National Electrical Code, the six fact-filled sheets cover a variety of topics, including appliance wattage, wire sizing, switch-installation schematics, cable-routing details, doorbell hookups, and many others. Sheets are bound together and color coded for easy reference. Glossary of terms included.

Only $14.95

Plan Your Home with Plan-A-Home™

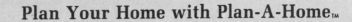

Plan-A-Home™ is a very useful tool. It's a simple product that will help you design a new home, plan a remodeling project or arrange furniture on an existing plan. Each package contains: more than 700 peel-and-stick *planning symbols* on a self-stick, vinyl sheet, including walls, windows, doors, furniture, kitchen components, bath fixtures, and many more; a reusable, transparent, ¼-inch-scale *planning grid* that can help you create houses up to 140x92 feet; *tracing paper;* and a *felt-tip pen,* with water-soluble ink that wipes away quickly. The transparent planning grid matches the scale of working blueprints, so you can lay it over existing drawings and modify them as necessary.

Only $24.95

Residential Construction Details

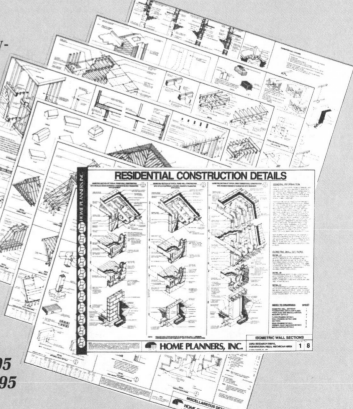

Home Planners' blueprint package contains everything an experienced builder needs to construct a particular plan. However, it doesn't show the thousands upon thousands of ways building materials come together to form a house. Prepared to meet requirements of the Uniform Building Code, these drawings—eight large, fact-filled sheets—depict the materials and methods used to build foundations, fireplaces, walls, floors, and roofs. What's more, where appropriate, they show acceptable alternatives. Bound together for easy reference.

Only $14.95

Get any two of Plumbing, Electrical, and Construction Details for just $22.95 (save $6.95). Get all three for only $29.95 (save $14.90).

To order, turn the page . . .

The Blueprint Price Schedule

The blueprint package you order will be an invaluable tool for the complete study of the details relating to the construction of your favorite design, as well as the master plan for building your home. Even the smallest of homes require much construction data and architectural detailing. As the house grows in size, so does the need for more data and details. Frequently, a house of only modest size can require an inordinate amount of data and detailing. This may be the result of its irregular shape and/or the complexity of its architectural features. In the pricing of its blueprints, Home Planners, Inc. has taken into account these factors. Before completing the blueprint order form on the opposite page, be sure to refer to the price schedule below for the appropriate blueprint charges for the design of your choice.

Schedule A: Single Sets, $125.00; Four Set Package, $175.00; Eight Set Package, $225.00. Additional Identical Sets in Same Order, $30.00 each. Sepia, $250.00.

Schedule B: Single Sets, $150.00; Four Set Package, $200.00; Eight Set Package, $250.00. Additional Identical Sets in Same Order, $30.00 each. Sepia, $300.00.

Schedule C: Single Sets, $175.00; Four Set Package, $225.00; Eight Set Package, $275.00. Additional Identical Sets in Same Order, $30.00 each. Sepia, $350.00.

Schedule D: Single Sets, $200.00; Four Set Package, $250.00; Eight Set Package, $300.00. Additional Identical Sets in Same Order, $30.00 each. Sepia, $400.00.

DESIGN NO.	PRICE SCHEDULE	DESIGN NO.	PRICE SCHEDULE	DESIGN NO.	PRICE SCHEDULE	DESIGN NO.	PRICE SCHEDULE	DESIGN NO.	PRICE SCHEDULE
T61060	D	T61852	C	T62162	A	T62558	A	T62683	D
T61075	A	T61858	C	T62172	C	T62559	B	T62684	C
T61104	A	T61868	B	T62174	B	T62561	B	T62685	C
T61106	B	T61870	B	T62176	B	T62563	B	T62686	C
T61107	A	T61880	C	T62181	C	T62565	B	T62687	C
T61115	B	T61882	B	T62183	D	T62569	A	T62688	B
T61149	B	T61884	C	T62184	C	T62571	A	T62689	B
T61163	B	T61887	B	T62185	C	T62572	B	T62690	C
T61170	B	T61890	B	T62188	C	T62575	D	T62691	B
T61174	C	T61900	C	T62189	B	T62585	B	T62692	C
T61186	B	T61901	A	T62191	C	T62596	B	T62694	C
T61191	A	T61902	B	T62192	D	T62597	B	T62700	C
T61196	A	T61903	B	T62209	C	T62598	A	T62704	B
T61208	A	T61904	B	T62211	B	T62600	C	T62707	A
T61222	B	T61906	B	T62216	C	T62603	B	T62713	C
T61239	C	T61907	B	T62221	C	T62609	B	T62718	C
T61241	A	T61911	D	T62223	B	T62610	C	T62722	C
T61242	C	T61916	D	T62225	D	T62614	C	T62724	C
T61265	C	T61920	B	T62230	D	T62615	D	T62726	D
T61269	B	T61924	C	T62237	D	T62616	B	T62727	C
T61285	B	T61927	C	T62250	C	T62617	B	T62731	B
T61304	B	T61929	C	T62253	C	T62621	C	T62733	B
T61308	A	T61930	B	T62259	B	T62622	A	T62739	D
T61317	B	T61931	C	T62264	C	T62623	B	T62742	B
T61337	B	T61933	B	T62283	C	T62625	C	T62751	B
T61339	B	T61935	B	T62284	B	T62627	A	T62752	B
T61346	B	T61939	A	T62285	A	T62631	B	T62757	C
T61348	B	T61945	B	T62301	D	T62632	B	T62762	C
T61358	A	T61946	B	T62313	B	T62633	C	T62766	C
T61365	A	T61949	B	T62316	B	T62634	B	T62767	D
T61366	A	T61950	B	T62320	C	T62635	A	T62768	D
T61372	A	T61955	B	T62333	B	T62636	A	T62769	C
T61394	A	T61956	A	T62338	C	T62638	C	T62774	B
T61701	B	T61961	C	T62342	D	T62639	C	T62775	B
T61705	B	T61964	C	T62344	C	T62640	B	T62776	B
T61711	D	T61967	B	T62360	B	T62641	C	T62777	B
T61718	B	T61970	C	T62367	B	T62642	B	T62778	C
T61719	A	T61974	C	T62395	B	T62643	C	T62783	D
T61721	C	T61977	B	T62396	B	T62644	B	T62784	C
T61728	C	T61980	B	T62397	C	T62648	B	T62786	B
T61736	B	T61981	B	T62398	B	T62649	C	T62787	B
T61739	C	T61985	C	T62399	B	T62650	B	T62799	A
T61747	C	T61986	B	T62488	A	T62651	C	T62808	C
T61761	C	T61987	B	T62500	B	T62652	C	T62826	B
T61766	B	T61996	B	T62501	B	T62653	C	T62839	C
T61767	C	T62014	C	T62505	A	T62654	A	T62840	C
T61768	B	T62020	B	T62510	A	T62655	A	T62841	B
T61770	A	T62024	B	T62513	C	T62656	B	T62842	B
T61773	B	T62025	C	T62514	B	T62657	B	T62849	C
T61777	B	T62051	B	T62519	C	T62658	A	T62852	A
T61780	B	T62052	B	T62520	B	T62659	B	T62853	A
T61786	C	T62101	B	T62521	B	T62660	D	T62867	C
T61787	C	T62103	B	T62522	C	T62661	A	T62869	B
T61788	C	T62107	A	T62524	A	T62662	C	T62870	A
T61790	C	T62108	A	T62527	C	T62663	B	T62878	B
T61791	B	T62109	B	T62531	B	T62664	B	T62880	C
T61793	C	T62124	B	T62533	B	T62665	D	T62888	D
T61794	C	T62125	B	T62535	B	T62666	B	T62889	D
T61796	D	T62131	B	T62538	B	T62667	B	T62890	C
T61814	B	T62132	C	T62539	B	T62668	B	T62891	B
T61816	C	T62133	D	T62540	B	T62672	B	T62897	C
T61822	C	T62139	B	T62542	D	T62673	C	T62898	C
T61829	B	T62140	C	T62544	C	T62675	C	T62899	C
T61835	B	T62144	C	T62547	C	T62676	C	T62907	B
T61849	B	T62145	A	T62550	B	T62680	C	T62908	B
T61850	B	T62146	A	T62553	C	T62681	B	T62909	B
T61851	C	T62157	C	T62556	C	T62682	A	T62921	D
								T63126	A
								T63189	A

Before You Order

1. STUDY THE DESIGNS . . . found in Home Planners and Heritage Homes plan books. As you review these delightful custom homes, you should keep in mind the total living requirements of your family — both indoors and outdoors. Although we do not make changes in plans, many minor changes can be made prior to construction. If major changes are involved in satisfy your personal requirements, you should consider ordering one set of sepias and having them modified. Consultation with your architect is strongly advised when contemplating major changes.

2. HOW TO ORDER BLUEPRINTS . . . After you have chosen the design that satisfies your requirements, or if you have selected one that you wish to study in more detail, simply clip the accompanying order blank and mail with your remittance. However, if it is not convenient for you to send a check or money order, you can use your credit card, or merely indicate C.O.D. shipment. Postman will collect all charges, including postage and C.O.D. fee. C.O.D. shipments are not permitted to Canada or foreign countries. Should time be of essence, as it sometimes is with many of our customers, your telephone order usually can be processed and shipped in the next day's mail. Simply call toll free 1-800-521-6797.

3. OUR SERVICE . . . Home Planners makes every effort to process and ship each order for blueprints and books within 48 hours. Because of this, we have deemed it unnecessary to acknowledge receipt

of our customers orders. See order coupon for the postage and handling charges for surface mail, air mail or foreign mail.

4. MODIFYING OUR PLANS . . . Slight revisions are easy to do before you start building. (We don't alter plans, by the way.) If you're thinking about major changes, consider ordering a set of sepias. After changes have been made on the sepia, additional sets of plans may be reproduced from the sepia master. Should you decide to revise the plan significantly, we strongly suggest that you consult an experienced architect or designer.

5. A NOTE REGARDING REVERSE BLUE-PRINTS . . . As a special service to those wishing to build in reverse of the plan as shown, we do include

an extra set of reversed blueprints for only $30.00 additional with each order. Even though the lettering and dimensions appear backward on reversed blueprints, they make a handy reference because they show the house just as it's being built in reverse from the standard blueprints — thereby helping you visualize the home better.

6. OUR EXCHANGE POLICY . . . Since blueprints are printed in response to your order, we cannot honor requests for refunds. However, we will exchange your entire first order for an equal number of blueprints at a price of $20.00 for the first set and $10.00 for each additional set. All sets from the previous order must be returned before the exchange can take place. Please add $3.00 for postage and handling via surface mail; $4.00 via air mail.

How Many Blueprints Do You Need?

Because additional sets of the same design in each order are only $30.00 each, you save considerably by ordering your total requirements now. To help you determine the exact number of sets, please refer to the handy checklist below.

Blueprint Checklist

__OWNER'S SET(S)

__**BUILDER** (Usually requires at least three sets: one as legal document; one for inspection; and at least one for tradesmen — usually more.)

__**BUILDING PERMIT** (Sometimes two sets are required.)

__**MORTGAGE SOURCE** (Usually one set for a conventional mortgage; three sets for F.H.A. or V.A. type mortgages.)

__**SUBDIVISION COMMITTEE** (If any.)

__**TOTAL NUMBER SETS REQUIRED**

BLUEPRINT HOTLINE

PHONE TOLL FREE: 1-800-521-6797.
Orders received by 3 p.m. (Eastern time) will be processed the same day and shipped to you the following day. Use of this line is restricted to blueprint and book ordering only.

KINDLY NOTE: When ordering by phone, please state Order Form Key Number located in box at lower left corner of the blueprint order form.

IN CANADA: Add 20% to prices listed on this order form and mail in Canadian funds to:
HOME PLANNERS, INC.
20 Cedar St. North
Kitchener, Ontario N2H 2W8
Phone: (519) 743-4169

TO: **HOME PLANNERS, INC., 23761 RESEARCH DRIVE FARMINGTON HILLS, MICHIGAN 48024**

Please rush me the following:

____ SET(S) BLUEPRINTS FOR DESIGN NO(S). . . . . $_____
Kindly refer to Blueprint Price Schedule on opposite page.

____ SEPIA FOR DESIGN NO(S). . . . . $_____

____ MATERIALS LIST @ $25.00. . . . . $_____

____ ADDITIONAL SPECIFICATION OUTLINES @ $5.00 each . . . . $_____

____ DETAIL SETS @ $14.95 ea.; any two for $22.95; all three for $29.95 . . . . $_____
☐ PLUMBING ☐ ELECTRICAL ☐ CONSTRUCTION

____ PLAN-A-HOME™ Design Kit @ $24.95 ea. (plus $3.00 postage) . . . . $_____

Michigan Residents add 4% sales tax $_____

FOR POSTAGE AND HANDLING PLEASE CHECK ✔ & REMIT	☐	$4.00 Added to Order for Surface Mail (UPS) – Any Mdse.	
	☐	$5.00 Added for Priority Mail of One-Three Sets of Blueprints.	
	☐	$8.00 Added for Priority Mail of Four or more Sets of Blueprints.	$_____
	☐	For Canadian orders add $2.00 to above applicable rates.	

☐ C.O.D. PAY POSTMAN (U.S. ONLY)

TOTAL in U.S. funds $_____

PLEASE PRINT
Name _____
Street _____
City _____ State _____ Zip _____

CREDIT CARD ORDERS ONLY: Fill in the boxes below

Prices subject to change without notice

Credit Card No.

Expiration Date Month/Year

CHECK ONE: ☐ *VISA* ☐ MasterCard

Order Form Key TB6BP

Your Signature _____

BLUEPRINT ORDERS SHIPPED WITHIN 48 HOURS OF RECEIPT!

TO: **HOME PLANNERS, INC., 23761 RESEARCH DRIVE FARMINGTON HILLS, MICHIGAN 48024**

Please rush me the following:

____ SET(S) BLUEPRINTS FOR DESIGN NO(S). . . . . $_____
Kindly refer to Blueprint Price Schedule on opposite page.

____ SEPIA FOR DESIGN NO(S). . . . . $_____

____ MATERIALS LIST @ $25.00. . . . . $_____

____ ADDITIONAL SPECIFICATION OUTLINES @ $5.00 each . . . . $_____

____ DETAIL SETS @ $14.95 ea.; any two for $22.95; all three for $29.95 . . . . $_____
☐ PLUMBING ☐ ELECTRICAL ☐ CONSTRUCTION

____ PLAN-A-HOME™ Design Kit @ $24.95 ea. (plus $3.00 postage) . . . . $_____

Michigan Residents add 4% sales tax $_____

FOR POSTAGE AND HANDLING PLEASE CHECK ✔ & REMIT	☐	$4.00 Added to Order for Surface Mail (UPS) – Any Mdse.	
	☐	$5.00 Added for Priority Mail of One-Three Sets of Blueprints.	
	☐	$8.00 Added for Priority Mail of Four or more Sets of Blueprints	$_____
	☐	For Canadian orders add $2.00 to above applicable rates.	

☐ C.O.D. PAY POSTMAN (U.S. ONLY)

TOTAL in U.S. funds $_____

PLEASE PRINT
Name _____
Street _____
City _____ State _____ Zip _____

CREDIT CARD ORDERS ONLY: Fill in the boxes below

Prices subject to change without notice

Credit Card No.

Expiration Date Month/Year

CHECK ONE: ☐ *VISA* ☐ MasterCard

Order Form Key TB6BP

Your Signature

MULTI-FAMILY HOME DESIGNS
TRADITIONAL

Some homes are especially designed to function as residence for more than one family, while retaining privacy for all. The Early American homes on the following pages certainly include room in their floor plans for such modern lifestyle needs.

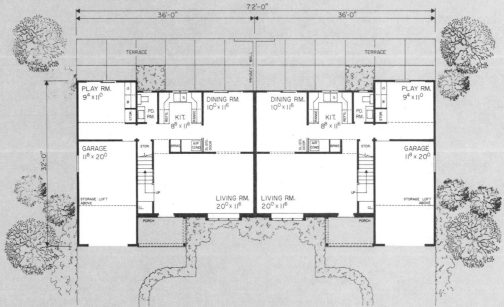

Design T62014
725 Sq. Ft. - First Floor - Each Unit; 624 Sq. Ft. - Second Floor - Each Unit; 13,613 Cu. Ft. - Each Unit

● A two-story duplex with a traditional plan and exterior styling. This plan provides both formal and informal areas on the first floor. The formal, L-shaped living and dining room will be ideal for entertaining. The informal play room and U-shaped kitchen will be appreciated by all family members. There are sliding glass doors leading to the private terrace in both the play room and dining room. Three bedrooms upstairs. Note the storage loft above the garage. Optional basement.

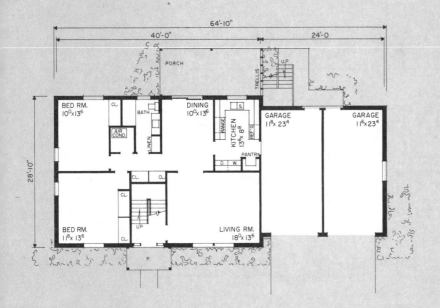

Design T62020

1,166 Sq. Ft. - First Floor
1,166 Sq. Ft. - Second Floor
23,996 Cu. Ft. - Each Unit

● Take a good look at this two-story Colonial. The exterior appeal is very delightful with its symmetrically placed windows, covered porch and side, two-car garage with cupola. From the street it looks like a single family home but immediately upon entering, one will know that this is an up-down duplex. Each unit is identical to the other in size and position. The dining room in each unit has a set of sliding glass doors, leading to a porch from the first floor unit and a deck on the second floor. Note that the washer and dryer are located in the efficient, U-shaped kitchen. The sleeping area consists of two bedrooms and a bath.

Design T62051

Three Bedroom Unit
 507 Sq. Ft. - First Floor
 572 Sq. Ft. - Second Floor
 14,571 Cu. Ft.
Four Bedroom Unit
 653 Sq. Ft. - First Floor
 653 Sq. Ft. - Second Floor
 17,794 Cu. Ft.

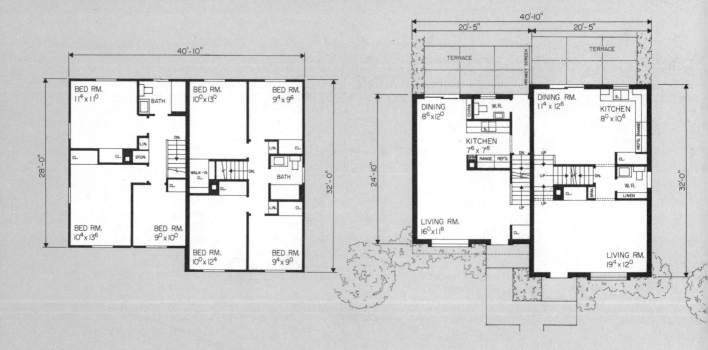

● This duplex is aimed toward those searching for a three or four bedroom home because this fine design offers both. Plus a choice of different elevations! Both elevations will be detailed in the blueprints so you need not decide now as to which one suits your preferences. The layout of each side is very different from the other. But they both have great livability. Now make your own comparison. Basement included for additional space in both three and four bedroom units.

● An adaptation reminiscent of Georgian styling. The narrow frontage of this series of two family designs means only a relatively small investment in land is required.

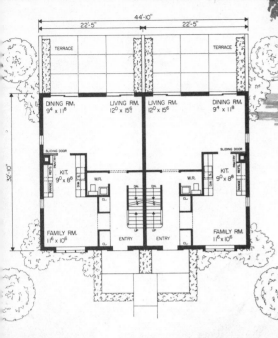

TERRACE   TERRACE

DINING RM. 9⁴ x 11⁸   LIVING RM. 12⁰ x 15⁶   LIVING RM. 12⁰ x 15⁶   DINING RM. 9⁴ x 11⁸

SLIDING DOOR   SLIDING DOOR

KIT. 9⁰ x 8⁸   W.R.   W.R.   KIT. 9⁰ x 8⁸

DN.   DN.
UP   UP

FAMILY RM. 11⁶ x 10⁶   ENTRY   ENTRY   FAMILY RM. 11⁶ x 10⁶

44'-10"
22'-5"   22'-5"
32'-10"

Design T62024
736 Sq. Ft. - First Floor - Each Unit
736 Sq. Ft. - Second Floor - Each Unit
21,712 Cu. Ft. - Each Unit

BED RM. 11⁰ x 11⁸   BED RM. 10⁰ x 11⁸   BED RM. 10⁰ x 11⁸   BED RM. 11⁰ x 11⁸

CL.   LIN.   CL.   LIN.   CL.

WALK-IN CL.   WALK-IN CL.

DN.   DN.

BATH   BATH

MASTER BED RM. 12⁶ x 13⁰   BATH   BATH   MASTER BED RM. 12⁶ x 13⁰

Design T62025
704 Sq. Ft. - First Floor - Each Unit
704 Sq. Ft. - Second Floor - Each Unit
20,768 Cu. Ft. - Each Unit

BED RM. 11⁰ x 11⁸   BED RM. 10⁰ x 11⁸   BED RM. 10⁰ x 11⁸   BED RM. 11⁰ x 11⁸

CL.   LIN.   CL.   LIN.   CL.

WALK-IN CL.   WALK-IN CL.

DN.   DN.

BATH   BATH

MASTER BED RM. 12⁶ x 13⁰   BATH   MASTER BED RM. 12⁶ x 13⁰

● Colonial version has all the appearances of a single family home. Pediment gable front porch adds a distinctive note. Second floor features three bedrooms, two baths.

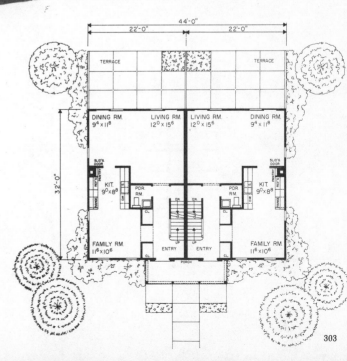

TERRACE   TERRACE

DINING RM. 9⁴ x 11⁸   LIVING RM. 12⁰ x 15⁶   LIVING RM. 12⁰ x 15⁶   DINING RM. 9⁴ x 11⁸

SLID'G DOOR   SLID'G DOOR

KIT. 9⁰ x 8⁸   PDR. RM.   PDR. RM.   KIT. 9⁰ x 8⁸

DN.   DN.
UP   UP

FAMILY RM. 11⁶ x 10⁶   ENTRY   ENTRY   FAMILY RM. 11⁶ x 10⁶

PORCH

44'-0"
22'-0"   22'-0"
32'-0"

Design T62052

507 Sq. Ft. - First Floor - Each Unit
531 Sq. Ft. - Second Floor - Each Unit
13,989 Cu. Ft. - Each Unit

● Along with design T62051 and T62050, this design also offers the use of different exterior materials for its construction. Whichever you choose, the materials will be detailed in the material list and blueprints for each.

. . .One will enter this home in the L-shaped living/dining room area. The convenient, inside kitchen will serve this area nicely. The private terrace is accessible by way of a sliding glass door in the dining room. Plus a rear door adjacent to the washroom. Nearby are stairs to the basement. Two good-sized bedrooms and a bath are upstairs.

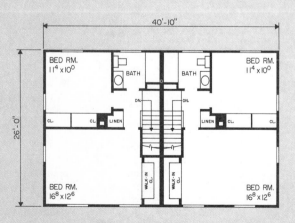

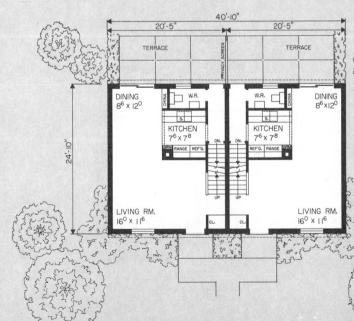

Some Helpful Terms

Our Design T62642 on Pg. 25 is fashioned after the timber-framed home of Boston's Paul Revere, built approximately 1676. This Medieval-style cottage featured second-story overhang and weatherboarding with wooden sideboards that sheathed the infilling. Revere House is the only structure remaining from 17th-Century Boston.

Our Design T62653 on Pg. 32 recalls the historic Boston home of Rev. Thomas Barnard, built in 1715. His house featured traditional salt box configuration and Georgian styling with symmetrically ordered windows and classically inspired exterior detailing.

Our Design T62638 on Pg. 180 is patterned after historic Gunston Hall, the 18th-Century Fairfax County estate of George Mason, author of the Virginia Declaration of Rights. The house reflected the classic forms popularized during Georgian Period. Its steeply pitched roof is broken by two tall chimneys at far ends and by pedimented dormers.

Recommended Reading:

- *A Field Guide to American Houses* by Virginia & Lee McAlester (Alfred Knopt, 1984), 525 pages, paperback.
- *The American House* by Mary Mix Foley (Harper & Row, 1981), 299 pages, paperback.
- *A Book of Cape Cod Houses* by Doris Doane (Chatham Press, 1970), 91 pages, hardback.
- *Early American Architecture* by Hugh Morrison (Oxford University Press, 1952), 619 pages, hardback.
- *The Eighteenth-Century Houses of Williamsburg* by Marcus Whiffen (Holt, Rinehardt, and Winston, 1960), 223 pages, hardback.
- *Dutch Houses in the Hudson Valley Before 1776* by Helen Wilkinson Reynolds (Dover Publications, 1965), 467 pages, paperback.

A
Architrave - Part of an entablature that rests on capital of a column and beneath frieze.

B
Baluster - Small column or pillar that supports a rail.
Base of Column - The part between shaft and pedestal or between shaft and plinth.
Brickwork - Header bricks are laid so ends appear on wall face, while stretcher bricks are laid so only sides show on face of wall. English bond employs alternating stretchers and headers. Flemish bond uses headers and stretchers laid alternately in same course. Heading bond calls for all headers.

C
Capital - Upper part of a column, pilaster, or pier.
Cloister - Covered, often vaulted, walk around an open space with a plain wall on one side and columns or piers on other.
Cornice - Projection at top of wall finished by a blocking course.

D
Dentil - One in series of small rectangular blocks arranged in row of "teeth" and projecting from lower part of cornices.
Detail - Part of a building, structural or ornamental, small in proportion to the whole.

E
Entablature - Assembly of horizontal, upper parts that are supported by a column. Three parts are architrave, frieze, and cornice.

F
Fluting - Vertical grooves on a shaft of a column, pilaster, or other surface. Also called stringes.
Fret - In Greek Revival, ornamental pattern of repeated combinations and straight lines.
Frieze - Portion of an entablature between cornice (above) and architrave (below).

G
Gable - Triangular portion of wall at the end of a ridge roof.
Gallery - A porch or verandah that extends entire length of house, usually on upper floor.

H
Hipped Roof - Roof that rises by equally inclined planes from all four sides of a building.

M
Modillion - Enriched block or horizontal bracket found under cornice or Corinthian entablature.
Mouldings - Projecting or recessed bands that decorate a wall or other surface.

N
Nogging - Use of brickwork or stone to fill spaces between studs or uprights in early timber-frame buildings.

O
Order - The columns with their entablature. Includes the Doric, Ionic, and Corinthian Greek orders, as well as Roman Tuscan and Composite orders.
Overhang - Projecting upper story of a building, sometimes called jetty.

P
Palladian - Architecture of Andrea Palladio revived in America in 18th Century.
Parapet - Dwarf wall along edge of a roof.
Pedestal - Square support of a column and the base of an order of a column.
Pilasters - Flat square columns, attached to a wall, behind a column, or along the side of a building, and projecting from the wall a fraction of their breadth.
Pillar - A detached upright support deviating in shape and proportion from the orders.
Portico - Entrance or porch with a roof supported by columns.

Q
Quoins - Large squared stones used for emphasis at corners of buildings.

S
Saddle-notched - Square-cut.

T
Temple Form - House styled after Greek temples. Forms are classified according to order of columns used.

W
Wainscot - Wood paneling.
Weatherboarding - Overlapping horizontal boards fixed on external wall or timber-framed building.
Weathering - Inclined surface at top of a projection to throw off rainwater. Sometimes called an offset.

Our Design T62659 on Pg. 38 echoes the historic Anthony, R.I., home of General Nathanael Greene, second in command to Washington. The Late Georgian manor, built in 1770, was a three-story, pitched-roof homestead with symmetrical windows and restrained yet elegant central entrance, flanked by pilasters and capped by bracketed pediment.

Our Design T62301 on Pg. 70 faithfully recalls the historic Charleston town house of William Gibbs, built in 1779. The house typifies the popular Georgian-style "double house" with centered main entry, central hall, and double file of rooms. It is sheathed in clapboard, instead of the brick usually used then in the South. The facade is distinguished by its unusually wide entry, graced by a combination of side lights, double pilasters, entablature, and pediments.

Our Design T62689 on Pg. 48 is reminiscent of historic Atwood House, an atypical Cape Cod home built in Chatham, Mass. in 1752. Most early Capes employed gabled roofs, while this featured gambrel roof. Note the typical small-panel windows and shingled siding. The easily fabricated rectangular shape of the full-size Cape Cod permits optimum use of space in a compact plan.

Our Design T62665 on Pg. 103 is patterned after the historic Mt. Vernon home of George Washington, built in 1787. The magnificent manor of Palladian styling combines the symmetry and ambience of imposing plantation dwellings. Flanking wings create a formal courtyard. Note the balance of porticoes, chimneys, and extensions.

HOME PLANNERS, INC.

ISBN 0-918894-60-3

$9.95
$11.95 Canada

- **Special Feature: Guide to Early American Styles**
- **Salt Box Homes & Adaptations**
- **Homes with Gambrel Roofs**
- **Georgian & Federal Versions**
- **Southern Colonial Homes**
- **Early American Farmhouses**
- **Traditional Style Variations**
- **Cape Cod Cottages**
- **Country Estate Houses**
- **1, 1½, 2 Stories & Multi-Levels**